CHICAGONOMICS

WORKS BY LANNY EBENSTEIN

The Greatest Happiness Principle:
An Examination of Utilitarianism

Great Political Thinkers: Plato to the Present (co-author)

Introduction to Political Thinkers (co-author)

Edwin Cannan: Liberal Doyen

Today's Isms: Socialism, Capitalism, Fascism,
Communism, Libertarianism (co-author)

Friedrich Hayek: A Biography

Hayek's Journey: The Mind of Friedrich Hayek

Milton Friedman: A Biography

The Indispensable Milton Friedman:
Essays on Politics and Economics (editor)

CHICAGONOMICS

THE EVOLUTION OF CHICAGO FREE MARKET ECONOMICS

LANNY EBENSTEIN

St. Martin's Press

New York

www.stmartins.com

Library of Congress Cataloging-in-Publication Data

Ebenstein, Alan O.
  Chicagonomics : the evolution of Chicago free market economics / Lanny Ebenstein.
    pages   cm
  Includes bibliographical references and index.
  ISBN 978-0-230-62195-4
  1. Chicago school of economics. 2. Economics—United States—History. I. Title.
  HB98.3.E235   2015
  330.15'53--dc23

2015008751

ISBN 978-0-230-62195-4 (hardcover)
ISBN 978- 1-4668-9112-8 (e-book)

Design by Letra Libre, Inc.

Our books may be purchased in bulk for promotional, educational, or business use. Please contact your local bookseller or the Macmillan Corporate and Premium Sales Department at (800) 221-7945, extension 5442, or by e-mail at MacmillanSpecialMarkets@macmillan.com.

First edition: October 2015

10 9 8 7 6 5 4 3 2 1

"The ideas of economists and political philosophers, both when they are right and when they are wrong, are more powerful than is commonly understood. Indeed the world is ruled by little else. Practical men, who believe themselves to be quite exempt from any intellectual influences, are usually the slaves of some defunct economist . . ."

—John Maynard Keynes

The General Theory of Employment, Interest, and Money

To Contemporary Libertarians

CONTENTS

Preface   ix

Introduction: Historical Background of
Chicagonomics   1

1 Rockefeller's University and the Department of
   Political Economy   19

2 Jacob Viner as Classical Liberal   38

3 Frank Knight before Chicago   53

4 Chicagoan and Austrian Economics in the 1930s   69

5 Henry Simons and Progressive Taxation   79

6 Cowles Commission and Keynes   92

7 The Chicago School of Economics   108

8 Chicago Economists in Academia   130

9 Law and Economics, and Political Philosophy   140

10 Hayek at Chicago: Philosopher of Classical Liberalism   154

11 Friedman as Economist and Public Intellectual   168

12 The 1980s Crescendo and Contemporary
    Libertarianism   184

    Conclusion: Current Applications of Chicagonomics   194

    Appendix: Interview with Milton Friedman on
    Friedrich Hayek   209
    Appendix: Letter from Paul Samuelson about Milton Friedman 218
    Bibliographical Essay   220
    Notes   242
    Index   268

Eight pages of photographs of Chicago economists appear between pages 208 and 209.

PREFACE

THIS WORK ON THE development of economic and political ideas emanating from the University of Chicago is my tenth book in the history of economic and political thought. I am pleased by the continuing gracious reception accorded these works. This is my fifth book specifically on Friedrich Hayek, Milton Friedman, or Chicago economics.

Times have changed much in the United States and internationally since I began this book in 2008. For this reason, I conclude with thoughts on the extension of the Chicago free market tradition in current circumstances. In a 1967 lecture on his former teacher and friend Henry Simons, Milton Friedman said: "Critical examination of a man's ideas is a truer tribute than slavish repetition of his formulas."[1] I therefore hope that the proposals offered here to achieve greater economic equality in the distribution of income and wealth in the United States through the restoration of progressive income and estate taxation will be looked on with interest and favor.

The policies recommended here are consistent with the contemporary application of traditional Chicagoan positive and normative economics. In many respects, I call for a return to earlier Chicagoans' views on appropriate government and economic policy, particularly Simons's views on the importance of greater equality and progressive taxation. The policies advocated here are essentially those that existed in the United States in the postwar era through 1980, when America was considered to be at its apex, domestically and internationally—particularly during the 1950s, when rates of progressive income taxation were highest.

In contrast to most previous scholarship, I distinguish between the younger and older Friedman and Hayek, and emphasize the radical, virtually neoanarchist positions that each took in his seventies and eighties, contrary to views they expressed earlier in their careers. Friedman's and Hayek's later views should be discarded for their younger and more moderate opinions. It is possible now to evaluate the careers of both with more distance, objectivity, and detachment than was possible even a few years ago. I hope that the distinction between the younger and older Friedman, in particular, will become standard in the literature. A number of authors, including Angus Burgin, Brian Doherty, and William Ruger, call attention to Friedman's progressive radicalization as he turned to policy advocacy.

I am very critical of contemporary libertarianism and to a lesser extent conservatism, though not, I hope, unreasonably or unfairly. I focus on streams of economic thought at Chicago with public policy emphases. Chicago economics has been most fruitful in its focus on public policy. Through the presentation of many economists' ideas over centuries, together with critiques of them, I hope to make an independent as well as derivative contribution to classical liberalism and the theory of free market capitalism. As historically understood at the University of Chicago, classical liberalism and capitalism require a strong egalitarian element achieved through progressive income and estate taxation.

The Chicago economists on whom I focus most include J. Laurence Laughlin, Jacob Viner, Frank Knight, Henry Simons, Milton Friedman, George Stigler, Aaron Director, and Friedrich Hayek. The discussion of their predecessors, from Adam Smith to William Graham Sumner, sets the stage, and, I hope, with the bibliographical essay, offers an accurate perspective on Adam Smith, consistent with contemporary literature. I emphasize Hayek and Friedman because of their importance and my familiarity with them, and because I hope I have new things to say about their thought and development.

I thank those who provided interviews for my previous works, which I have incorporated here. I thank Lester Telser, Thomas Sowell, Sam Peltzman, Stephen Stigler, and Edwin Meese. I also interviewed Milton and Rose Friedman, Ronald Coase, Gary Becker, Allen Wallis, D. Gale Johnson, Larry Sjaastaad, Larry Hayek, and Arthur Seldon, all of whom have passed away. I exchanged correspondence with Paul Samuelson, James Meade, Robert Fogel, and others who have also passed away. I recently had the opportunity to interview George Shultz and talk with David Stockman. I have reviewed archives, particularly relating to Friedrich Hayek and Milton Friedman at the Hoover Institution on War, Revolution, and Peace at Stanford University.

In addition, I thank the many scholars who have plowed the same field, and from whose works I benefit, including Angus Burgin, Ross Emmett, J. Daniel and Claire Hammond, George Nash, Johan Van Overtveldt, Robert Leeson, Philip Mirowski, Robert Van Horn, Thomas Stapleford, Sherryl Kasper, Mark Skousen, Malcolm Rutherford, Donald Winch, Robert Skidelsky, and the late Warren Samuels and Henry Spiegel. My monthly breakfast associates—John Busby, Bob Casier, John Kay, Peter MacDougall, and Stan Roden—provided helpful thoughts on the conclusion, as did my old professor Tom Schrock, Nelson Lichtenstein, and Jerry James. I would also like to thank Alan Bradshaw for his work on the manuscript. None of these good people is responsible for this work's errors and inaccuracies, and many will disagree with the relative merits of classical liberalism, contemporary libertarianism, and contemporary conservatism presented. I hope to persuade, or be persuaded by, them.

Lanny Ebenstein
Santa Barbara, California
July 20, 2015

CHICAGONOMICS

INTRODUCTION

HISTORICAL BACKGROUND
OF CHICAGONOMICS

IF WE WERE TO DIG as deeply as possible into the temporal roots of Chicago free market economics, we would find some of the most important to be in the eighteenth century and first decades of the nineteenth—in the works of the Scottish moral philosopher and economist Adam Smith (1723–1790) and the British political philosopher and founder of utilitarianism Jeremy Bentham (1748–1832). Both Smith and Bentham have dominated economic and political thought, and Bentham took much of his inspiration from Smith. Together with the great John Locke (1632–1704) and John Stuart Mill (1806–1873), Smith and Bentham were two of the four greatest economists and political philosophers in the original classical liberal line of Whig and liberal authors and thinkers in the late seventeenth through mid-nineteenth centuries.

With Smith's work, the fields of economics and political economy really come into view for the first time. There was, in Smith's work, an appreciation for the national economy as a self-sustaining and autonomous institution—shaped, but by no means determined or directed, by government—that was not present in earlier writers. Smith's brilliant insights included the ideas that when two parties engage in trade, both benefit from it; that enlightened self-interest is a surer basis for society than altruism; that the division, or specialization, of labor allows vastly greater production than a less complex economy; and that economic activity, income, and wealth are morally beneficial. Smith was thoroughly modern in his approach. As Bentham would state the basic postulate of utilitarianism and classical liberalism: "It is the greatest happiness of the greatest number that is the measure of right and wrong."[1]

Crucially, Smith and Bentham affirmed that individuals are equal in their capacities to experience happiness. For this reason, they supported democratic polities (Bentham more than Smith) and an economic system in which wealth is maximized both totally and in the amount of wealth and income that each person receives. Both Smith and Bentham were modest to moderate egalitarians. They were not extremely egalitarian, but they saw greater equality of income and wealth than existed in their day as vital to increased human happiness. They lived in and saw a social world in which a substantial aristocratic class was unproductive and undeserving, and they meant to change that world and the conditions of that class. They were on what today would be considered the political left. Smith sought the wealth of nations—their whole peoples—not of a small class.

Smith and especially Bentham were not afraid to use government to do good, like most (though not all) of their successors at the University of Chicago. They understood that government is necessary for an increased standard of living for all, and they supported government activity to create this standard. They advocated government public works and schools. They thought that government has a crucial role to play in monetary institutions. They approved of nascent welfare state activities. The portrayal of Smith, Bentham, and classical liberals generally as extreme opponents of government activity, though widespread, is mistaken.

Jacob Viner, who was among the greatest historians of economic thought, believed that in the *Theory of Moral Sentiments* (1759), Smith "develops his system of ethics on the basis of a doctrine of a harmonious order in nature guided by God,"[2] and that in the *Wealth of Nations* (1776), he applied this idea to the economic realm. Smith, like others in the classical liberal tradition, saw a universe in which God attempts to create the greatest happiness.

Smith's great insight in *The Wealth of Nations* was the division, or what we would today call the specialization, of labor. His celebrated example of pin-making remains illustrative and may be considered the start of quantitative economics. If one person had to perform all of the functions required by this trade, "he could scarce make one pin in a day, and certainly could not make twenty." But when this enterprise is divided into many branches, "ten persons . . . could make among them 48,000 pins in a day."[3] The division of labor—more than any other single factor—is what allows the wealth of nations to emerge. In less developed economies, with less specialization, individuals' productive capacities are more limited.

The most effective division of labor requires, moreover, a free market and significant private property rights. Where there is not a free market, individuals are restricted in trading with others and the economy is not as productive as it would otherwise be. Similarly, unless there are significant (though by no means total, whatever that would be) private property rights, individuals do not have the incentive to innovate and be as productive as possible. As much as is feasible, markets should be free or open on both domestic and international bases. The larger the market, the greater the possibilities for specialization of labor and production—and the higher the standard of living for all.

A free market in labor and capital tends to direct resources to those who use them most effectively and productively—those who can best serve others at a particular task or in producing a particular object at the lowest possible cost. The market does not work perfectly or all the time, but it works most of the time or more of the time than any other institution that has yet developed or evolved. Like democracy, the free market is an imperfect institution, but it is the best institution we have for producing the greatest diversity and highest quality of goods and services in the most efficient manner.

Smith's genius was to see that economic production is usually encouraged just by allowing people to exchange goods and services with one another: "It is not from the benevolence of the butcher, the brewer, or the baker, that we expect our dinner, but from their regard to their own interest. We address ourselves, not to their humanity but to their self-love."[4] There is a natural harmony of interests in society whereby as individuals become more productive they serve others more, and society becomes wealthier and more economically prosperous in general.

Crucially, for Smith it was important that wealth and income are spread as equitably as possible in a society, as the wealth of a nation is nothing other than the wealth of the individuals who compose it. Unless it is necessary to create more total production—and a higher average and distribution of income and wealth for all—Smith's system does not sanction inequality. He was at one with the great Enlightenment and classical liberal thinkers on the essential equality of all persons. He especially opposed laws regarding the inheritance of land that result in the concentration of wealth. He remarked in *The Wealth of Nations:* "All for ourselves, and nothing for other people, seems, in every age of the world, to have been the vile maxim of the masters of mankind."[5] He commented throughout *The Wealth of Nations* on the morally suspect nature of the business, land-owning, and aristocratic classes.

He supported government activity that aimed at benefitting the people as a whole rather than a small group among them. For Smith, wrote Viner: "Government activity is natural and therefore good where it promotes the general welfare, and it is an interference with nature and therefore bad when it injures the general interests of society."[6] The areas in which Smith sanctioned a government role in *The*

Wealth of Nations included involvement with the monetary system; certification of certain productive practices such as the "sterling mark upon plate and the stamps upon linen and woolen cloth"[7]; labor regulations requiring workers to be paid in cash, not kind; regulation of monopoly of various sorts; sanitary standards, including the cleaning of streets; promotion of public hygiene to prevent the spread of disease; public works, including the construction and operation of highways, bridges, canals, and harbors; government ownership and operation of public parks; patent and copyright laws; regulation of mortgages; regulation of interest rates (he thought the maximum rate of interest should be 5 percent); operation of a postal service; and provision of public education.

Viner observed that in "many instances Smith supported government restrictions on private initiative where neither justice nor defense was involved, and where the sole aim was to improve upon the direction which private initiative gave to the investment of capital, the course of commerce, and the employment of labor."[8] Smith approved of using the tax code to discourage certain activities, including the consumption of hard liquors, and he supported a higher road toll on luxury carriages than freight wagons so that "the indolence and vanity of the rich [may be] made to contribute in a very easy manner to the relief of the poor."[9] He advocated detailed regulation of rental agreements and higher-than-average taxation of land whose value had been increased by government. He sanctioned progressive taxation. He wrote in *The Wealth of Nations:* "It is not very unreasonable that the rich should contribute to the public expense, not only in proportion to their revenue, but something more than in that proportion."[10] The Smithian "invisible hand" of natural and spontaneous order to maximize general happiness included significant government activity, including to promote the common welfare and equality.[11]

It would be inaccurate, though, to portray Smith merely or mostly as a welfare statist in embryo, though he undoubtedly was one. His primary contribution was to elucidate the system by which, absent government control and direction, the greatest economic productivity and production can occur. He lived and wrote before the French Revolution—he died in its first year. He did not contemplate the practical changes in society which that event signaled, and he surely would have supported further extensions of government had he lived longer. Smith was admired by early leaders of the French Revolution. He favored the American Revolution. Like other classical liberals, he was not a religious dogmatist. He was a gentle deist. He sought the maximization of happiness and the standard of living (the two were almost synonymous in his mind) in this life, not in a life to come.

The great challenge in Smith's time was to reduce the role of government and tradition. Prohibitions by government and custom with respect to economic activities greatly reduced productive opportunities. Smith saw his goal primarily as to elucidate a natural system of liberty founded on private property, free exchange, and a considerable government role in which economic production would be maximized and distributed equitably. His focus was government. Through the right mix of policies and activities, government could bring about the best living circumstances possible.

Smith's most recent and perhaps best biographer, Nicholas Phillipson, writes: "Smith believed that it was . . . possible to develop a genuine Science of Man based on the observation of human nature and human history; a science which would not only explain the principles of social and political organization to be found in different types of society, but would explain the principles of government and legislation that ought to be followed by enlightened rulers who wanted to extend the liberty and happiness of their subjects and the wealth and power of their dominions."[12] In no way did Smith merely favor government doing nothing or next to nothing. Chicagoans Thomas Sowell and James Buchanan share this view. According to Sowell: "Egalitarianism is pervasive in Smith."[13] According to Buchanan: "A returned Adam Smith would be a long distance from the modern libertarian anarchists."[14]

John Maynard Keynes observed that "the phrase *laissez faire* is not to be found in the works of Adam Smith, of Ricardo, or of Malthus.

Even the idea is not present in a dogmatic form in any of these authors."[15] The concept of extreme antigovernmentism is more similar to the French rationalist tradition (Hayek's "false"[16] individualism) than the British and American historical and pragmatic traditions. The great British political philosophers and economists, up to Herbert Spencer, all called for a healthy and positive government role, especially for their time. They were all on the left religiously—agnostics, gentle deists, atheists, or modest Christians. They all considered themselves to be scientists (who originally were called "philosophers"), of a sort, who would follow the truth where it led. They were rationalists. There was not a dogmatist among them.

Smith wrote in *The Theory of Moral Sentiments,* establishing himself unequivocally as a utilitarian:

> The idea of that divine Being, whose benevolence and wisdom have, from all eternity, contrived and conducted the immense machine of the universe, so as at all times to produce the greatest possible quantity of happiness, is certainly of all the objects of human contemplation by far the most sublime. . . . The administration of the great system of the universe, . . . the care of the universal happiness of all rational and sensible beings, is the business of God and not of man. To man is allotted a much humbler department, but one much more suitable to the weakness of his powers and to the narrowness of his comprehension, the care of his own happiness, of that of his family, his friends, his country.[17]

Like later utilitarians, Smith sought the greatest happiness of the greatest number.

Jeremy Bentham was, if anything, even more influential than Smith. The British utilitarians, whom Bentham inspired and headed, were Smith's greatest proponents. They championed, popularly and in Parliament, economic reforms that Smith had advocated, and they were largely successful in their efforts. Utilitarian and other reformers successfully established free choice of occupations, free exchange of land, domestic free trade, and free trade in foreign commerce in the first decades of the nineteenth century.[18] Among other momentous legislative acts, the Corn Laws were reformed to eliminate prohibitive import duties on foreign grains and the English Poor Laws were reformed to reduce the expense of assistance to the poor.

Among Bentham's greatest efforts was to extend voting to as many people as possible. He considered the expansion of democracy and of good government to be virtually synonymous. The great Reform Act of 1832, which provided representation to new urban areas, took seats away from "rotten boroughs" with small populations, and expanded the franchise, passed Parliament just days before he died. Democracy and a significant role for government have gone hand in hand with a free market and the greatest economic production in history.

Unlike Smith, Bentham, writing some years later, was more full-throated in his support of government activity to promote the greatest happiness of the greatest number. Viner, again, is the best as well as the leading Chicago authority:

> The list of reforms in England which derive largely from Bentham is a truly impressive one, and I present it here only in part: fundamental law reform in many of its branches; prison reform; adult popular suffrage, including woman suffrage; free trade; reform in colonial government; legalization of trade unions; general education at public expense; free speech and free press; the secret ballot; a civil service appointed and promoted on merit; repeal of the usury laws; general registration of titles to property; reform of local government; a safety code for merchant shipping; sanitary reform and preventive medicine at public expense; systematic collection of statistics; free justice for the poor.[19]

Viner said that Bentham was a "successful social reformer, more successful perhaps than anyone in history except Karl Marx."[20]

Other Chicagoans have shared Viner's high opinion of Bentham. Henry Simons wrote that "Smith, and Bentham especially, stand out . . . as the great political philosophers of modern democracy."[21] George Stigler referred to "the great Bentham."[22] Hayek remarked on "a thinker of the stature of Jeremy Bentham."[23] Commenting on the spread of Smith's ideas in England, Friedman wrote: "Bentham, Ricardo, James Mill, and John Stuart Mill were actively engaged in spreading these ideas and promoting them politically."[24] Simons said of his own policy approach: "Perhaps everything I have tried to say was better said by Bentham and the Benthamites."[25]

Essential in and central to Bentham's schema was the concept of utility. Utility was the sun around which his other ideas, like planets, traveled. "Happiness," he wrote in an early manuscript unpublished in his lifetime, "is the end of every human action, of every human thought. How can it, or why ought it to be otherwise? This is for those to say, who sometime seem to struggle to dispute it."[26] He famously wrote in commencing *An Introduction to the Principles of Morals and Legislation* (1789): "Nature has placed mankind under the governance of two sovereign masters, *pain* and *pleasure.* It is for them alone to point out what we ought to do, as well as to determine what we shall do. . . . They govern us in all we do, in all we say, in all we think."[27]

Like his Chicago successors and almost all economists today, Bentham emphasized secular utility maximization—the maximum human well-being. Indeed, Bentham may be considered to be the founder of modern economics, as the principle of quantifiable utility maximization underlies modern economic theory.

John Stuart Mill quoted "Bentham's dictum" as "everybody to count for one, nobody for more than one."[28] Equality truly was—and is—basic in the classical liberal schema. The classical liberal economic ideal was not and is not a society divided into a very few, ultra-wealthy makers and creators and a great mass of impoverished workers and indigents, though this may rapidly be approaching the American reality for tens of millions—and, indeed, this reality is rapidly attaining the status of an ideal for many contemporary libertarian writers and thinkers. A radically unequal economic order is becoming, for perhaps the first time in American history, the implicit or even explicit goal of one of the two major political parties. To the extent that a society practices or experiences extreme inequality, however, it is ipso facto not a classical liberal one, though it may be a contemporary libertarian or contemporary conservative society—that is, contemporary libertarians and many conservatives seek inequality as among their highest practical goals.

In the words of contemporary libertarianism's greatest avatar, Ayn Rand, in a soliloquy by one of her characters gazing out over and describing a great city's lights:

> Look at it. A sublime achievement, isn't it? A heroic achievement. Think of the thousands who worked to create this and of the millions who profit by it. And it is said that but for the spirit of a dozen men, here and there down the ages, but for a dozen men—less, perhaps—none of this would have been possible. And that might be true. If so, there are . . . two possible attitudes to take. We can say that these twelve were great benefactors, that we are all fed by the overflow of the magnificent wealth of their spirit, and that we are glad to accept it in gratitude and brotherhood. Or, we can say that by the splendor of their achievement which we can neither equal nor keep, these twelve have shown us what we are, that we do not want the free gifts of their grandeur, that a cave by an oozing swamp and a fire of sticks rubbed together are preferable to skyscrapers and neon lights—if the cave and the sticks are the limit of our own creative capacities.[29]

Many, perhaps most, contemporary libertarians are vitally influenced by Rand and her radically inegalitarian views. Accordingly, their and their conservative allies' opinion of the appropriate and optimal society is one in which income and wealth are very unequally received and held, such as, for example, the contemporary United States. One hears nary a word on behalf of equality across the political spectrum—indeed, one is much more likely to hear criticism of government redistribution of income and wealth, especially from contemporary libertarians and conservatives, as inequality in the reception of income and the possession of wealth has skyrocketed.[30] The view of Rand and her followers on the desirability of inequality is not a part of the classical liberal tradition. Friedman and Stigler in their younger years, as well as Simons, were advocates of substantial progressive income and estate taxation to lessen economic inequality.

Following Smith and the great line of British classical liberal economists and political philosophers, Chicago economists have typically advocated public policies that are intended to result in the highest standard of living possible for all people—not a small group among them. The goal of free market economists from Smith to the present is to maximize everyone's happiness, with everyone's capacity to experience happiness being considered to be equal. Even in old age, Friedman could occasionally express egalitarian sentiments. He commented in a 1996 interview, when inequality in income and wealth was substantially less than it has become, that the "greatest problem facing our country is the breaking down into two classes, those who have and those who have not. . . . We really cannot remain a democratic, open society that is divided into two classes."[31]

Perhaps more students have been introduced to classical liberalism through John Stuart Mill's *On Liberty* (1859) than any other work. Mill was born in 1806 and died in 1873. He was the son of James Mill, a leading political economist in his own right. Both Mills were students and disciples of Bentham.

John Stuart Mill's works were dominant in politics, philosophy, and economics in the second half of the nineteenth century. His *Principles of Political Economy* (1848) was the standard work in the emerging college-university system—either directly or at a remove through texts influenced by it. *On Liberty* was, as it continues to be, the best argument for free speech and expression and a noble paean for individualism. *Considerations on Representative Government* (1861) helped to influence parliamentary reform. As a member of Parliament, Mill introduced legislation to give women the right to vote half a century before similar legislation ultimately passed. Mill's *Autobiography* (1873) influenced social reform. The early members of the British Fabian Society, which started in 1884 and became one of the most influential think tanks ever, all read Mill. *Utilitarianism* (1861) remains an inspiring ethical essay.

Mill insisted emphatically on the importance of genius. He believed that there are few people in comparison with the whole of humankind whose experiments would be any improvement over established practice. But these few are the salt of the world, without whom the human race would become a stagnant mass.

In addition to his emphasis on genius, which has tended to be shared by great Chicagoans, Mill was a proponent of the highest standard of living possible for all people and ultimately all sentient life through the application of the principle of secular utility maximization. He truly was a utilitarian, and his followers at the University of Chicago have, for more than 120 years, been true to this creed. Whatever their technical, philosophical, or other differences, Chicago economists, as economists generally, have been overwhelmingly utilitarian in outlook.

Mill foresaw a vastly higher standard of living for all people as possible and even inevitable. He wrote presciently in 1861:

> No one whose opinion deserves a moment's consideration can doubt that most of the great positive evils of the world are in themselves removable, and will, if human affairs continue to improve, be in the end reduced within narrow limits. Poverty, in any sense implying suffering, may be completely extinguished . . . [T]hat most intractable of enemies, disease, may be indefinitely reduced . . . ; while the progress of science holds out a promise for the future of still more direct conquests over this detestable foe. . . . All the grand sources, in

short, of human suffering are in a great degree, many of them almost entirely, conquerable by human care and effort.[32]

Mill was a genuine individualist, and he believed that societies could be persuaded through rational conversation. He was one of the first public intellectuals. He exerted much influence on public opinion, though he was not much involved for most of his career in direct political activity. Rather, he influenced public opinion through his moral and empirical arguments presented in many works on many subjects—philosophy, economics, politics, ethics, and religion.

In addition to Smith, Bentham, and Mill, many other writers and thinkers exerted influence during the eighteenth and nineteenth centuries. Perhaps the strongest influence in the last decades of the nineteenth century was from science. The work of Charles Darwin in *The Origin of Species* (1859) burst onto the intellectual firmament in a way that few books ever have. Perhaps only the Bible and Koran are of comparable influence. Darwin challenged the conception of a God-centered universe. Rather, he argued, all of the living universe can be accounted for through natural processes. According to Keynes: "The economists were teaching that wealth, commerce, and machinery were the children of free competition—that free competition built London. But the Darwinians could go one better than that—free competition had built Man. . . . The principle of the Survival of the Fittest could be regarded as a vast generalization of the Ricardian economics."[33]

Richard Hofstadter wrote in his classic *Social Darwinism in American Thought* (1955): "The United States during the last three decades of the nineteenth and at the beginning of the twentieth century was *the* Darwinian country. England gave Darwin to the world, but the United States gave to Darwinism an unusually quick and sympathetic reception."[34] Hofstadter added: "Herbert Spencer, who of all men made the most ambitious attempt to systematize the implication of evolution in fields other than biology itself, was far more popular in the United States than he was in his native country."[35]

Darwin imbued human consciousness with a completely new conception of the cosmos. Previously, it had been thought that God proximately created the living things of the earth in their final forms as species. It was believed that the animal and plant species that humankind had known throughout its existence were for the most part the only species there have ever been. Gradually, though, through the early modern period—from the 1500s through the 1800s—more and more fossils and other remains of extinct species were found. In addition, geologists and others identified different past climates in locales and speculated that the earth was far older than the 6,000 or so years presented in Genesis. What was the answer?

Darwin's contribution was so immense that it is hard to conceptualize or grasp. Others were close to and even expressing ideas of natural evolution, but it was Darwin's work that was the most encompassing, persuasive, and original. Darwin became famous around the world, and the *Origin of Species* was translated into scores of languages.[36]

It was not long before Darwin's ideas were applied to society. Herbert Spencer was the philosopher who most espoused, on Darwinian premises, a limited role for government in the nineteenth century, a different position than most of his predecessors in the British classical liberal and free market line. Spencer was born in 1820 and died in 1903. Both his paternal and maternal ancestors were English and French nonconformists, dissenters, and rebels, and Spencer traced in his autobiography his disregard of political, religious, and social authority to the tradition of independence and dissent so long cherished by his family. He was a subeditor of the *Economist* from 1848 to 1853 before he became a full-time freelance author and public intellectual.

With respect to John Stuart Mill's influence, Spencer wrote on his death in 1873: "To dilate upon Mr. Mill's achievements, and to insist upon the wideness of his influence over the thought of his time, . . . seems to me scarcely needful. The facts are sufficiently obvious, and are recognized by all who know any thing about the progress of opinion during the last half-century."[37] British economist Henry Fawcett wrote two years earlier: "Anyone who has resided during the last twenty years at either of our universities must have noticed that Mr. Mill is the author who has most powerfully influenced nearly all the young men of the greatest promise."[38] Darwin himself remarked in his *Descent of Man* (1871) that Mill was "so profound a thinker."[39]

In discussing the functions of government, Spencer was concerned with what the state ought not to do, rather than what it should do. In his view, the maintenance of order and the administration of justice were the only two proper activities of government. Their purpose is merely to defend the natural rights of person and property. The state has no business to promote religion, regulate trade and commerce, encourage colonization, aid the poor, or enforce sanitary laws. Spencer was the most extreme nineteenth-century laissez-faire advocate.

Spencer was influenced by Darwin, and it was, indeed, Spencer who coined the phrase "survival of the fittest," not Darwin. Spencer's Darwinian idea applied to society was that natural selection was already at work in social life. Those who were wealthier were, in Spencer's eyes, naturally more fit than those who were not as well off (an argument revived with vigor in the United States in recent years). It was the natural merits of the wealthy that led and lead them to prosper—and it was the natural demerits of the poor that led and lead them to fail. To give aid to the poor or support them in any way would only propagate lesser human beings. As Keynes remarked, "socialistic interferences" with the market became "not merely inexpedient, but impious, as calculated to retard the onward movement of the mighty process by which we ourselves had risen . . . out of the primeval slime."[40]

John D. Rockefeller, who founded the University of Chicago, was influenced by the milieu of ideas surrounding Spencer. Rockefeller once explained that the "growth of large business is merely a survival of the fittest. . . . The American beauty rose can be produced in the splendor and fragrance which bring cheer to its beholder only by sacrificing the early buds which grow up around it. This is not an evil tendency in business. It is merely the working-out of a law of nature and a law of God."[41] According to Spencer himself: "I am simply carrying out the views of Mr. Darwin in their application to the human race. . . . Only those who *do* advance . . . eventually survive . . . [These] must be the select of their generation."[42]

William Graham Sumner was Spencer's leading academic disciple in the United States. Sumner wrote:

> The struggle for existence is aimed against nature. It is from her niggardly hand that we have to wrest the satisfaction for our needs, but our fellow-men are our competitors for the meager supply. Competition, therefore, is a law of nature. Nature is entirely neutral; she submits to him who most energetically and resolutely assails her. She grants her rewards to the fittest, therefore, without regard to other considerations of any kind. If, then, there be liberty, men get from her just in proportion to their works, and their having and enjoying are just in proportion to their being and their doing. . . . If we do not like it, and try to amend it, there is only one way in which we can do it. We can take from the better and give to the worse. We can deflect the penalties of those who have done ill and throw them on those who have done better. . . . We shall thus lessen the inequalities. We shall favor the survival of the unfittest, and we shall accomplish this by destroying liberty.[43]

Sumner also said: "The millionaires are a product of natural selection . . . the naturally selected agents of society for certain work. They get high wages and live in luxury, but the bargain is a good one for society."[44]

The social Darwinists believed that successful businesses were a manifestation of the survival of the fittest. Unsuccessful workingmen were the nonsurvival of the unfit. Larger economic circumstances or contingency played virtually no role in economic success or failure. To interfere in the rewards and punishments occurring through laissez-faire was to transgress both moral and physical laws. It simply could not be done. Efforts at amelioration or to increase the standard of living of the less fortunate through government would merely increase their numbers and condemn even more to poverty. Similarly, to give fewer resources to the successful would result in them having less with which to do their good works. The writings of Darwin and Spencer were the scientific and social credo of economically conservative interests in the United States during the last decades of the nineteenth century and first decades of the twentieth as the University of Chicago was founded and instantaneously established.

The utilitarian and classical liberal philosophers and political economists in England and elsewhere in the eighteenth and nineteenth centuries were overwhelmingly secular in outlook. The purpose of life is to maximize human happiness in the world. For this reason, they tended not to ground their justifications of the market in natural rights terms—rather, all political and economic rights are human-made.

Mill expressed this idea well in *On Liberty* when he said that "I forego any advantage which could be derived to my argument from the idea of abstract right, as a thing independent of utility. I regard utility as the ultimate standard on all ethical questions."[45] Ludwig von Mises, the great Austrian libertarian economist who was a mentor of Hayek, stated the material aspect of liberalism as well as anyone in his *Liberalism in the Classical Tradition* (1962): Classical liberalism "has nothing else in view than the advancement of outward, material welfare."[46] Brian Doherty, a senior editor at *Reason* magazine, comments on this passage that the vision of classical liberalism is "utilitarian; Mises does not support economic and personal liberty out of any spiritual or metaphysical doctrine of rights, but because he believes it can be demonstrated, both in theory and by observation, that liberalism ensures the greatest wealth and physical abundance for all."[47]

In contemporary American society, economists who continue to carry the banner for traditional, classical liberalism—the school of Adam Smith and Jeremy Bentham, John Stuart Mill, John Locke,

Alfred Marshall, Edwin Cannan, John Maynard Keynes, Wesley Mitchell, Jacob Viner, Frank Knight, Lionel Robbins, Henry Simons, Paul Samuelson, Herb Stein, and the younger and middle-aged Hayek and younger Friedman—include Joseph Stiglitz, Paul Krugman, Larry Summers, Robert Reich, James Heckman, Ben Bernanke, and Janet Yellen. By way of contrast to the great classical liberal tradition, the virtually neoanarchist positions of the late Hayek and especially Friedman should be considered a radical departure in both policy and method—the "constructivist rationalism" that Hayek criticized so harshly elsewhere in his work. In terms of the scope of desired change in society and the economy they sought, though not direction, the older Hayek and Friedman were closer to Marxists than to classical liberals.

Neither Hayek nor particularly Friedman made any bones in old age about being a radical. They rejected the course of gradual, incremental change and substituted in its place revolutionary proposals to reorganize society comprehensively, often with little attention to transition issues. In the virtually neoanarchist society that Friedman advocated later in life, he returned to ideas that were more popular a century before, at the University of Chicago's founding.

1

ROCKEFELLER'S UNIVERSITY AND THE DEPARTMENT OF POLITICAL ECONOMY

DURING THE LAST DECADE of the nineteenth century and to the present, the University of Chicago has established itself as the world's leading research institution. More Nobel Prize recipients are or have been affiliated with it as students, researchers, or teachers than with any other institution in the world, particularly in Nobel Prizes in Economics and Physics. Milton Friedman said in tongue-in-cheek advice to would-be laureates: "Go to the University of Chicago."[1]

The university emerged as fully developed as any institution of higher learning and research ever has. Founded in 1891, it opened its doors in 1892. Its first president was William Rainey Harper, a Bible scholar and canny academic administrator who enjoyed the strong support of the university's primary benefactor and founder, John D. Rockefeller, the president of Standard Oil Company.

Rockefeller was born in 1839 in Richford, New York. His family was well-off and he attended high school when few did. He wrote in a school essay in 1854 of "cruel" southern masters who worked slaves "beneath the scorching sun. . . . How under such circumstances can America call herself free?"[2] He voted for Abraham Lincoln for president in 1860. He founded Standard Oil in 1870. After an extremely controversial career during the next two decades as he became the wealthiest man in America, he began to turn his focus to philanthropic endeavors. A devout Christian, he thought that among the most productive contributions he could make would be to medical research, science, and education. At the time, there was not the breach between science and religion that now exists. Indeed, the deeply religious often were among those who supported scientific research most.

This was an era of college development and establishment. The later 1800s was one of the waves of expansion in American higher education. Rockefeller had been interested in founding a major college or university affiliated with his faith for a number of years when he was contacted by the Baptist Union Theological Seminary in Chicago in 1877 to revive a college that previously had been located there. Central in Rockefeller's decision to establish a major institution of higher education and research in Chicago was Harper, then thirty-one and a scholar of the Old Testament at Baptist Union. Rockefeller immediately fell for the younger man. He said later of Harper that, as a "friend and companion, in daily intercourse, no one could be more delightful than he."[3] In 1887, Harper wrote Rockefeller that there was "no greater work to be done on this continent than . . . establishing a University in or near Chicago."[4]

Why the interest particularly in Chicago? Chicago is the quintessentially American city. Not founded by the English, Dutch, French, or Spanish, Chicago incorporated in 1837. By 1890, it was the second-largest city in the nation, following New York, with a population of more than one million. Site of the famous World's Fair of 1893 celebrating the 400th anniversary of Columbus's first trip to the Americas,

Chicago would become even more famous during the twentieth century through the University of Chicago, which is located on part of the World's Fair show grounds. Rockefeller feared that to found a university in the East would lead it to stick to conventional intellectual ways. In Chicago, on the other hand, he thought that an institution would "strike out upon lines in full sympathy with the spirit of the age."[5]

Rockefeller gave the University of Chicago $35 million in its early years, which would be equivalent to $1 billion or more today. He was concerned that it should not appear that he was involved in the university in any way with respect to academic management. He rarely visited the campus, did not sit on the board of trustees, and adopted a hands-off policy on academic matters. It nevertheless could not have been the Gilded Age that the wealthiest man in the country could give vast sums to a new institution without it attracting great interest, and attack.

In the public mind, the University of Chicago was Rockefeller's university. Early cartoons showed the school with Rockefeller dropping wads of cash on it. Rockefeller biographer Ron Chernow notes that "reams of press coverage presented the university as Rockefeller's hobbyhorse. In 1903, *Life* magazine ran a cartoon of Ye Rich Rockefeller University, showing a lady holding aloft a lamp marked Standard Oil, her robes checkered with dollar signs."[6] Together with Robert Maynard Hutchins, who was the university's president and chancellor from 1929 to 1951, and Friedman, who was on the faculty from 1946 to 1976, Rockefeller was one of the three individuals most associated with the University of Chicago in the public mind in its history to date.

Located in south Chicago near downtown and Lake Michigan, the university opened its doors on October 1, 1892. No ceremonies were held to mark the occasion. The university started classes as if it had already been in operation. Harper was instructed and given the funds by Rockefeller to create a great university ab initio. Hutchins biographer Harry Ashmore said: "Free of the tradition that imposed parochial collegiate obligations upon its elder brothers to the east, and of the political considerations that shaped the more recently founded state institutions, Chicago was modeled on European centers of higher learning that placed primary emphasis on scholarly research. Its declared mission was to advance the frontiers of human knowledge."[7]

American higher education was tiny at this time compared to what it would become, particularly after World War II. In 1900, only about 4 percent of 18-to-21-year-olds in the United States were in college.[8] Harvard and Yale had merely about 1,500 students each. One of the major purposes of colleges was to prepare men for the ministry. There were several hundred colleges in the United States in the late 1800s—mostly local and very small state institutions, agricultural colleges, teachers colleges, technical institutes, and general education colleges that were state-sponsored, denominational, or private. Almost none had graduate programs and thus they were not referred to as (or even named yet) a "university." In 1850, there were only eight graduate students in the entire country. This grew to 5,700 in 1900, 47,000 in 1930, and 224,000 in 1950.[9]

Harper created an extraordinary faculty with Rockefeller's money. Chicago could offer higher salaries than almost any other institution of higher education. It was explicitly a "university"—one of the first in the nation. Mortimer Adler, perhaps Hutchins's closest associate, remarked in 1941 in a popular magazine article titled "The Chicago School" (with no reference to economics) that the University of Chicago was "popularly thought of as one of America's youngest institutions. In truth it is one of the oldest, if we discriminate between an undergraduate college and a university, a place for graduate study and research."[10] Adler went on to note that only Johns Hopkins University and Clark University preceded Chicago as universities in the United States. In the second half of the nineteenth century, many Americans pursued graduate studies in Germany because there were so few opportunities at home.

The University of Chicago emphasized graduate programs and research from the start. Harper developed a comprehensive institutional program—the University of Chicago Press was founded, libraries were emphasized, departments were encouraged to start journals, and top faculty were recruited from around the nation. Chernow writes that Harper "raided so many Ivy League faculties . . . that his ransacked rivals complained of foul play."[11] Nine college presidents were on the first faculty. Additionally, the University of Chicago did not discriminate against Jews. Though the only available data are from a somewhat later period and pertain to undergraduates rather than graduate students, close to one-third of Chicago undergraduates during the 1930s were Jewish. As a result of quotas limiting Jews elsewhere, this was "the sociological fact that made the College of the University of Chicago unique in the country,"[12] according to university historian William McNeill. The university was coed from the beginning, which was the emerging direction in higher education. African Americans and Asians were not prevented from enrolling, but constituted less than 2 percent of enrollment by the early 1930s.[13]

Adler also noted that in 1895, Harper said:

> It is not enough that instructors in a university should merely do the class and lecture work assigned them. This is important, but the university will in no sense deserve the name, if time and labor are not also expended in the work of producing that which will directly or indirectly influence thought and life outside the University. . . . The true university is the center of thought on every problem connected with human life and work, and the first obligation resting upon the individual members who compose it is that of research and investigation.[14]

As Adler then said: "Steadfast devotion to and brilliant performance of this mission brought Chicago fair renown in the first ten years of its existence."[15]

The first chair of what originally was the Department of Political Economy was James Laurence Laughlin. An outstanding teacher, he believed that the goal of education should be "acquisition of independent power and methods of work . . . rather than specific beliefs."[16] He was a strong proponent of the gold standard. He provided significant academic, practical, and popular support for the Federal Reserve Act of 1913. He had close links with the Republican Party.

According to Chicago school of economics historian Johan Van Overtveldt: "Laughlin's foundation of economics were the classical views of Adam Smith, David Ricardo, and above all, John Stuart Mill."[17] Laughlin received his PhD from Harvard, where he taught from 1878 to 1888, establishing himself as a staunch opponent of government intervention in the economy and as a proponent of laissez-faire. He founded a Political Economy Club at Harvard—among its members was Sumner.

Laughlin edited an abridged version of Mill's *Principles of Political Economy* in 1884. This edition of Mill's *Principles* contributed to Mill's interpretation in the United States as almost a strictly conservative economist. In Britain, on the other hand, through the Fabian Society and for other reasons, the more socialist of Mill's views became more emphasized. The importance of *Principles of Political Economy,* which was first published in 1848 and the sixth and final edition of which appeared in 1868, should be properly estimated. Though Mill tends to be remembered today more for *On Liberty* and *Utilitarianism,* he perhaps exerted his greatest influence in the nineteenth century through *Principles of Political Economy.* It was and is one of the great classics in world economics literature.

In his abridged edition of Mill's work, Laughlin stressed the importance of Smith's *Wealth of Nations.* Laughlin prepared a "Sketch of the History of Political Economy" which he used to introduce Mill's *Principles.* Laughlin here said that a "connected and comprehensive grasp of principles was the great achievement of Adam Smith," and that the *Wealth of Nations* had been the "basis of all subsequent discussion and advance in political economy."[18] He said further that a "new period in the history of political economy . . . begins with Adam Smith."[19] With respect to Mill's work, he wrote that it "remains one of the most lucid and systematic books yet published which covers the whole range of the study" of political economy and that the *Principles* was the "best systematic treatise"[20] of the subject.

In several respects, Laughlin's edition of Mill's work looked to the future of the discipline of political economy rather than to the past. The book was prepared for an American audience, and it was specifically geared toward college students. Interestingly, Laughlin's work introduced twenty-four charts of a statistical nature to elucidate and expand Mill's views to concern American circumstances. Regarding the then-nascent mathematization of economic theory, Laughlin had little positive to say. In his introduction, he remarked concerning Mill and others that "Professor W. Stanley Jevons put himself in opposition to the methods of the men just mentioned, and applied the mathematical process to political economy, but without reaching new results."[21] The relatively nonmathematical presentation of economic theory—as distinct from the presentation of statistical data—has remained a distinctive hallmark of most of the Chicago economists considered here.

According to Laughlin, Smith held that a "plan for the regulation of industry by the Government was indefensible, and that to direct private persons how to employ their capital was either harmful or useless. He taught that a country will be more prosperous if its neighbors are prosperous."[22] A free market requires a large private sector. A free market, however, is not inconsistent with, and indeed has usually coincided with, a substantial role for government. The free market and a large, but not all-encompassing, government role have historically gone hand in hand in democratic societies during the industrial and more recent eras.

With Rockefeller setting the reputation of the University of Chicago among the general public and Laughlin as the head professor in the Department of Political Economy for its first twenty-four years, it is little wonder that Chicago developed a conservative reputation in the emerging academic discipline of economics. Like many of his outstanding successors at Chicago (though from a different perspective), Laughlin emphasized the importance of money in economic activity. He perceptively observed in his historical introduction to Mill's *Principles of Political Economy* that it is "worth notice that the first glimmerings of political economy came to be seen through . . . discussions on money, and the extraordinary movements of gold and silver"[23] to Europe as a result of Spanish and Portuguese colonization of the Americas.

Laughlin taught in and chaired the Department of Political Economy at Chicago until 1916, and continued scholarly and public activities until his death in 1933. He stood aloof for a number of years from the fledgling American Economic Association, which helped create an early professional separation between Chicago and the rest of the profession that continued at different times in different ways, although this is no longer the case. Among the influential economists he gathered or who emerged at Chicago during his tenure were Thorstein Veblen, Wesley Clair Mitchell, John M. Clark, and Jacob Viner—all of whom became leading American economists during the first half of the twentieth century.

Laughlin strongly advocated a business school at Chicago and founded the *Journal of Political Economy.* He was a Christian, and remarked in his early economics textbook, *The Elements of Political Economy* (1887): "Christian character lies at the basis of industrial progress. To obtain self-mastery, to learn how to adapt one's powers to a given end, to regard the higher and unseen good of the future as above the lower and seen enjoyment of the present . . . —this will enable one to reach a place far above that from which one started out in life."[24] According to historian of economic thought Richard Ebeling, Laughlin "set the tone for much of the department for the next hundred years."[25]

The use of the name "Department of Political Economy" rather than "Department of Economics" merits notice. Though treatises on politics have existed since at least Plato's *Republic,* major works on economics did not really come into existence until the 1600s or so. Thomas Hobbes put forward in his great *Leviathan* (1651) that the purpose of social life and community order is "commodious living"—essentially the utilitarian standard of happiness. John Locke, too, in his revolutionary *Second Treatise of Civil Government* (1689), grounded the purpose of social order in personal happiness, provided the best justification of private property to this day, and enunciated the labor theory of value, among other contributions. But Hobbes's and Locke's works were mostly on politics.

As nation-states emerged in the sixteenth through nineteenth centuries, and, vitally, the spirit of the age became more secular, individualist, industrial, and urban, consideration of economic topics proceeded apace. The word "economics" derives from two Greek words—*eco*, meaning house, and *nomos,* meaning law. Economics originally referred to the art of household management. In time, the term took on a more general connotation, and in 1767 the first work in English to use "political economy" in its title appeared, Sir James Steuart's *Inquiry into the Principles of Political Economy.* Nine years later, Smith's *The Wealth of Nations* was published.

Smith's work was followed by others in the same direction, including works by Jeremy Bentham, John Stuart Mill, James Mill, David Ricardo, and Thomas Malthus. All of these figures wrote on political economy, which was pictured as intimately connected to and concerned with public policies and the general welfare. It was Malthus who, more than anyone else, gave economics its dour cast, believing as he did that poverty was inevitable for the great mass of people as a result of overpopulation and limited resources.[26] Darwin was influenced by Malthus in developing the ideas that only some individuals propagate and that there is a struggle for existence. Economic theory was almost exclusively verbal at this time, rather than mathematical or geometric (though Ricardo pointed in a mathematical direction), and focused on national policies. The goal of classical economics was to free emerging economies from the shackles of government and social regulations, traditions, and taxes that inhibited the free exchange of goods and services.

As it developed in the 1800s, economics was an international discipline, comprising many economists from Germany, France, elsewhere in continental Europe, and, later in the century, America, as well as Britain, which was the acknowledged leader in economic theory. Following the "marginal revolution" of the 1870s, economic thought became more explicitly mathematical and was also presented geometrically. As the nineteenth century passed to the twentieth, the phrase "political economy" became replaced by "economics," denoting a change in the subject from what today we call macroeconomics to microeconomics and to the increasing mathematization and professionalization of the field. By the 1930s, "economics" ruled and "political economy" was dead.

The University of Chicago's Department of Political Economy, in addition to being one of the first graduate programs in the nation, was the first separate economics department in North America. Prior to this time, political economy was joined with history and political or social science. Laughlin wrote in the era of the transition from political economy to economics. His work retained more of a practical, public policy emphasis, as does that of some of his best Chicago successors, than that of many economists since his time.

From its beginning, many of the most prominent economists in America were associated with the University of Chicago. Thorstein Veblen was quite probably the most famous American economist in the first quarter of the twentieth century. He taught at Chicago longer than at any other institution during his tumultuous career, which was littered with sex scandals—Veblen had an eye for women (and traveled, to great criticism, unchaperoned with one across the Atlantic while at Chicago). Nonetheless, he achieved intellectual prominence, particularly through the *Theory of the Leisure Class* (1899), a blistering attack on commercial advertising, the rich, and "conspicuous consumption."[27] He was the first managing editor of the *Journal of Political Economy*. He was considered one of the leaders in, as well as inspirations of, the emerging institutional movement in economics, which adopted a more historical and sociological, rather than theoretical and mathematical, approach.

Veblen was very opposed to the existing order of his day, which he saw as rigged for the rich and against the poor. He wrote in *The Vested Interests and the Common Man* (1919) that the "ownership of large wealth controls the markets and thereby controls the conditions of life for those who have to resort to the markets to sell or to buy." He noted as well that "the population of . . . civilized countries now falls into two main classes: those who own wealth . . . and those who do not."[28] Perhaps more than anyone else in America, he criticized the notion that the rich are entitled to or merit their great wealth, or spend it wisely. He also introduced the idea of the wastefulness of advertising, which formed an important part of the negative critique of capitalism in the middle decades of the twentieth century. Social writer Stuart Chase wrote in 1934 of Veblen that his "thesis is simple. People above the line of bare subsistence . . . do not use the surplus, which society has given them, primarily for useful purposes. They do not seek to expand their own lives, to live more wisely, intelligently, understandingly, but to impress other people with the fact that they have a surplus."[29]

Veblen was highly regarded in the early decades of the twentieth century, even though his contributions are now appraised very differently and his popular fame is almost nonexistent. Business editor Virgil Jordan said in the early 1930s that Veblen's "influence upon the present economic, political, and social situation and upon current governmental policies has probably been greater than that of any other American thinker. No one can fully understand what is happening today in this country without knowing something about Veblen and his thought."[30] A number of Franklin Roosevelt's top academic advisers were familiar with or had read Veblen.

Among those who influenced Veblen were Spencer and Sumner, who was Veblen's teacher. Darwin's views of evolutionary change had descended on the academic mind like a thunderclap. Veblen wrote in *The Theory of the Leisure Class:* "The life of man in society, just like the life of other species, is a struggle for existence, and therefore it is a process of selective adaptation. The evolution of social structures has been a process of natural selection of institutions. The progress which has been made and is being made in human institutions . . . may be set down, broadly, to a natural selection of the fittest habits of thought."[31] Unlike social Darwinists, though, economic institutionalists such as Veblen emphasized the role of human agency in determining social ways and norms, and did not see the results of a social order as necessarily reflecting the natural order.

Wesley Clair Mitchell was a commanding figure in American economics and more generally in the social sciences in the first half of the twentieth century. One of Laughlin's doctoral students and a young instructor at Chicago, he later moved to Columbia University and founded the National Bureau of Economic Research, two institutions that have been closely interconnected with economists who also studied or have taught at the University of Chicago. Mitchell was born in 1874 and made contributions in several fields and to several institutions. His most significant association was with the National Bureau of Economic Research, where he served as director of research for many years. In his role with the National Bureau, he guided many economists in their research programs. He influenced them toward his methodological approach stressing empiricism and measurement, usually through statistics.[32] His primary field of personal research was economic fluctuations, in which his *Business Cycles* (1913) was a leading work for years. He was also a great historian of economic ideas. He died in 1948.

Mitchell provided one of the best justifications of free market capitalism, discussing the use of money:

> It is the foundation of that complex system of prices to which the individual must adjust his behavior in getting a living. . . . Individuals who possessed superior aptitude for making money came to the fore in all walks of life. . . . The new leaders found many chances to

exploit others and took advantage of them; but, broadly speaking, men who are trying to make money are the servants of consumers—that is, of the whole society. . . . In this sense, the money economy gradually put the task of making goods under the directions of men who provided most efficiently what solvent consumers wished to buy, and whose continued leadership depended on maintaining their efficiency."[33]

The justification of capitalism, in Mitchell's view, is its technical efficiency. It is a purely utilitarian system.

To a greater extent than most in the profession, a number of Mitchell's intellectual descendants at Chicago were not enamored with standard neoclassical theory. As Thomas Stapleford remarks: "One of Mitchell's more famous methodological statements was his 1924 presidential address to the American Economic Association in which he dismissed neoclassical theory as an unrealistic creation of armchair philosophers and outlined a new vision for economics founded on extensive empirical study."[34] Both Hayek and Friedman were students of Mitchell—Hayek when he was a graduate student in New York for a year from Vienna in 1923–1924 and Friedman in the 1930s and 1940s when he studied at Columbia and later was affiliated with the National Bureau of Economic Research. Mitchell opposed the mathematization of economic theory, though he employed statistical data to great effect. There is a great and real difference between the use of numerical and statistical data in economic arguments and the mathematical (as distinct from verbal) presentation of economic *theory*.

It merits emphasis again that "classical liberalism" is not "libertarianism" as the latter term is used today. It is important to be crystal clear on this point. Both Hayek and Friedman—the two greatest classical liberals and libertarians in the twentieth century—used the word "libertarianism" to denote the classical liberal view put forward here for much of their careers, although each became significantly more radical with age, particularly Friedman. Whereas contemporary political and economic libertarianism has come to mean the virtual elimination of government, classical liberalism does not typically refer to a certain extent of government, although it favors less government rather than more, direct services at the local level rather than indirect services at the national level, and private initiative rather than state control, as well as government activity at the national level. Classical liberalism recognizes that there is a wide and appropriate area for government activity in a prosperous and just modern society. Classical liberalism affirms the value of greater equality in properly ordered economies and societies, and attempts to foster equality.

By way of contrast, contemporary libertarianism too often denotes cranky obscurantism, intolerance, irrelevance, and, frankly, poor scholarship and the manipulation of data, although these are not always the case or unique to it. Contemporary libertarianism is a dead dogma. It is hostile to new ideas. There is an official creed, and there are heretics to it. Many of the arguments and positions of contemporary libertarians have not changed an iota for decades. There is little value placed on new ideas or different outlooks. Practicality often means little, if anything—indeed, many contemporary libertarians are proud to consider their beliefs impractical or of little relevance. There is no reason to compromise on anything. They are utopians working toward and often living in a mythical land, "Libertania."

New information or new circumstances hardly affect many contemporary libertarians' views at all—different perspectives rarely merit consideration or engagement. Moreover, that some ideas are of enduring worth does not mean that all public policy positions are carved in stone, as many contemporary libertarians appear to believe. Many contemporary libertarians are, it must be said, ideological crackpots and even charlatans. They impugn the motives and character of their opponents and present caricatures of their views. Their works, even when intended otherwise, are essentially polemical rather than scholarly and empirical. They are one-sided in presentation, and emotional rather than intellectual in substance if not tenor.

James Heckman, perhaps the leading Chicago economist today in the classical liberal tradition, writes of some economists:

> A great weakness of many bright people is their frequent inability to distinguish between agreement with their personal views and genuine intelligence and creativity. A second-tier group of people at Chicago, selected more for their agreeability than their creativity or originality, left much to be desired. Often rabidly political, they were careless with data and careless with theory. However, they concurred with the masters and were valued as disciples or co-religionists to spread the truth.[35]

According to the conservative author Russell Kirk in 1981: "The representative libertarian of this decade is humorless, intolerant, self-righteous, badly schooled, and dull."[36] Political scientist and Senator John East wrote: "The new ideological libertarianism is anti-state and seems bent on excursions into the mindless, chaotic, and disoriented world of anarchy."[37] Brink Lindsey, perhaps the most open-minded and tolerant of contemporary libertarians, remarks specifically of the Libertarian Party: "Far too rationalistic and utopian ever to appeal to mass tastes," it "quickly sank into crankish obscurity and irrelevance."[38]

These are hard words, but it is the mark of a living and vibrant doctrine that it seeks to engage with alternative perspectives and, as accurate, incorporate them. "Toleration," according to the great John Locke, is the "chief characteristic mark of the true Church."[39] A vibrant and living doctrine—particularly one in the realm of economic and political thought—does not pretend to be 100 percent right all the time on all issues, and it is not dogmatic. By way of contrast, it is dead dogmas that require no new light. All thought evolves and develops.

To many, perhaps most, contemporary libertarians, the thought that other ideas, values, or perspectives might have worth or should be considered would be quite foreign and strange. The intellectual conformity and intolerance of contemporary libertarianism toward new ideas and information, and disdain for relevance, were not always such. Classical liberals once genuinely, respectfully, and thoughtfully evaluated and debated ideas other than their own or minor variants from them, and considered relevance to practical circumstances to be among the most important elements of theories and public policies.

The purpose of this extended discussion of contemporary libertarianism is to emphasize how different in policy and, especially, spirit it is from the classical liberalism of most historical Chicago economists. "Classical liberalism," as the term is used here, is very different than "contemporary libertarianism." It is possible for intelligent people of good will to differ and change their minds. They do all the time.

Henry Simons wrote in *A Positive Program for Laissez Faire* (1934):

> Liberals cannot wisely or hopefully oppose all "socialistic" experimentation; they should not fear its possible successes. . . . Libertarian prophecies of impending doom, save from global war, are as romantic as adolescent-radical notions of how all social problems can be solved. The development of political-economic institutions, if not altogether like that of language, is not altogether different either. Hysteria is unbecoming of liberals; they must have faith in social process and in the durability of liberty; for their kind of society simply cannot be promoted by revolutions and counterrevolutions. A liberal screams (or despairs) only as an apostate.[40]

John Maurice Clark was the son of John Bates Clark, who was the leading American economist during the last decades of the nineteenth century and first decades of the twentieth. John B. Clark was sometimes referred to as the "American Marshall," after the British economist Alfred Marshall, usually considered to be the leading economist in the world at the time. Both Marshall and John B. Clark were neoclassicists. They incorporated modern marginal utility theory into an essentially classical liberal political point of view, supporting a substantial role for government. John M. Clark taught at Chicago from 1915 to 1926, before joining his father at Columbia, where the son became a leading institutionalist who combined his work with traditional economic theory. It is a reflection of early economics at Chicago that Cornell economist Paul Homan identified the three leading American economists in 1928 as John B. Clark, Thorstein Veblen, and Wesley Mitchell,[41] each of whom (John B. Clark at a remove) had substantial Chicago connections.

Other economists affiliated early with the University of Chicago included Herbert Davenport, Charles Hardy, Alvin Johnson, Robert Hoxie, Leon Marshall, and Walton Hamilton. Marshall was the chair of the Department of Political Economy from 1916 to 1928 following Laughlin's retirement in 1916. His focus was business. Davenport was an early Chicago student and teacher with sound theoretical proclivities. He introduced subjectivist elements to price theory. Hardy was another student and teacher at Chicago; like Davenport, he influenced the emerging Frank Knight theoretically. Johnson, another teacher at Chicago, became a leading figure in the social sciences on the moderate left. Hoxie was a labor economist on the far left. Hamilton was an early institutionalist.

Other prominent scholars in other fields associated with the University of Chicago in its early years included philosopher and education reformer John Dewey, social psychologist and philosopher George Herbert Mead, astronomer George E. Hale, archaeologist and historian James Breasted, physicist Albert Michelson (the first American Nobel Prize winner in the sciences), sociologist Robert Park, and political scientist Charles Merriam. The university's campus over time became located on the equivalent of about 25 blocks separated in two parts by the "Midway," a long, eight-to ten-block park area, with major thoroughfares running through it. The bulk of the campus is on the northern side of the Midway. About 10,000 students, disproportionately graduate students, have typically attended the university—which has many Gothic-style, impressive, and oversized buildings—once it became established.

According to economic historian John Nef (who later founded and ran Chicago's Committee on Social Thought), the Department of Political Economy obtained its commitment to ideological and philosophical diversity from Laughlin. Nef wrote in 1934:

> A very considerable portion of all the men who have made an important mark in economic thought between 1895 and 1930, beginning with Thorstein Veblen and coming down to Jacob Viner . . . , were connected at one time or another, as members or students, with the Department of Political Economy. . . . Laughlin frequently chose the best men when they were of very different persuasions from his own. . . . And so it came about that one of the most conservative heads of an economics department in the country had politically the most liberal and economically the least orthodox department.[42]

Historian of economic thought Malcolm Rutherford observes that for "most economists the terms 'Chicago economics' and 'institutionalism' denote clearly antithetical approaches to the discipline." However, Rutherford also writes, in the "period up to 1918 the Economics Department at Chicago contained, at various times, virtually all of those individuals most closely associated with the founding of the institutionalist movement"—including Veblen, Hoxie, Mitchell, Hamilton, and John M. Clark—and thus Chicago has a "strong claim to be seen as the birthplace of what became known as institutionalist economics."[43]

According to historian of economic thought A. W. Coats, during Laughlin's long tenure as head of the Department of Political Economy at Chicago from 1892 to 1916, the department became a "leading center and breeding ground of economic heterodoxy."[44] Stigler, too, emphasized intellectual diversity as among the department's early features.[45] The evidence is clear that the economics department at Chicago historically has been a very diverse place. This came about, Friedman argued, because of an insistence from the start that "intellectual quality and intellectual quality alone be the basis of appointments to the faculty."[46]

In addition to his emphasis on intellectual quality, Laughlin stressed research and teaching. Intellectual quality, intellectual diversity, focus on practical issues and public policy, and quality teaching were all parts of Laughlin's legacy to Chicago economics from the perspective of the Department of Economics. His contribution to the perception of conservatism in economics at Chicago derived from his severe economic liberalism and ties to the Republican Party. Coats noted Chicago's "early reputation as a center of economic conservatism,"[47] as a result of Rockefeller and Laughlin, despite the actual intellectual heterogeneity of its economics faculty.

The University of Chicago became perhaps the greatest university in the world during the twentieth century. In a rare address at Chicago in 1897, Rockefeller said of his contributions to the university: "It is the best investment I ever made in my life."[48] At its centennial in 1991, more than sixty individuals affiliated with the university had received Nobel Prizes, including more than twenty-five in physics. Since then, more than twenty additional individuals associated with the University of Chicago have received Nobel Prizes. The official number of Chicago Nobelists, as of 2014, is eighty-nine, with representation in all of the six Nobel categories. Twenty-eight Chicago students, researchers, and faculty have received the Nobel Prize in Economic Sciences since it was first given in 1969. More great minds and scholars in many disciplines have been associated with the University of Chicago than with any other institution. Especially in economics, the University of Chicago has dominated the field.

It bears emphasis that Nef wrote as early as 1934 that Chicago economics, to that time, had consisted of many leaders in economics. From its inception, the University of Chicago has dominated economics in the United States; and in time, the world.

2

JACOB VINER AS CLASSICAL LIBERAL

JACOB VINER, known to his friends as Jack and to his family as Jake, was born in Montreal in 1892. His parents were Jewish immigrants to Canada from Romania. He attended McGill University in Canada as an undergraduate and then went to Harvard for graduate work, where he became a favorite student of Frank Taussig, one of the leading lights in economics of the era. Viner began to teach at the young age of twenty-four at the University of Chicago in 1916. Following the United States' entry into World War I in 1917, he worked at the US Tariff Commission in Washington, DC, under Taussig, and then at the US Shipping Board until 1919, when he returned to Chicago. Viner was marked as an economics up-and-comer from a young age. As historian of economic thought Henry Spiegel commented, though Viner worked and consulted for government agencies throughout his career, he was "foremost an academic." Spiegel also perceptively noted that the economics profession during the earlier part of Viner's career was "essentially a 'wasp' establishment."[1]

Viner's works comprise a broad array of contributions from the 1920s through the 1960s in economic theory and the history of economic thought. He was a true classical liberal and internationalist. He was raised on a diet of classical, Millian, and Marshallian economics. Unlike some of his successors at Chicago, he believed that liberalism, and economics more generally, is not a stationary but an evolutionary creed, and that institutions and policies that are beneficial in one era may not be in others. Moreover, and vitally, he sanctioned a greater positive role for government than some of his most prominent Chicago successors. Viner had no doubt that there was no alternative to a substantial government presence in modern societies. He was in no way what is here called a contemporary libertarian—an advocate of neoanarchism. Indeed, Viner consistently and repeatedly rejected, throughout his career, the position of contemporary libertarianism, which he considered to be almost unworthy of an economist or genuine liberal.[2]

Paul Samuelson—who was the first American to win the Nobel Prize in Economics in 1970, the second year the award was given—was an undergraduate at Chicago from 1931 to 1935. In a 1991 remembrance of Viner on the University of Chicago's hundredth anniversary, Samuelson wrote that there was not one but "two Chicago schools. The first Chicago school was that of Knight, Viner, and Simons. It advocated use of the market, but recommended redistributive taxes and transfers to mitigate the worst inequalities of the *laissez faire* system. It pragmatically favored macroeconomic policies in the areas of credit and fiscal policies to attenuate the amplitude of cyclical fluctuations."[3] James Buchanan, who was a graduate student at Chicago immediately after World War II and received the Nobel Prize in Economics in 1986, made reference to "the original, or pre-Friedman, 'Chicago School.'"[4]

The first Chicago school—though no explicit "Chicago school" in economics was identified until after World War II—had a very different perspective from the view that emerged starting in the late 1940s. According to social scientist Dieter Plehwe: "A specific Chicago version of young and radical neoliberalism emerged during the 1950s, which differed markedly . . . from the liberalism of the older generation of Chicago-based scholars."[5] According to Don Patinkin, who was an undergraduate and then doctoral student at Chicago from 1941 to 1947, Viner and Knight were "less doctrinaire" in their views than some of their "younger colleagues and followers."[6] Later work of some Chicagoans should be considered in significant ways a departure from rather than continuation of historical Chicago views. Historically, in the person of Viner and others, Chicago was imbued with the classical liberal outlook, philosophy, policies, and spirit.

Viner embraced classical liberalism. Eugene Rotwein wrote in 1983 that there was a "significant difference between the early—or principally prewar—and the postwar Chicago school (whose most prominent spokesmen have been Milton Friedman and George Stigler). . . . [O]n the whole the position of the early group is . . . more moderate and eclectic than that of later Chicago."[7] Rotwein called attention to a number of statements by Viner that established him in the classical liberal camp. Especially because many contemporary libertarians take their extreme antigovernment positions for granted (or, in some cases, amazingly, derive them from self-evident, deductive premises— Ludwig von Mises's "praxeology"), it is worthwhile to review Viner's thoughts on the appropriate comprehensive role of government, as well as for their intrinsic merit.

Viner delivered a lecture in 1927, "Adam Smith and *Laissez Faire*," to commemorate the 150th anniversary of the *Wealth of Nations*. In this lecture, Viner—already "world-famous"[8] in the economics profession, according to Samuelson—summarized Smith's position, also giving his own:

> Adam Smith was not a doctrinaire advocate of *laissez faire*. He saw a wide and elastic range of activity for government, and he was prepared to extend it even farther . . . He attributed great capacity to serve the general welfare to individual initiative applied in

competitive ways to promote individual ends. . . . But even in his own day . . . Smith saw that self-interest and competition were sometimes treacherous to the public interest they were supposed to serve, and he was prepared to have government exercise some measure of control over them . . . He did not believe *laissez faire* was always good, or always bad. It depended on circumstances . . . In these days of contending schools, each of them with the deep . . . conviction that it, and it alone, knows the one and only path to economic truth, how refreshing it is to return to the *Wealth of Nations* with its eclecticism, its good temper, its common sense, and its willingness to grant that those who saw things differently from itself were only partly wrong.[9]

He said later, speaking at the second Henry Simons Lecture at the University of Chicago Law School in 1959:

There is a great variety of species and degrees of liberty, interrelated in complex and changing patterns of mutual dependence, of mutual reinforcement, of rivalry, of conflict . . . and particular species of liberty can have widely different significance for individuals differing in their psychological make-up and in their material circumstances. Even if liberty in some general sense were the one supreme and absolute good for all men, it would still remain necessary—and often difficult—to seek light on whether the establishment or retention of a particular liberty added to or subtracted from the system of liberties as a whole. . . . Particular liberties may clash, moreover, not only with other liberties, but with other values than liberty, as, for example, individual or national security, prosperity, internal peace and order, equity. The tragic element in decision-making arises often, not from the conflict of good with evil, but from the conflict of true values with each other.

He also said here: "I will carefully avoid using the term *laissez faire* to mean what only unscrupulous or ignorant opponents of it and never its exponents make it mean, namely, philosophical anarchism, or opposition to any government power or activity whatsoever."[10]

Viner strongly affirmed the intrinsic value of democracy:

> If freedom means freedom from coercion, freedom is not of this earth. But if the coercion is to be consistent with liberalism, it must come from natural forces or if it is exercised through particular persons or institutions wielding "authority," whether political or economic, that authority must be derived by what we would regard as democratic political processes from the individuals against whom it is exercised, must be subject to withdrawal by these individuals at their pleasure in the aggregate, and therefore has to be exercised within the limits and restraints imposed by this necessity of constantly obtaining popular approval or consent.[11]

He was not among those who see private property as the only distinguishing mark of a free society—democracy, too, is essential. In this respect as well, Viner differentiated himself from some contemporary libertarians, who are increasingly tepid supporters of democracy.

Viner was more moderate in both economics and politics than some of his Chicago successors. He also wrote:

> There is another important field for government activity which was not stressed sufficiently, I believe, by the founders of economic liberalism, which is urgent even in the United States, and which for countries like China and India probably constitutes the most important single element in the planning of a sound liberal society; that is, to overcome the inertia of individuals where that inertia is the result of inadequate education, of bad health, of bad nutrition, of regional isolation, of bad traditions, and above all of the operation of the great vicious circle of modern society, poverty breeding poverty, bequeathing it to the children, and thus cutting off their access to health, to knowledge, to reasonable education . . .

> It is the major positive economic function of the liberal state to discover the pockets (and they may be more than pockets; they may be great areas) of undeveloped productive capacity on the part of individuals and by non-coercive methods to raise their serviceability to themselves and to society. This calls for education, for health work, for guidance and subsidization . . . [12]

Historians of economic thought Robert Van Horn, Philip Mirowski, and Thomas Stapleford write in their introduction to *Building Chicago Economics* (2011): "The founders of the postwar Chicago school (including Friedman, Stigler, and Aaron Director) departed quite sharply from the classical liberalism that had animated their mentors at the university."[13] According to Ross Emmett, the leading Knight scholar: "The [Chicago] school is largely a postwar phenomenon."[14] Friedman scholar J. Daniel Hammond writes: "Within a short time after the end of the Second World War the University of Chicago economics faculty was transformed."[15] According to David Laidler, another historian of economic thought: "When all is said and done, the Chicago monetary tradition of the late 1960s was more homogeneous, more distinctive, and more the product of the ideas and energy of one man [Friedman] than anything that had been seen in the interwar years,"[16] again belying notions of continuity and homogeneity between prewar and postwar economics at Chicago.

Historian Angus Burgin writes in his excellent *The Great Persuasion: Reinventing Free Markets since the Depression* (2012) that, in contradistinction to the contemporaneous opinions of Friedrich Hayek, Lionel Robbins (who later in his career changed his views), and others at the London School of Economics—who put forward an Austrian theory of economic fluctuations during the Great Depression—Chicago economists, including Viner, Knight, and Simons, "developed a more moderate response to the events of the time. All three were quick to denounce the excesses of *laissez faire,* and they varyingly embraced the prospect of public works projects, progressive taxation, social insurance, and vigorous antitrust policies."[17] Martin Bronfenbrenner, who was a graduate student in economics at Chicago in the middle 1930s, wrote as early as 1962, prefiguring Samuelson's later remarks: "There are not one but two Chicago schools; the departure of Jacob Viner and the passing of Henry Simons are the watersheds between them."[18]

With respect to his membership in a Chicago school of economics before his 1946 departure to Princeton, Viner said in a 1969 letter to Patinkin:

> It was not until after I left Chicago . . . that I began to hear rumors about a "Chicago School" which was engaged in *organized* battle for *laissez faire* and "quantity theory of money" and against "imperfect competition" theorizing and "Keynesianism." I remained skeptical about this until I attended a conference sponsored by University of Chicago professors in 1951. . . . From then on, I was willing to consider the existence of a "Chicago School" (but one not confined to the economics department and not embracing all of the department). . . . But at no time was I consciously a member of it.[19]

In another letter in 1969, to Bronfenbrenner, Viner recalled: "I had little discussion with my colleagues, and absolutely none with my students, about what my colleagues taught, and in fact I had only vague notions of the drift of their teaching. . . . [L]ack of participation and interest then and lapse of memory since make me an ill-equipped reporter on the beginnings of the 'Chicago School.'"[20] In a 1967 letter, Viner wrote that when he was at Chicago: "I do not think that I was ever conscious of a 'Chicago School,' and I certainly was not conscious of being a member of any 'school,' except that I was very much in the 'neoclassical' tradition."[21]

Emmett, commenting on Viner's 1969 letter to Patinkin, says: "The notion of an organized school of thought at Chicago could, at best, only be said to be gradually emerging prior to 1945." Emmett also holds that the "term 'school' is really only applicable to Chicago in the post-war, and perhaps even post-1950, period,"[22] and that economics at Chicago has been "far more diverse than common descriptions of the Chicago school allow."[23] Economist Arthur Bloomfield, who was a graduate student at Chicago in the late 1930s, recalled: "When I was at Chicago I never heard of, nor suspected the existence of, a 'Chicago school' of economics. On the contrary, I was then impressed by the diversity of thinking and interests of the individual faculty members."[24] According to historian of economic thought Donald Winch, who was a student of Viner at Princeton, Viner "cannot be assimilated within any of the obvious doctrinal or ideological groupings"—Winch notes in particular that Viner was not "a member of what has become known as the 'Chicago School.'"[25]

The fact of the matter is that there was no Chicago school of economics before the return of the 1930s graduate students Milton Friedman, Aaron Director, and Allen Wallis to the University of Chicago as faculty in the fall of 1946. The birth of the Chicago school of economics may be dated to that time. Had Friedman, in particular, never returned to Chicago, there never would have been a Chicago school of economics in the popular and academic minds.

Burgin provides this description of the views of Viner, Knight, and Simons during the 1930s, juxtaposing them with less temperate opinions elsewhere. The three Chicagoans were

all eager to distance their approach from the more extreme views associated with their colleagues in Austria and London. . . . Knight made his opinion clear in a review of Robbins' *Economic Planning and International Order* in 1938 . . . "We confront a picture of *laissez faire* bordering on the conception of a world-wide anarchist utopia," [Knight] remarked, "a vision of universal freedom and brotherhood, if only governments would cease from troubling and politicians go out and die, except for police functions." . . . In a letter to Walter Lippmann in 1937, Henry Simons put his dissatisfactions in still stronger terms. Ludwig von Mises' and Lionel Robbins' "notions regarding the proper spheres of governmental action [...] are often fanatically extreme," he wrote, "and their contribution to the liberal cause, on balance, is probably a disservice." Viner's friendship with Robbins softened his tone, but he, too, expressed concerns in private correspondence about the need for a "stabilizing influence" at the LSE to counteract its economists' "doctrinaire tendencies with respect to methods of analysis and selection of premises." . . . Viner referred to Mises' work as "really eccentric or crank economics," and Knight found it "slightly impatient and dogmatic" and often simply "contrary to facts."[26]

Viner, Knight, and Simons were classical liberals, and it is vital to be clear here. Viner's position was different from the prevailing views on both the left and the right. Most Democrats and contemporaneous liberals were calling for government management and regulation of the economy. This was the purpose of Franklin Delano Roosevelt's "alphabet agencies" in the early New Deal, including the National Industrial Recovery Act (NIRA) and Agricultural Adjustment Act (AAA). Both the NIRA and the AAA gave unprecedented powers to government to control and regulate much private economic decision making. Pursuant to NIRA, industries and businesses were not able to cut prices, increase production, or reduce wages. Essentially, price and production decisions in large sectors of the economy were taken away from the private sector and transferred to the government. Similarly, the AAA established prices and production for agricultural goods. This was the part of the New Deal that Viner, Knight, and Simons opposed so vigorously. They understood that freely fluctuating prices and profits are essential to optimal economic activity. They knew that government cannot run a productive economy and that excessive government control of economic decision making is counterproductive not only to economic output but to personal freedom.

When it came to activist national fiscal and monetary policies in the face of the Great Depression, however, it was an entirely different matter. Here, Chicago economists, including Viner, joined with practically the entire economics profession in the United States and throughout Europe in calling for activist and stimulative fiscal and monetary policies. J. Ronnie Davis, the foremost historian of Chicago economic views in the early 1930s, writes: "Frank H. Knight, Henry Simons, Jacob Viner, and their Chicago colleagues, argued throughout the early 1930s for the use of large and continuous deficit budgets to combat the mass unemployment and deflation of the times."[27] In their advocacy of activist government fiscal and monetary policies, Chicago free market economists differed markedly from their colleagues in London and Vienna, who adopted a do-nothing or hands-off approach by government during the severe political and economic crisis of the Great Depression, which was worse in the United States than elsewhere. Moreover, Viner and others at Chicago were free-traders. They opposed and saw as counterproductive the imposition of tariffs by all nations.

Viner was prescient. Though there is some scholarly debate over the extent to which his views on the Great Depression were similar to those Friedman would enunciate later, Viner said in February 1933 of then-current objections to a more expansionary monetary policy that at no time "since the beginning of the depression has there been for so long as four months a net increase in the total volume of bank credit outstanding. On the contrary, the government and Federal Reserve bank operations have not nearly sufficed to countervail the contraction of credit on the part of the member and non-member banks. There has been no net inflation of bank credit since the end of 1929. There has been instead a fairly continuous and unprecedentedly *great contraction* of credit during this entire period [emphasis added]."[28] As early as 1933, Viner referred to the period from 1929 to 1933 as a "great contraction." This later became Friedman's preferred description for the period.

In 1932, Viner said that the Federal Reserve had "revealed to the outsider no greater capacity [than other national central banks] to formulate a consistent policy, unless a program of drift, punctuated at intervals by homeopathic doses of belated inflation and deflation and rationalized by declarations of impotence, can be accepted as the proper constituents of central bank policy."[29] He also said that while the New York Federal Reserve Bank had "made more effort than any other central banking institution to develop a program and a technique of credit control with a view to stabilization, it has at critical moments found itself at cross-purposes with . . . [the] Federal Reserve Board."[30] This was almost exactly Friedman's later description of the roles of the Federal Reserve and the New York Federal Reserve Bank. "Can," Friedman later asked, "anyone who knows my work read Viner's comments and not see the direct links between them . . . and my *Monetary History* . . . [A]s I have read Viner's talk . . . I have . . . been amazed to discover how precisely it foreshadows the main thesis of . . . *Monetary History* for the depression period."[31]

Friedman recalled being especially influenced by courses with Viner: "Without question, one of the greatest intellectual experiences of my life was the first-quarter course in economic theory with Jacob Viner. This opened my eyes to a world I had not realized existed. I was made aware of both the beauty and the power of formal economic theory,"[32] mostly microeconomic theory. Viner was a "great teacher," Friedman recollected. "He made me realize that economic theory was a coherent, logical whole that held together, that it didn't consist simply of a set of disjointed propositions."[33]

Samuelson remembered Viner's "famous" graduate course in economic theory: "By reputation it was considered the best course in economic theory being given in the America of those days."[34] Samuelson also wrote: "When I attended the University of Chicago in the early 1930s, it had the best department of economics in the country";[35] and: "There has never been a greater neoclassical economist than Jacob Viner."[36]

Viner was completely a part of the great British-American classical liberal political and economic tradition, which argues that a mostly private sector economy combined with efficient and effective government is the best polity attainable, though it is not completely consistent intellectually or perfect in its structure or outcomes. Viner's emphasis on the price system and its coordinating function in his course on price theory was pathbreaking for its time. He was a leader in the micro-economic movement in early twentieth-century economics, though he later did not keep up with the mathematical revolution in economic theory. He tended to be suspicious of the overmathematization of economic theory and emphasized actual, real-life empirical relevance.

Viner remained at Chicago through the winter quarter of 1946, when he moved to Princeton in part so that he and his wife would be closer to their children. At Princeton, he became interested in religion, somewhat as Knight was at Chicago, but in a different and more systematic manner. Viner's last major work was *Religious Thought and Economic Society,* the first four chapters of which were posthumously published in 1978.

In this work, he traced the history of Christianity and its influence on economics from the early Christian fathers to the link between Protestantism and the rise of capitalism. He emphasized the otherworldliness of early Christian thought. With respect to more modern developments, he noted: "Protestantism, through its emphasis on freedom of individual conscience in interpreting the message of the Gospel, not only placed great emphasis on education, but fostered the development of habits of free examination—all of which was conducive to the growth of civil freedom and economic and cultural progress."[37]

According to Winch, Viner "emerged as the leading economist-scholar of his generation."[38] A popular 1950 account of leading economists in the United States said Viner had the "reputation for being the most brilliant and vitriolic controversialist of the profession."[39] In a reminiscence after Viner's death, Lionel Robbins called him the "outstanding *all-rounder* of his time in our profession."[40] Viner was not a specialist in one field—rather, his domain covered much of the terrain of twentieth-century economics.

Robbins remembered his first personal interaction with Viner, in the later 1920s: "This was a new sort of economist for me: equal to the acutest I had known in speculative thought but with a range of erudition and practical information and a respect for the complexity of fact which I had not met before." Robbins also said that Viner made "significant contributions to pure analysis. He enriched the literature of applied economics. He served his tour of duty as a public servant and adviser. He was a great teacher and a great scholar."[41] Robbins added in his autobiography: "If I were asked to assess his personal qualities, I do not know which I should wish to stress more, his integrity and independence, his argumentative zest and wit, or the catholic moderation of his judgment. In the continuous dialogue which goes on whenever we meet, I am sure that I have learnt more of scholarship and practical wisdom from him than from any other colleague of the last forty years."[42]

Gary Becker, who received the Nobel Prize in Economics in 1992 and was one of Viner's undergraduate students at Princeton, said: "The person who influenced me the most [at Princeton] was a professor who had been at Chicago before, Jacob Viner, who was a very famous economist at the time. He . . . taught graduate courses at Princeton. I took a lot of graduate courses there, even though I was still doing undergraduate studies. So I took two graduate courses taught by Viner and liked them a lot."[43] Becker added that Viner "may have had the greater long-run impact [than Knight] through his emphasis on the empirical relevance of microeconomic theory, and on the necessity of testing a theory with historical and other empirical evidence."[44]

According to Emmett, Viner was "one of America's premier economic theorists in the twentieth century."[45] Emmett also calls Viner a "master economist" and notes that Viner's "contributions to the history of economic thought stretch from re-evaluation of Adam Smith's adherence to a strict *laissez faire* to a reconsideration of the relation between religion and economics."[46] According to historian of economic thought Mark Blaug, Viner was "quite simply the greatest historian of economic thought that ever lived."[47] According to Spiegel, Viner was "without peer"[48] in his work in the history of economic thought.

Rotwein perceptively observes that "unlike the later Chicago school, which treats government as the principal enemy of freedom, Viner (recognizing that freedom from coercion is itself a product of restraints imposed by government) is at least equally concerned with protecting the individual from coercion by other individuals or private agencies." Rotwein observes the "basic incompatibility" between Viner's views and those of later Chicagoans in "their respective perceptions of the economic world and of society in general." He adds: "Viner's general perspective is . . . thoroughly uncongenial to the setting of highly restrictive limits to governmental activity."[49]

Viner served as Bloomfield's dissertation supervisor. He recalled:

> There have always been some differences of opinion about Viner as a person. Many of those who attended his famous course on price theory at the University of Chicago may still remember him mainly for his rough handling . . . of students (although he was not at all like that, I understand, in his Princeton classes, by which time he had mellowed considerably). Some have regarded him as rather arrogant and as one who often antagonized people by his unnecessarily sharp comments or unduly critical remarks. Most of those who knew him well personally, however, take a quite different position. As for myself, I can state quite simply that I regard Jack Viner as one of the kindest, most considerate, most stimulating, and wisest men that I have ever known.[50]

William Baumol, who knew Viner as a colleague at Princeton and who is a past president of the American Economic Association, remembers him as "kindly, warm, witty, and above all, willing to give his energy and time unsparingly to help others in their work."[51] It is a measure of the esteem in which Viner has been held that he has been so highly regarded by so many leading economists. As a valued colleague, he maintained extensive correspondence with many of the most prominent economists in the world for decades.

In addition to his work in academia, he was a consultant to the United States Treasury and State Departments and Federal Reserve for many years. He advised on the establishment of Social Security and trade issues, among other areas. He served as president of the American Economic Association in 1939 and received its prestigious Francis A. Walker Award—given only once every five years, prior to the commencement of the Nobel Prize in Economics—in 1962. Viner served for eighteen years as co-editor with Knight of the Chicago-based *Journal of Political Economy.* It is interesting to observe that unlike most of his Chicago libertarian successors who typically served in or were appointed by Republican administrations, Viner served primarily in Democratic administrations, those of Franklin Roosevelt and Harry S Truman.

In a 1964 essay, "The United States as a 'Welfare State,'" he concluded that the welfare state is "really worth fighting for and dying for as compared to any rival system . . . because, despite its imperfections in theory and practice, in the aggregate it provides more promise of preserving and enlarging human freedoms, temporal prosperity, the extinction of mass misery, and the dignity of man and his moral improvement than any other social system."[52] In a 1965 essay on Adam Smith, he noted that in the *Theory of Moral Sentiments,* Smith referred to "the greatest and noblest of all characters, that of the reformer and legislator of a great state."[53] Like Keynes, Hayek, and others, Viner believed in the power of intellectuals' ideas to change the world.

He characterized his vision of optimal social order as a "society with as completely free and competitive a market as was attainable in the setting of a welfare state in which mass poverty had been eliminated, the business cycle tamed, and opportunity made as equal as was consistent with the survival of private property, the family, and biological differences, as between men, in capacities and motivations. Such a Utopia would be nearer to the modern 'welfare state' than to *laissez faire.*"[54]

3

FRANK KNIGHT
BEFORE CHICAGO

IT IS, IN TRUTH, difficult (at least for this writer) to understand the very high esteem in which Frank Knight—usually considered to be the dean or progenitor of the postwar Chicago school of economics—was, and to some extent still is, held by some of his former students and others. As a colleague, Knight was a bear. His mocking and derisive consideration of others' work was intemperate, counterproductive, and inconsiderate. Although he was unquestionably intelligent, even brilliant, there is no real doctrine or specific public policy proposal that can be attributed to him; his work was more philosophical than in economic theory or public policy. He had a good sense of humor. He was an indifferent family man. He must have been more impressive as a direct teacher than through his writings. There is little in his published work that at least to this writer has lasting or substantial value.

Among the best depictions of Knight as a teacher was by Don Patinkin, who was a graduate student at Chicago in the mid-1940s. He wrote on Knight's death in 1972:

> What is the mark of a great teacher? It is first and foremost the qualities he conveys by his very presence in the classroom: his personal integrity and his intellectual curiosity and stimulation; his humility and his breadth of interests.
>
> And it is, secondly, the insights and understanding—the new way of looking at things—that he transmits to his students. Frequently these insights are original to him; but even when they are not, they reflect his judgment as to what is important in the existing body of knowledge, and hence worthy of emphasis. And it is the mark of a great teacher that the insights he thus passes on to his students do indeed remain important: that they continue to guide their thinking many years later; and that these students in turn consider the insights so important as to wish to pass them on to their own students as well.
>
> In all of these ways Frank Knight was a great teacher.[1]

Little is known of Knight's forebears. His son Horace wrote that his father came from a "family that had some ministers,"[2] who were among the most educated men of their time. Knight's two brothers also went to college at a time when this was unusual (and later became professors of economics, at the University of California at Berkeley and Dartmouth). Their mother knew Greek, in which she instructed her sons for college admission.

Knight's childhood was deeply religious, but he became a devout skeptic. Throughout life, including in childhood and adolescence (though from a somewhat different perspective than would later be the case), he was strenuously anti-Catholic. While growing up, he was a member of the fundamentalist and evangelical Plymouth Brethren, sometimes also called the Christian Church and associated with the Disciples of Christ. With respect to theology, it was and is among the strictest conceptions of Christianity. The Bible is the inerrant, literal word of God. Every word in the Bible is factual and true. Every moment of life should be dedicated and devoted to the Lord and His way.

Knight was too intelligent and too much of a skeptic to adopt a devout, fundamentalist view of the world. His reaction to religion was that of a rationalist in an era bursting with scientific advance. He to some extent retained the absolutism of fundamentalist Christianity, but turned this to a scientific perspective of the world. He did not adhere to the ethical teachings of Christianity. He was a philosophical hedonist who saw the maximization of pleasure or happiness as life's purpose. He was a part of the English-speaking tradition of political philosophers and economists, starting with Hobbes, who created many of the most important societal concepts of modern life.

The story is frequently told how once, after Knight and his younger brothers and sisters had signed pledges in church to be faithful in church attendance for the rest of their lives, he led them to a site behind the family barn and instructed them to burn the pledges, because pledges made under duress are not binding. This story is open to more than one interpretation. It could be and usually is interpreted as depicting what an irreligious youth Knight was. But other interpretations are possible. Knight possessed a highly Protestant conception of free will. He likely attended church every Sunday until college, and even afterward he and his first wife and children were members of the Unitarian Society. Though the story speaks loudly and clearly as to his lack of respect for religious, as other, authority, it also exemplifies a passionate Protestant point of view. Free will and choice are everything.

Knight went to high school for a year and a half in preparation for going to college in the fall of 1905 as he turned twenty. He was something of a late bloomer. He did not receive his PhD until his thirty-first year and did not go to the University of Chicago permanently to teach until turning forty-two. This was at a time, moreover, when these distinctions were more likely to be attained at a younger age than later became the case.

He initially attended college at American University in Harriman, Tennessee. The college was undistinguished. Horace Knight wrote that when his father was enrolled, its "professor of astronomy was a dentist, and its home economics teacher was someone's housekeeper."[3] American did have one chief asset, Frederick Kershner, its dean and professor of the Bible school and modern languages. Religiously conservative, Kershner was politically liberal. Kershner had significant influence on Frank and, indeed, the whole Knight family. After American University closed during Frank's time as a student there (it had "grandiose plans with inadequate funds,"[4] according to Horace Knight), Frank followed Kershner to the latter's new academic position at Milligan College in Tennessee. Later, Frank's younger brother Melvin studied with Kershner, and even, somewhat like Frank, followed Kershner from Milligan to Texas Christian University, when Kershner moved to it. Frank's other brother, Bruce, also attended Texas Christian.

Kershner was an intellectual figure of note in the Disciples of Christ. The Disciples were a part of the restoration movement in nineteenth- and twentieth-century America, seeking to re-create the original church of the decades immediately following Jesus's ministry. Some of Kershner's writings are on the websites of the Disciples today, including a chapter on "The Place of Christian Baptism"; a book, *The Christian Union Overture;* an interpretation of *The Declaration and Address of Thomas Campbell,* the founder of the Disciples; and the foreword to a work on Campbell. These writings reveal Kershner to have been thoughtful, tolerant, and well educated. He had a master's degree in history from Princeton at a time when an advanced degree was rare, and almost had received a fellowship to work on a PhD. As well as his work in theology, he taught foreign languages, including German and French. He was, above all, a religious man.

Knight studied at American University for two years, from 1905 to 1907. Expenses were $125 per year, and rooms were $1 per month. In addition to his classes, he was an assistant in math and science and secretary to the faculty. While at American, he took two courses, in physics and trigonometry, by correspondence from the University of Chicago, his first contact with the university. After his two years at American, he served as secretary to the director of works at the Jamestown, Virginia, exposition.

In 1908, he entered Milligan College, also in Tennessee, to which Kershner moved when American shut its doors and of which he now was president. According to Joseph Dorfman, a leading historian during the middle decades of the twentieth century of American economic thought, Knight was a "one-man Business Department,"[5] teaching bookkeeping, shorthand, typewriting, and commercial law, though he was primarily a student. Knight met the woman who would become his first wife and the mother of his first four children, Minerva Orlena Shelburne, at Milligan in 1908. They married in 1911 on his graduation. Their son, Horace, visited Milligan years later and had these observations: "The college occupies 135 acres and the campus is beautiful. They have strict conservative Christian standards for the behavior of men and women students, and for alcoholic beverages."[6] Undoubtedly, these standards were even more stringent when Frank and Minerva were students.

Milligan offered programs in literature, science, and philosophy when Knight was a student, and he and Minerva took courses in philosophy together. Horace called his parents "brilliant students."[7] Like American University, Milligan was associated with the Disciples of Christ. In the 1910–1911 course catalog, Knight was listed as taking Latin, English, French, math, philosophy, Old and New Testament history, and Christian doctrine and polity. As at American, he worked as a secretary to the faculty.

He first took economics in 1910 at Milligan. The text was Charles Jesse Bullock's well-known *Introduction to the Study of Economics*. Bullock was one of the leading economists at Harvard during the first decades of the twentieth century. In all courses he took at American and Milligan, Knight received very high grades, including in deportment.

His notes from a harmony of the Gospels he possessed at this time provide a fascinating look into his views in his later undergraduate years. Though these indicate that he was a skeptic or doubter, they do not necessarily indicate that he was an atheist, at least not at this time. Knight clearly was wrestling with these issues. The following lines from the New Testament are followed by Knight's handwritten comments:

> Mark 8:34: "If a man would come after me, let him deny himself, and take up his cross, and follow me." How does this bear on the individual and the race? Utilitarian versus idealistic standards of good. Is there any standard of ideals beyond the utilitarian standard? [Knight's underlining]

> Matthew 7:12: "Whatsoever ye would that men should do unto you, even so do ye also unto them: for this is the law and the prophets." But it is not the whole of the Bible nor the best of it . . .

> Matthew 14:20: "And they did all eat, and were filled: and they took up that which remained over of the broken pieces, twelve baskets full." None wasted. Christ economical.

> Luke 19:44: "And they shall not leave in thee one stone upon another: because thou knewest not the time of thy visitation." Punishment for ignorance the same as deliberate transgression. Is there an ultimate distinction between sin and error?

> John 15:12: "This is my commandment, that ye love one another, even as I have loved you." Christ gave no real commandments (Thou shalts).[8]

From an early age, Knight heavily annotated and underlined what he read.

On graduating from Milligan, Kershner wrote on Knight's behalf: "From the standpoint of quickness of perception, or of that rare capacity, which enables a person to 'see through things' almost at a glance, he is the best student I have had." He added that Knight was the best-read student in the college, a top stenographer, and possessed "practical business capacity as well as technical knowledge."[9]

Knight's next academic stop was the University of Tennessee, to which he and Minerva moved for the 1911–1912 academic year, where both were students. Frank received a master's degree there in 1913 at the age of twenty-eight. He majored in German and wrote a master's thesis on Gerhart Hauptmann, a German dramatist who received the Nobel Prize in Literature in 1912 and initiated the naturalist movement in modern German literature. A professor of Knight's remembered him years later as a "brilliant young man, but too pessimistic, too much influenced by Schopenhauer."[10] His one course in economics and two in philosophy in 1912–1913 emphasized the history of economic thought, Adam Smith, Thomas Malthus, David Ricardo, and John Stuart Mill.

Knight was obviously very interested in Germany, and hoped to spend time studying there after receiving his master's degree. However, hoped-for financial support did not materialize. He received a scholarship to study philosophy at Cornell in the fall of 1913 instead, soon transitioning from philosophy to economics. He received his PhD in 1916. He intellectually blossomed at Cornell. The "depth of the knowledge of economic theory that Knight acquired in these few years is simply incredible,"[11] according to George Stigler.

The story of Knight's shift from philosophy to economics, as reported by one of his economics professors, Alvin Johnson, who had previously taught at Chicago, has often been repeated:

> Knight came up from Tennessee, where border-state diet had endowed him with dyspepsia and a graven expression of pessimism. . . . I found him the keenest student of theory I had ever had. When I was elaborating some theoretical subtlety, he would turn on me that gray light of his skeptical eyes, seeming to say, "I don't believe

a word of that." Sometimes he would attack my position, very competently . . .

One day in the spring Knight came to me with an unusually sad face. "Doctor," he said, "I thought . . . I was doing pretty well in my philosophy major. But [James] Creighton called me in and gave me the most frightful hauling over the coals. Said I was totally unfit to study or teach philosophy; indeed, that I ought to drop the idea of teaching anything, for with my attitude I'd do more harm than good. I went to [Frank] Thilly for comfort, and he gave it to me still worse."

I was astonished. Could two such clear-headed philosophers make such a mistake about so promising a student as Knight? I couldn't believe it, I went straight to Creighton.

"Knight?" he said bitterly. "It isn't that he is devoid of ability. But with his ingrained skepticism he repudiates all the values of philosophy. As a teacher or writer he will . . . destroy the true philosophic spirit wherever he touches it . . . We in philosophy will have nothing to do with him."[12]

Johnson was a leading figure in the social sciences and a public intellectual during the first decades of the twentieth century. In addition to teaching, he was editor of the *New Republic* and co-founder of the New School for Social Research in New York, an organization which aided many Jewish intellectuals in emigrating to the United States in the period leading up to World War II. Knight wrote Johnson asking for further details, after the latter's autobiography was published, in which the reminiscence above appeared. Johnson wrote back: "I knew your type. You came out of a malodorous environment where every man with a mind doubts everything. You doubted every statement I made, but that was alright with me . . . But your major professors . . . didn't like it."[13]

Richard Howey emphasized Johnson's role in Knight's development. Knight took two classes with Johnson during the 1913–1914 academic year, "The History of Economic Thought" and "Value and

Distribution." According to Howey, Knight "could and did appreciate Professor Johnson's lectures," noting that the

> topics of these two courses became the ones that Knight taught most often during his own professorial career . . . As Knight did later, Johnson often treated his students to digressions on a range of issues. He never belabored the economic theory of the past: He assigned textbooks in three languages for that purpose. He gave his students their money's worth in . . . his own outspoken memorable remarks—not a presentation that they could come upon elsewhere, even in his own books, where greater discretion prevailed.[14]

Knight took more than one hundred pages of typed, single-spaced notes merely in Johnson's "History of Economic Theory." Excerpts include:

> Man loves to look on his fellow man as a sort of historical document which it is impractical if not impossible to decipher.
>
> The root of all our difficulties is that we profess to regard all men as theoretically equal. Middle Ages avoided this by the happy concept of status.
>
> Hume a philosopher of the fine old type that did not pride itself on not knowing anything. Of all men who ever wrote English prose, Hume the most worth reading. Uses plain English. Makes few assumptions or pretensions. Theory of money stated fairly complete in about 16 pages.
>
> Mill and Adam Smith the only great writers of classical economics. . . . Still true that all the best in classical economics from Smith to 1850 is in Mill.[15]

The major project of Knight's graduate career at Cornell was his dissertation, "The Theory of Business Profits,"[16] which—he wrote in the preface to the rewritten, published version, *Risk, Uncertainty and*

Profit (1921)—was suggested as a "suitable topic for a doctoral dissertation in the spring of 1914 by Dr. Alvin Johnson. . . . The study was chiefly worked out under the direction of Professor Allyn A. Young,"[17] following Johnson's departure from Cornell. Young was an economist of note who was president of both the American Statistical Association and the American Economic Association. He taught at Stanford, Harvard, and the London School of Economics, among other places, as well as at Cornell. He wrote Knight after receiving the final dissertation: "This is by all odds the ablest thesis that has passed through my hands. I suspect that it ought to go a long way toward establishing your reputation as an economist. I have read it with admiration and enjoyment, and really got quite a good deal of intellectual stimulus from it."[18] Knight wrote Young on publication: "Thanks again for your generous words respecting the book; also renewed assurance of my keen realization that whatever merit it has is largely owed to you and that it would have been better if conditions had allowed me to make fuller use of your suggestions. These, however, are not lost by any means as to whatever I do in the future will show their influence."[19] Young later wrote Knight: "I am more and more impressed with the fundamental soundness of the position we both take, namely that the social sciences must be art as well as science, and rather more so."[20]

Risk, Uncertainty and Profit was accepted at Cornell in June 1916, and the next year Knight submitted it to a leading competition of the day among dissertations in economics, in which it received second place. After graduating with his PhD from Cornell, he taught there for one year as an instructor, and then taught at the University of Chicago from 1917 to 1919 as an instructor in economics. Since he had grown up a mere one hundred miles from Chicago, he undoubtedly had been long aware of the University of Chicago and may have been targeting it as his preferred academic location.

Perhaps more important than the teaching experience he then gained was the opportunity to revise his dissertation. He wrote in the published version's preface that he rewrote it entirely at Chicago under the editorial supervision of John M. Clark, then at the university, and that he benefited from discussions there with Charles Hardy. Knight also thanked Viner: "Professor Jacob Viner, of the University of Chicago, has kindly read the proof of the entire work."[21]

Apparently, there never was any professional jealousy or rivalry between Viner and Knight, but neither were they personally close. According to Burgin: "When Knight was at the University of Iowa in the 1920s, they [Viner and Knight] engaged in a notably warm correspondence . . . By 1927, however, Viner began to criticize Knight's increasing preoccupation with the assumptions that lay at the foundations of social-scientific analysis. . . . They were not close personal friends and communicated rarely in the years after Viner's postwar transfer to Princeton."[22] Viner was among those who strongly supported offering Knight a position at Chicago in 1927 to replace John M. Clark.

Risk, Uncertainty and Profit led to Knight's prominence in the economics profession. According to Hayek, the work "became, and for many years continued to be, one of the most influential textbooks on economic theory, although it had not originally been designed as such."[23] According to Emmett, the book established Knight's reputation as one of the best theorists in America.[24] Knight attempted to modify and develop economic theory, examining and explaining how profit arises. His leading idea was that profit is not a result of the cost of production or even risk. Rather, the source of profit is uncertainty, which is indeterminate—unlike risk, which is knowable, measurable, and insurable. Profit comes from guessing right in circumstances of uncertainty.

Following an American economic tradition stemming from American business history, Knight emphasized the vital role of the entrepreneur: "The particular technical contribution to the theory of free enterprise which this essay . . . make[s] is a fuller and more careful examination of the role of the entrepreneur or enterpriser."[25] The successful entrepreneur possesses effective economic insight over time, which is the source of his or her profit.

Knight considered himself to be, like Mill, "an empiricist," maintaining that experience is fundamental to all reasoning. Knight also said he was a "radical empiricist in logic, which is to say, as far as theoretical reasoning is concerned, an agnostic on all questions beyond the fairly immediate facts of experience."[26] Just as some of Friedman's work in monetary theory is prefigured in Viner's work, some of Friedman's work in methodology is adumbrated in Knight's writings. Thirty years before Friedman outlined his approach in "The Methodology of Positive Economics," Knight wrote in *Risk, Uncertainty and Profit*: "The aim of science is to predict the future for purpose of making our conduct intelligent," noting the importance of "mak[ing] actual predictions."[27] Friedman's parallel statement was: "The ultimate goal of a positive science is the development of a 'theory' or 'hypothesis' that yields valid and meaningful (i.e., not truistic) predictions about phenomena not yet observed."[28] Knight held that it is a "matter of life and death for economics as a science in the limited sense possible to keep the desired and desirable separate,"[29] which was also similar to Friedman's view.

Knight similarly prefigured Friedman's perspective on the appropriate place of mathematics in economics. Speaking on the "difference of opinion rife among economists as to the meaning and use of theoretical outlooks," Knight said: "At one extreme we have mathematical economists and pure theorists to whom little if anything outside of a closed system of deductions from a very small number of premises assumed as universal laws is to be regarded as scientific at all. At the other extreme there is certainly a strong and perhaps growing tendency to repudiate abstraction and deduction altogether, and insist upon a purely objective, descriptive science. And in between are all shades of opinion."[30] He also said that "mathematical economists have commonly been mathematicians first and economists afterward, disposed to oversimplify the data and underestimate the divergence between their premises and the facts of life. In consequence, they have not been successful in getting their presentation into such a form that it could be understood, and its relation to real problems recognized, by practical economists."[31] Knight, like others at Chicago, resisted the mathematization of economics. Writing in 1921, he inaccurately forecast: "Mathematical economics . . . seems likely to remain little more than a cult, a closed book to all except a few of the 'initiated.'"[32]

He was certainly an intellectual elitist: "The one thing clear . . . is that crowds 'think' very little if at all, in the sense of impartial analysis or criticism. . . . Anything that appeals to the crowd-minded must be simple and romantic; its favorite formula is *credo quia impossibile* ['I believe it because it is impossible'], its favorite policy, witch-hunting."[33] According to Rose Friedman, two-thirds of the students in Knight's classes had little to no idea what he was talking about.[34]

His reading was broad. Though he considered economists from continental Europe, most of his sources were in the British and American economic traditions. The economists he cited the most included Mill, Alfred Marshall, and John B. Clark. Knight provided brilliant historical analysis and insight. For example, while observing the growth of the concept of profit in economic theory, he commented that this was tied largely to the actual increased making of profits through new forms of business organization, often using new technology, in the nineteenth century. He remarked that the first "notable development in the field of profit theory in America was the work of General Francis A. Walker,"[35] who was a nineteenth-century president of the Massachusetts Institute of Technology and the first president of the American Economic Association.

The upshot of Knight's views was to support the free market. His emphasis on the entrepreneur led him to support the system in which entrepreneurs flourish, free market capitalism. He was by no means dogmatic in his support for laissez-faire. He acknowledged a large role for government not only in providing the libertarian minimum of a night watchman state, but also in a wide range of areas, imperfectly determined by imperfect men and women through discussion and imperfect institutions. His skepticism and elitism led him to doubt that democratic government would provide very good answers to societal ills, but he also believed that, given human shortcomings, democracy and freedom of expression were likely to attain whatever progress is possible. Moreover, concentration of power in the state is inefficient and dictatorial.

Knight's view of Smith was similar to Viner's. Knight wrote in a later essay:

> The *laissez faire* economists of the straightest sect made exceptions of a sort which opened the way to much wider departures from the principle. . . . This applies particularly to the great apostle of the movement, Adam Smith. All liberal individualists have recognized the necessity for restriction on individual freedom, and also for action by the state. . . . The state was to be supported, of course, by taxation, and the liberal notions of tax policy always inclined rather to equalizing. . . . Moreover, liberalism has always accepted without question the doctrine that every member of society has a right to live at some minimum standard, at the expense of society as a whole. . . . Adam Smith and other liberals recognized as a legitimate function and task of the state, provision for the education of the youth, and, in varying degrees, for activities designed to promote the diffusion of knowledge and the advancement of science, art, and general culture.[36]

Knight also said that "Smith was no doctrinaire advocate of a hands-off policy by government in respect of economic matters . . . What his attitude would have been under the later conditions of the nineteenth and twentieth centuries toward the factory acts, social insurance, and particularly measures intended to foster equality of opportunity, we cannot tell. But there is nothing in the aims of these newer types of legislation which runs counter to his principal conventions or is inconsistent with his general economic philosophy."[37] In a 1946 essay, he wrote: "The alternative to dictatorship is simply democracy in general as we have known it, struggling to solve its problems, along lines already familiar. It means cooperation in thinking and acting to promote progress, moral, intellectual, and esthetic, with material and technical progress as the basis of all, and all under the limitation of gradualism and 'seasoned' with humor and play. The combination is the meaning of liberalism"[38]—a fine statement of the liberal creed.

He no doubt hoped that *Risk, Uncertainty and Profit* would assist him professionally. In 1919, before its publication, Knight became an associate professor in the Department of Economics at the University of Iowa, teaching the history of economic thought. In 1922, after *Risk, Uncertainty and Profit* was published, he became full professor.

The relationship among Knight, Viner, and Henry Simons is interesting to know. It is difficult to argue that the three self-consciously formed a school. Burgin is again the best authority:

> Although some of their students would go on to ascribe a retrospective coherence to their time at Chicago, Knight, Viner, and Simons demonstrated only limited affinity for one another and little sense that they considered themselves members of an ideological community. . . . Chicago economists in the interwar years were fashioned into a group through the loose reflections of certain students, colleagues, and successors, but one can accept the term only by denying the contrary impressions of its ostensible members.
>
> In their personal interactions they expressed little mutual warmth, virtually no belief that they held allied perspectives, and some skepticism about one another's worldviews. . . .
>
> As early as 1925, Viner was expressing reservations about Simons' capabilities. . . . After Simons and Knight made the transition from Iowa to Chicago, Viner's impressions of his younger colleague solidified. . . . On at least one occasion he [Viner] voted not to grant Simons tenure. . . . [39]

With respect to religious views, correspondence from Knight to Kershner in 1922 sheds light on Knight's views at this time:

I am reading King's *Ethics of Jesus* and want to go through a lot of this stuff. I can't get away from the fact that the spirit of western civilization is the antithesis of christianity [*sic*], nor see how it would be western civilization if it weren't The problem to me is how far one can go toward christianity without giving up material and scientific progress which I am not willing to do. I wish the world were so mature and organized that one could live on christian principles and at the same time live fairly decently . . . , but I cannot see that it is so.

I am committed to casting my fortunes with the local Unitarian association. I want some sort of religious connection, and while these people are really about as dogmatic and opinionated as any . . . , at least they stand theoretically for a truth seeking attitude.[40]

His perspective could not have been more clear. He was completely of this world, secular, rational, and utilitarian. This life is all there is. One should seek to maximize happiness, or secular utility, in it. The advance and progress of knowledge and science is the master key to improving human life. Democratic government is justified—not because it is the best, but because it is the least bad, form of government. Christian, as other, dogma is an old wives' tale, a fable, a superstition. Humankind is far better off to look at the truth completely, clearly, and accurately than ever to resort to any sort of untruth or misstatement. Humankind is diverse. In the battle of faith and reason, Knight took the side of reason.

4

CHICAGOAN AND AUSTRIAN
ECONOMICS IN THE 1930s

WHEN HARRY JOHNSON CAME to teach economics at the University of Chicago in 1959, it was, he later recalled, still "dominated by the memory of the great 1930s days of Frank Knight and Jacob Viner, though in fact Milton Friedman was already clearly in the ascendant, along with George Stigler."[1] Economics at the University of Chicago would reach increasingly greater heights for decades. Yet, at the time, the 1930s seemed the most exciting period ever, with a cornucopia of great teachers and great students. In addition to Viner and Knight, outstanding and influential teachers included Paul Douglas (later a US senator) and Henry Simons. Students included Milton Friedman, Paul Samuelson, George Stigler, Aaron Director, and Allan Wallis. It was a stellar group—the second tiers of teachers and students were barely less prominent and talented.

Knight came to the University of Chicago as a professor in 1927, eleven years after Viner. Knight was seven years older than Viner. As a result of Knight's *Risk, Uncertainty and Profit,* he was highly sought-after as an academic property. According to Samuelson, "reliable rumor"[2] had it that Harvard was interested in him as well as Chicago. Knight and Viner were an outstanding duo. Rose Friedman remembered that they sometimes taught the same course, and students would take both because their approaches were so different. Viner was the clear-headed economist and teacher. Knight was the charismatic philosopher and skeptic.

Edward Shils was a leading sociologist at Chicago and a student of Knight during the early 1930s. He had these recollections. Knight could be

> querulous and as persistent in discussion as a bulldog; he was sharp and subtle and had an exceptional acumen in detecting contradictions in others' and in his own positions. While he always complained about the errors of others, he never ceased to confess his own ignorance. He had an exasperated certainty when he referred to what was unlikely to be true, but when it came to the truth of his own assertions he was modest to the point of humility.

Shils also remembered a talk Knight gave in 1932: "The main point of his lecture was an affirmation of the principles of liberalism—individual freedom, rational choice and action, rational discussion to settle political disagreements, the functioning of the competitive model as the most productive, the freest, and the socially most beneficial mode of organization of economic life."[3]

According to his student James Buchanan, who received the Nobel Prize in Economics in 1986, "nothing was sacrosanct" to Knight, "not the dogmas of religion, not the laws and institutions of social order, not the prevailing moral norms, not the accepted interpretations of sacred or profane texts. Anything and everything was a potential subject for critical scrutiny, with an evaluative judgment to be informed by, but ultimately made independently of, external influence." Buchanan also characterized Knight as willing to "question any authority."[4]

Both Viner and Knight were free market economists, but from somewhat different methodological and argumentative points of view. They co-edited the *Journal of Political Economy*, with Viner taking the leading role. Though neither was the chair of the economics department, they intellectually presided over a continuing broad mix that included modern liberal and future senator Paul Douglas, statistician and econometrician Henry Schultz, Knight follower and classical liberal Simons, monetary instructor Lloyd Mints, department chair and labor economist Harry Millis, economic historian John Nef, and Knight disciple Aaron Director.

J. Ronnie Davis, in his authoritative *The New Economics and the Old Economists* (1971), presents the view of Chicago economists as essentially Keynesian in public policy recommendations during the 1930s. Indeed, they were more Keynesian at times than Keynes himself. Whereas Keynes tended to look to monetary policy for the solution to the economic slump in the early 1930s, they tended to focus on fiscal policy more at this time. Concerning both fiscal and monetary policies, economists at Chicago, as elsewhere, recommended budget deficits, increased government spending, and an expansive monetary policy. However, Chicago economists were less inclined to view these as permanent policies (seeing them as justified temporarily by the exigencies of the Great Depression), favored budget deficits through tax cuts rather than spending increases and tax receipts equal to government expenditures over the course of the business cycle, and opposed more regulation of the economy through New Deal agencies. These continued to be Chicago policy recommendations for many years. The expansive fiscal and monetary actions that Chicago and other economists recommended in fact became the policies implemented around the world to combat the Great Depression. Chicago economists were in the mainstream in the 1930s—they were not a school apart from the rest of the discipline.

The issue of a business cycle was more emphasized in the first decades of the twentieth century in economics than in the later decades. Before World War II, the economy was more unstable than it subsequently became, particularly during the period between 1983 and 2008—when the global economy appeared to have banished any sort of a regular business *cycle,* as opposed to mere *fluctuations* in economic activity, from existence.

Viner, Knight, and others at Chicago were not at all doctrinaire concerning their policy responses to the Great Depression. A dozen economists at Chicago—Garfield Cox, Aaron Director, Paul Douglas, Harry Gideonse, Frank Knight, Harry Millis, Lloyd Mints, Henry Schultz, Henry Simons, Jacob Viner, Chester Wright, and Theodore Yntema—endorsed a 1932 memorandum on economic policy calling for budget deficits to combat the Depression and countercyclical budget surpluses to lessen the extremes of the business cycle. In 1931 and 1932, economists from around the country and world met in Chicago. John Maynard Keynes attended the first conference. He was largely in agreement with the policy recommendations of the paper presenters. "I think that this analysis," he remarked after one presentation, "is extraordinarily good and most helpful. . . . I have very little to add to the . . . scope of this, or to criticize."[5]

In 1933, Henry Simons and others at Chicago came forward with what became known as the "Chicago Plan" for monetary reform, which encompassed a 100 percent reserve requirement in banking and a fixed expansion of the money supply according to a rule each year. It attracted some attention, and several articles were written on the Chicago plan. In Simons, Knight had an able follower. Simons had been a student of Knight's at the University of Iowa and followed him to the University of Chicago when Knight went there to teach in 1927. Simons published *A Positive Program for Laissez Faire: Some Proposals for a Liberal Economic Policy* in 1934, raising the banner of laissez-faire in its title and seeking to preserve the traditional meaning of "liberal" at a time when the New Deal was at high tide. At home, national planning was ascendant.

Abroad, liberal, capitalist democracy was under attack from Communism, fascism, and Nazism.

It really was with *A Positive Program for Laissez Faire* that a self-consciously "Chicago" group of graduate students began to look at their perspective as a distinct view. Though *A Positive Program for Laissez Faire* would appear, from the standards of a later time, to make excessive concessions to the appropriate range of government activities, Simons got the main point right that so many of his contemporaries got wrong: economic liberty is an essential part of freedom comprehensively understood. Private property is as fundamental to liberty as free speech and the right to vote. Allen Wallis remembered *A Positive Program for Laissez Faire* as a work that "although small, was inexhaustible."[6] Simons's approach, and that of the Chicago tradition at its best, incorporates a strong empirical component. Facts matter. It is possible to separate facts from values. Economics is potentially scientific to the extent it can separate facts from values. Economic theory should correspond to events in the real world. Facts illustrate theories and lead to new hypotheses. Prediction is the pith of empiricism.

Empiricism leads to pragmatism. Looking at the world and making predictions about it, formal and informal, one quickly realizes that one's outlooks are often inaccurate and incomplete. A pragmatic view, one that does not rest on absolutely certain precepts or perspectives, has much to recommend it. "The real enemies of liberty in this country are the naive advocates of managed economic or national planning,"[7] Simons wrote. In the extreme circumstances of the Great Depression, he did not advocate a hands-off approach by government—whatever that would be. Of course, every action of government affects the economy. The questions are empirical—What are these effects?—and ethical—What should these influences be?

Government establishes the institutional framework within which other activities in a society take place, including economic activity. Government cannot simply *not* intervene. Both Hayek and Friedman were clear on this point, at least earlier in their careers. Every action by government, even seeming nonaction, has influence. There are both empirical and ethical disagreements with respect to what the effects of government are and should be. The Chicago approach at its best emphasizes the empirical nature of economic inquiry in theory and constructive, incremental, and practical proposals in public policy. The Chicago view is that normative recommendations should be based upon as accurate empirical observations of the world as possible. If our recommendations are built upon inaccurate, irrelevant, or nonfactual empirical predictions, they are unlikely to be of much value or use and can be counterproductive.

The Chicago approach, in technical economics, was much closer to Keynes's views during the early Great Depression than to the positions of economists from the Austrian school. Friedman recalled that once, in a debate with Abba Lerner shortly after World War II, he came to realize what some of the differences between the Chicago and Austrian approaches in economics were.[8] At the London School of Economics, where Lerner was a graduate student in the 1930s, the dominant view, under the influence of Hayek and Robbins, was that the Depression was the result of prior bad investments. There was nothing to do but allow these "malinvestments" to work themselves out through liquidation. There was little that government monetary or fiscal policies could do positively.

Hayek went further. He introduced a complex and complicated system of capital production and interest rates in which even stable prices result in periodic busts.[9] He wrote in the June 1932 preface to *Monetary Theory and the Trade Cycle* that there could,

> of course, be little doubt that, at the present time, a deflationary process is going on and that an indefinite continuation of that deflation would do inestimable harm. But this does not, by any means, necessarily mean that the deflation is the original cause of our difficulties or that we would overcome these difficulties by compensating for the deflationary tendencies by forcing more money into circulation.

> There is no reason to assume that the crisis was started by a deliber-
> ate deflationary action on the part of the monetary authorities, or the
> deflation itself is anything but a secondary phenomenon, a process
> induced by the maladjustments of industry left over from the boom.[10]

This was a very inaccurate analysis. Far from it being the case that
there was, as Hayek maintained, a "deliberate policy of credit expansion"[11] between 1929 and 1932, the Federal Reserve pursued a deflation-
ary policy. He also inaccurately maintained in an April 1934 journal
article that the Federal Reserve "succeeded, by means of an easy-money
policy, inaugurated as soon as the symptoms of an impending reaction
were noticed, in prolonging the boom for two years beyond what would
otherwise have been its natural end. And when the crisis finally occurred
[in 1929], for almost two more years, deliberate attempts were made to
prevent, by all conceivable means, the normal process of liquidation."[12]

Hayek's Austrian economic perspective, perhaps especially its
methodology, prevented him from seeing economic activity during the
Great Depression clearly. At the heart of his methodological views,
following Mises, was the amazing thought that facts, in Friedman's
words, "are not really relevant in determining, in testing, theories.
They are relevant to illustrate theories but not to test them, because
we base economics on propositions that are self-evident. And they are
self-evident because they are about human beings, and we're human
beings. So, we have an internal source of final knowledge, and no tests
can overrule that. . . . 'Praxeology.'"[13] Hayek did not believe there were
facts that could refute his theory of the trade cycle—that was not the
role of empirical information in theories. There was no alternative but
to do nothing in the face of tens of millions out of work and destitute.

By way of contrast, both Keynes and Chicago called for activist
government monetary and fiscal policies. There were few differences
in policy recommendations between the Keynesian and Chicagoan
approaches during the catastrophe of the Great Depression. The Austrian view, on the other hand, recommended no or little action by

government. Its mistaken opinion was that government monetary and fiscal policies could do no good—they could only do harm.

In retrospect, the Austrian position in economic theory, as opposed to political philosophy or public policy, has been almost universally discarded by the economics profession. Lionel Robbins wrote late in his career:

> Whatever the genetic factors of the pre-1929 boom, their *sequelae,* in the sense of inappropriate investments fostered by wrong expectations, were completely swamped by the vast deflationary forces sweeping away all those elements of constancy in the situation which otherwise might have provided a framework for an explanation in my terms. The theory was inadequate to the facts. . . . Confronted with the freezing deflation of those days, the idea that the prime essential was the writing down of mistaken investments and the easing of capital markets by fostering the disposition to save and reducing the pressure on consumption was completely inappropriate. . . . [T]o treat what developed subsequently in the way which I then thought valid was as unsuitable as denying blankets and stimulants to a drunk who has fallen into an icy pond, on the ground that his original trouble was overheating. I shall always regard this aspect of my dispute with Keynes as the greatest mistake of my professional career . . . it will always be a matter of deep regret to me that . . . I should have so opposed policies which might have mitigated the economic distress of those days.[14]

Hayek's views of economic activity and appropriate government policy during the Great Depression were not in accord with the facts. He was empirically in error when he held that the Federal Reserve Board in the United States practiced expansionary monetary policies in the early 1930s, when, in fact, the Fed repeatedly and disastrously raised interest rates. After the Great Depression, the Austrian school as a recognized entity in economic theory (as distinct from political philosophy) was hardly heard from or of again until the mid-1970s and the rise of the New York University—and more recently, George Mason University—modern American Austrian movement.

Herbert Stein, who was the chairman of the Council of Economic Advisers under Presidents Richard Nixon and Gerald Ford and who received his PhD in economics from the University of Chicago, had a positive estimate of Simons's influence and a beneficial conception of his recommended public policies: "Simons visualized a division of labor between the government and the market. The market would determine what gets produced, how, and for whom. The government would be responsible for maintaining overall stability, for keeping the market competitive, and for avoiding extremes in the distribution of income." Stein also said that Simons "emphasized the use of the progressive income tax as a means of reducing inequality both because reducing inequality was important and because the progressive income tax was a way of reducing inequality that was much more compatible with a free economy than other measures commonly proposed for that purpose."[15] Stein remarked as well that the "principle that seems to me to require the least qualification is that government should not intervene in the heart of the market—in the determination of relative prices and the allocation of labor and capital among various industries."[16]

In the 1934–1935 academic year, Milton Friedman, George Stigler, Allen Wallis, and Homer Jones—another Knight student, who played a key role in making it possible for Friedman to attend Chicago and who was later an important Federal Reserve System official—edited a collection of Knight's essays. Stigler commented in his memoirs that Knight was "famous for a brilliant book on economic theory (*Risk, Uncertainty and Profit,* 1921), and also for a set of highly provocative philosophical essays,"[17] *The Ethics of Competition,* in 1935.

Other students, of course, than Friedman, Wallis, Stigler, Aaron Director, Paul Samuelson, Herb Stein, and Homer Jones attended Chicago during this period. Some of the more exceptional included Rose Director (Aaron's younger sister, who married Milton Friedman),

Albert Hart, Kenneth Boulding, and Gregg Lewis, and slightly later Martin Bronfenbrenner and D. Gale Johnson. Hart taught at Columbia after graduating from Chicago, and sought a more equitable income tax code. Boulding became president of the American Economic Association and taught at the University of Colorado at Boulder. Lewis taught at the University of Chicago from 1939 to 1975, and then at Duke. Bronfenbrenner had a diverse career both as to interests and as to the institutions at which he taught; he was known for teaching. Johnson had a long tenure at Chicago, from 1944 until his death in 2003—he was one of the foremost authorities in agricultural economics and served in various administrative positions at Chicago, including provost.

The 1930s were an exceptional time economically and in the discipline of economics. Following World War II, Keynes and Keynesianism reigned throughout the discipline, with the signal exception of Chicago. It is important to emphasize again that virtually all economists called for a more expansive and interventionist government role in the exigencies of the Great Depression. What distinguished economists at Chicago from those elsewhere was that they saw this increased government activity as temporary, an aberration from the natural and beneficent order of things in a fundamentally free market economy. As time went on and economic conditions improved, Chicago economists became identified as anti-Keynesian and pro–free market. Historically, Chicago economists would not have been considered against government in general or in the abstract.

There was no "Chicago school of economics" during the 1930s. Viner never considered himself a part of any school, nor did Knight. Simons was the one who most attempted to build a group of like-minded classical liberal economists at Chicago, but he had not succeeded in this effort by his premature death in 1946. It was the postwar return of 1930s graduate students that spurred the creation of a definite Chicago school of economics in the 1950s, 1960s and 1970s. At the end of the 1930s, there was no telling in what direction economics at Chicago would turn.

5

HENRY SIMONS AND
PROGRESSIVE TAXATION

AS A RESULT OF OPPOSITION in the Department of Economics, Henry Simons began to teach in the law school at Chicago in
1939. When he became an associate professor in 1942, it was to teach
both economics and law. Simons played the largest role in laying the
groundwork for an explicit "school" of economics at Chicago, in part
through nurturing the personal ties upon which a school rests. In a
1981 discussion among thirty current and former Chicago faculty and
students, some of the participants recalled his contributions:

> ALLEN WALLIS: Simons had considerable influence directly on in-
> dividuals. I was a graduate student around there, as were Mil-
> ton and George. . . . He knew a lot of people and had a lot of
> personal influence. I think that's probably at least as important
> as what happened in the courses.

AARON DIRECTOR: I never took a course from him, but I was
    greatly influenced by him.
WALTER BLUM: I got to know him as a result of drinking beer with
    him in Hanley's tavern about once a week . . .
MILTON FRIEDMAN: That is a very important element. Henry was
    a very gregarious fellow. He had a great deal of influence in
    these social interactions.[1]

Born in 1899, Simons played a key role in bringing together the
individuals who would comprise the Chicago school of economics after World War II, as Milton Friedman, Aaron Director, and Allen
Wallis returned to Chicago. Together with Knight, Lloyd Mints, Ted
Schultz, and others, these individuals formed the core of the emerging
libertarian-conservative wing in the economics department and elsewhere at Chicago. Friedrich Hayek joined the Committee on Social
Thought at the University of Chicago in 1950—Friedman and Knight
attended Hayek's seminar. Stigler returned to Chicago in 1958.

Alas, Simons himself was not on the scene when the Chicago
school began to form, as he died of an overdose of sleeping pills in
1946. His death has often been called a suicide, but this may be a
mistake. Simons left no suicide note. After a long bachelorhood, he
had married in 1941. In 1944, he and his wife had a daughter. According to historian of economic thought Sherryl Kasper: "Beginning
in 1945, Simons had problems with stomach ulcers and insomnia."[2]
Hayek, in a 1983 interview, commented that some said Simons had
"the habit, every time he woke up, to take more [sleeping pills]. This
happens."[3] Burgin reports that Simons's wife "informed the coroner
that he had been taking pills for severe insomnia in increasing doses
in the months before his death, and that she did not believe that he
had taken an overdose willfully."[4] Chicago-area newspapers called the
death an accident.

Simons, more than anyone else, sought to create a school at Chicago that was explicitly classical liberal in nature. He identified himself

with the great classical liberal line in political philosophy and economics. In the introduction to his posthumously published *Economic Policy for a Free Society* (1948), he said that his "underlying position may be characterized as severely libertarian or, in the English-continental sense, liberal. The intellectual tradition is intended to be that of Adam Smith, . . . Mill, Menger, Brentano, Sidgwick, Marshall, Fetter, and Knight, and of Locke, Hume, Bentham, Humboldt, Tocqueville, Burckhardt, Acton, Dicey, Barker, and Hayek."[5]

According to Burgin, Simons was the "first significant economist to refer to himself as a 'libertarian.'"[6] In his essay on his "political credo" written in 1945, Simons titled a section "Libertarian Socialism" and provided these thoughts:

> Modern socialism has been deeply sobered by the first meager efforts to become something more than a negative, revolutionary movement. Its intellectuals have finally begun to face the task of drafting positive proposals and an intelligible platform for action beyond the revolution. Their positive prescriptions are usefully and paradoxically epitomized in the name "decentralized socialism." . . .
>
> Socialism, of necessity, has been deeply corrupted by liberalism and conversely, for they have been contemporaries in a world of free discussion and have been catalyzed by the same evils and guided by much of the same aspirations. Indeed, it is not hard to see how socialists and libertarians can long sustain substantial intellectual differences, save by avoiding all discussion.
>
> Modern socialism is avowedly concerned mainly about inequalities of wealth (and power?) and about industrial monopoly—both major concerns of libertarians.[7]

In Simons's view, Smith's and Bentham's "special insight" was that "political and economic power must be widely dispersed and decentralized in a world that would be free; that economic control must, to that end, be largely divorced from the state and effected through a cooperative process in which participants are relatively small and anonymous."[8] What Smith and Bentham failed adequately to see, not being able to predict contemporary circumstances, is that the institutions of advanced free market economies, as they have developed, devolve great resources on a relatively few positions. Unless government steps in to equalize income and wealth, free market capitalism turns into crony, plutocratic capitalism, which is neither efficient nor just.

Smith, Bentham, Mill, and Simons all criticized, in different ways, the rich. Smith was, as previously noted, admired by early leaders of the French Revolution. He referred in a letter in 1780 to *The Wealth of Nations* as "the very violent attack I had made upon the whole commercial system of Great Britain."[9] Bentham was even more disdainful of the powerful. He wrote in 1822 that the theory of utility was "dangerous . . . to every government which has for its actual end or object, the greatest happiness of a certain one, with or without the addition of some comparatively small number of others,"[10] which he considered to be the object of most governments. Mill, who was the original socialist-libertarian, affirmed egalitarian sentiments (what economists now call "declining marginal utility") in the *Principles of Political Economy* (1848) when he said: "The difference to the happiness of the possessor between a moderate [economic] independence and five times as much, is insignificant when weighed against the enjoyment that might be given . . . by some other disposal of the four-fifths."[11] Simons emphasized competition. It is by breaking down the power of the rich and, within reason, redistributing their resources that a competitive society can be achieved.

George Stigler said of Simons that "much of his program was almost as harmonious with socialism as with private-enterprise capitalism."[12] Simons recognized much similarity between the visions of true classical liberals and socialists.[13] Each outlook seeks the utilitarian end of the greatest good for the greatest number, with the human good for classical utilitarians defined as happiness—the greatest surplus of the highest-quality pleasures over the lowest-quality pains.

Each individual's happiness is valued equally. Classical liberalism, in the hands of Simons and its other masters, is an egalitarian creed and program.

Simons's most-recognized contemporaneous work, *A Positive Program for Laissez Faire,* was written at the height of the Great Depression and the onset of the New Deal. This helps explain its concessions to more government activity than later generations would sanction. It was essentially a counterprogram to the New Deal. At the same time, Simons also saw that the classical liberal process of discussion and debate ultimately results in greater agreement and compromise in society, including among those who previously had very different views.

In late December 1934, Allen Wallis and George Stigler wrote a letter to the editor of the *New York Times* on *A Positive Program for Laissez Faire,* referring to Simons's "brilliant and suggestive" work. They had noted in a letter to the *Times* two weeks before, published as the lead letter, that Simons's book contained "concrete and practical proposals for social policies."[14] Wallis and Stigler gave their location in both letters as the University of Chicago. In their second letter, they noted that Simons's work was a University of Chicago Public Policy Pamphlet and that it could be obtained from the University of Chicago Press.

It is thus possible that some young Chicagoans and others began to refer to an explicit Chicago school of economics in the 1930s. However, there was then a hiatus in further development until 1946 and the simultaneous return to campus of Friedman, Director, and Wallis, all of whom had left Chicago by 1936. It should be noted that the young Chicagoans were primarily on the moderate left when they started at Chicago as graduate students in the early 1930s—they were Norman Thomas (mild) socialists. Friedman remarked in a 2000 interview that when he was an undergraduate, "I probably would have described myself as a socialist, who knows."[15] They supported President Roosevelt's general approach, if not all of his specific policies. They read the *New Republic, Nation,* and similar publications. Indeed, in their original letter to the *New York Times,* Wallis and Stigler mentioned "imperfect competition" theorizing twice and praised "Robinson, Chamberlain, Yntema, Sraffa, Harrod, and others,"[16] who were on the political and economic left. The young Chicago economists were not doctrinaire classicists at the time.

Many writers on economics at Chicago emphasize that there was a difference between the work of Viner, Knight, and Simons and that of the postwar Chicago school of economics led by Friedman, Director, and Stigler. Viner, Knight, and Simons each allowed government intervention in the economy in ways that their Chicago successors did not. Each of the earlier trio was concerned with problems of equality in society and of imperfect and monopolistic competition. As late as 1960, Viner, then at Princeton, said: "Monopoly is so prevalent in the markets of the western world today that discussion of the merits of the free competitive market as if that were what we were living with or were at all likely to have the good fortune to live with in the future seems to me academic in the only pejorative sense of that adjective."[17] There was not the focus on monetary policy that became the hallmark of the later Chicago school of economics.

Simons and his colleagues, in what Paul Samuelson and others have called the "first" Chicago school, were far more inclined toward considerations of equality in their public policy recommendations, as well as to greater government involvement in society and the economy generally, than their successors; and, indeed, their successors were themselves more inclined to these traditional Chicago classical liberal positions earlier in their careers. Simons proclaimed the virtues of social, political, and economic equality. He wrote that a "free-exchange society . . . involves and permits progressive mitigation of inequality; indeed, it affords the largest possibilities of substantial equality."[18]

Crucially, for Simons, government should undertake its equalizing action after the private sector has created wealth: "What is important, for libertarians, is that we preserve the basic processes of free exchange and that egalitarian measures be superimposed on those processes, effecting redistribution afterward and not in the immediate course of production and commercial transactions."[19] Virtually all of the pre–World War II economists at the University of Chicago supported greater economic equality as an important and appropriate, if not paramount, governmental and societal goal.

Egalitarianism is part of classical liberalism, though not of contemporary libertarianism. Indeed, contemporary libertarians most often see massive inequality as one of the most crucial marks of a successful and prosperous society (wherein income and wealth are being directed to job- and wealth-creators) and would, if anything, like to see even more inequality in the United States than is currently the case. Through their emphasis on the importance of the inheritance of great wealth, contemporary libertarians and conservatives take a position that is completely at odds with that of Adam Smith and the other great classical liberals of the seventeenth through nineteenth centuries. They urged greater equality in society especially through laws regarding inheritance and extolled middle-class societies without extremes of rich and poor.

This is not at all to say that Smith, Simons, and other classical liberals favor complete economic equality in a society, for surely they have not and do not. Equality is one value among others—*classical liberalism does not favor complete equality of result*. However, as a general rule, it supports institutions that minimize inequality and that promote meaningful equality of opportunity. True classical liberalism looks at the gross inequality that constitutes current American society with horror and revulsion. By way of contrast, it favors the sort of income and wealth distribution that characterized the 1950s and 1960s in the United States—an era of great growth, limited government, strong families, and high marginal income and estate tax rates.

Simons argued that strict ideas of "commutative" (or procedural) justice are and ought to be "radically modified in all societies, especially free-exchange societies, by private charity and governmental outlays at the bottom and, notably, by taxation at the top."[20] Simons and others in the "first" Chicago school supported progressive income taxation superimposed on a free private market to achieve greater equality. "Redistribution" of income and wealth was not, in their lexicon, a dirty word or concept. Rather, they supported redistribution of income and wealth from the rich to the poor and middle class within a system of the private creation and management of economic resources.

Simons was emphatic throughout *A Positive Program for Laissez Faire* that inequality in income and wealth was a major economic and social ill and that it is largely up to government—primarily through progressive income and estate taxation—to right it:

> A substantial measure of inequality may be unavoidable or essential for motivation; but it should be recognized as evil and tolerated only so far as the dictates of expediency are clear. . . . [A] cardinal sin of government against the free enterprise system is manifest in the kind of institution of property which the state has inflicted upon that system. It has lain within the powers of the political state, in defining rights of property and inheritance, to prevent the extreme inequality which now obtains; and the appropriate changes might still be effected without seriously impairing the efficiency of the system. In a practical sense, there is not much now wrong with the institution of property except our arrangements with respect to taxation.[21]

The third of his five enumerated "main elements in a sound liberal program" was: "Drastic change in our whole tax system, with regard primarily for the effects of taxation upon the distribution of wealth and income."[22] He maintained:

> Our proposal with reference to taxation is based on the view (1) that reduction of inequality is *per se* immensely important; (2) that progressive taxation is both an effective means and, within the existing framework of institutions, the only effective means to that end;

(3) that, in a world of . . . competition, the gains at the bottom of the income scale can be realized without significant loss to persons of large income, so long as their rank in the income scale is unchanged; and (4) that drastic reduction of inequality through taxation is attainable without much loss of efficiency in the system and without much impairing the attractiveness of the economic game.[23]

He footnoted at this point: "Some students would justify the reduction of inequality on the ground that it is essential to the political stability of the system; others, on the ground that it is important for the reduction of unemployment and for the mitigation of industrial fluctuations,"[24] though these were not the main arguments he used to advocate more egalitarian policies. Simons supported the "establishment of the personal income tax as the predominant element in our whole fiscal system" and "drastic alteration in the rate structure of the personal income tax, with more rapid progression."[25] He had similar views concerning estate taxation.

With respect to government expenditures, he took the classical liberal view. He noted concerning the provision of government services: "On the expenditure side, we may look forward confidently to continued augmenting of the 'free income' of the masses, in the form of commodities and services made available by government . . . There are remarkable opportunities for extending the range of socialized consumption (medical services, recreation, education, music, drama, etc.) and, especially, for extending the range of social welfare activities."[26] Near the end of *A Positive Program for Laissez Faire,* he again held: "The designing and building of a mighty engine of income and inheritance taxation is an undertaking big enough and hard enough to occupy the capable people who are really concerned about inequality. There are endless possibilities for increasing and improving the community's 'free income' in the form of governmental services, especially through extension of social welfare activities."[27] He was a true classical liberal.

Simons thundered in concluding *A Positive Program for Laissez Faire:* "No diabolical ingenuity could have devised a more effective agency for retarding or preventing recovery (or for leading us away from democracy) than the National Recovery Act and its codes." Government management of the economy is the problem—progressive taxation is a big part of the solution. With respect to the measures he put forward, he acknowledged that there "cannot, of course, be general agreement in detail on the measures here proposed. No reader is likely to find all of them acceptable," noting, "I must confess to serious misgivings myself at many points."

He was no doctrinaire ideologue:

> This tract is submitted in the hope of promoting a consensus of opinion within a group which might now perform an invaluable service in intellectual leadership. The precious measure of political and economic freedom which has been won through centuries may soon be lost irreparably; and it falls properly to economists, as custodians of the great liberal tradition out of which their discipline arose, to point the escape from the chaos of political and economic thought which warns of what impends.[28]

As early as 1934, Simons sought to bring a "consensus of opinion within a group" of economists at and affiliated with the University of Chicago. This was the view, in opposition to New Deal policies, that the private sector should essentially be allowed to work, not be regulated, and that income redistribution through taxation and extensive government services could be provided without impairing or impinging on a free market order. Simons also explained that, by way of contrast to his views on increased progressive income and estate taxation, he opposed "widespread unionization, reduction of hours, and increase of wage rates"[29]—regulation—for their pernicious effects on the private economy. He believed that extensive taxation and provision of government services are not just consistent with but essential to a functioning and vibrant free market order. Progressive government taxation of income and estates provided the only hope, in Simons's view, of maintaining a democratic and fair productive market society.

Hayek thought well of *A Positive Program for Laissez Faire.* He wrote in a 1934 letter to Simons: "I have the greatest sympathy for the general spirit which it expresses and I feel that it does raise the problems which economists ought to discuss to-day more than others."[30] At the same time, he did not agree with all of Simons's particular approaches on issues, a criticism which Simons acknowledged. In 1945, when Hayek traveled to the United States to promote *The Road to Serfdom,* which had been published by the University of Chicago Press in America the year before, Simons became "my great friend in Chicago,"[31] Hayek later recalled.

On that same trip, Hayek appeared on a memorable University of Chicago radio roundtable program with Maynard Krueger and Charles Merriam, both professors at Chicago. Krueger had been the socialist party candidate for vice president in 1940. Here, Hayek remarked in response to criticism that the society he advocated was one in which government would not do anything: "There are a good many people . . . who oppose planning who do not mean by that opposition that they think that there ought not to be any government at all. They want to confine the government to certain functions." What Hayek primarily opposed was government management of the economy: "Whenever the government is asked to decide how much of a thing is to be produced, who is to be allowed to produce it . . . that is a kind of social system which is an alternative to the competitive system and which cannot be combined with it." He sanctioned at this time, to an extent, legislation with respect to working conditions, minimum wages, social insurance, and aspects of one of the most prominent New Deal agencies, the Tennessee Valley Authority. He observed: "I have always said that I am in favor of a minimum income for every person in the country." He opposed the Agricultural Adjustment Act and "nearly all" of the National Recovery Act. He opposed "government direction of production"[32]—the centralization of economic decision making in the state.

Hayek and the early Chicagoans were at one with respect to the inefficiency and inadequacy of government planning and involvement in particular economic decisions. They also agreed that excessive government regulation or ownership of the economy was inherently repressive. Whether through regulation as in the United States or through nationalization as in Europe, government is inherently inefficient and ineffective when it attempts to manage the details of production. These should be left to a largely private market, both Hayek and the early Chicagoans believed—separating them from the majority of the economics profession. At the same time, both Hayek and classical liberal Chicago economists favored a significant, positive role for government, asserting that it should provide many services, stabilize the economy, and create a more equitable society.

Historians of economic thought William Breit and Roger Ransom provide this generous estimation of Simons's influence: "His obscurity as a public figure belied the influence which Henry Simons exerted on the shaping of economic thought in the turbulent years of the Roosevelt era. While the students at Cambridge—and increasingly elsewhere in the United States—were pondering the advantages of Keynesian Doctrine, a generation of students at the University of Chicago listened to Simons' articulate defense of the *laissez faire* philosophy and neoclassical economic theory."[33]

Herb Stein recalled:

After World War II . . . national discussion and, to some extent, policy turned to Simons's direction. There was no possibility of reverting to the negative conservatism of the prewar years. But with a greatly enlarged federal budget and debt, and with the experience of inflation, the naive expansionism of Keynes's American disciples was no longer an acceptable policy. In this gap, Simons's ideas filled a need. A "modern conservatism" emerged that accepted government responsibility for general economic stability, was strongly anti-inflationary, . . . relied on tax changes rather than expenditure changes when positive fiscal measures were needed, opposed protectionism, . . . and accepted the progressive personal income tax as the main source of federal revenue.[34]

There is nothing inconsistent between classical liberalism and income and wealth equalization—indeed, classical liberalism requires substantial income and wealth equalization through progressive income and estate taxation, while retaining incentives and differential rewards for different kinds of labor, endeavor, and the taking of risk. Simons advocated a society and economy in which government would, within reason, adopt policies that advance equality (or, at least, minimize inequality). Classical liberalism demands progressive taxation.

As will be discussed further in the Conclusion, the American economy grew faster in the 1950s, 1960s, and 1970s—when top marginal income tax rates were high—than in the 1980s, 1990s, and 2000s—when top tax rates were low. This would appear to argue against a straight-line correlation between lower top marginal rates and faster economic growth, because the empirical relationship is in precisely the opposite direction. Moreover, this is an international trend. In Europe as well as the United States, economic growth has declined and family structure weakened since top marginal tax rates on the very wealthy were substantially reduced and payroll and sales taxes were increased.

Simons thoroughly rejected the idea that government should play little to no role in society and the economy. Together with other earlier Chicagoans, he considered this notion to be far-fetched—and that a society with the extent of government envisioned by today's libertarians would be a nightmarish place. As with other classical liberals, including Locke, Smith, Bentham, and Mill, Simons stood with the people, not the masters.

6

COWLES COMMISSION
AND KEYNES

NOTWITHSTANDING THE OUTSTANDING economists who went through Chicago in the university's first half-century, economics there reached a peak during the late 1940s and early 1950s, when the Cowles Commission of econometricians was located with the economics department. Founded in 1932, the Cowles Commission was intended to tie economics to mathematics. At one point, thirteen future Nobel laureates in economics and a dozen current and future presidents of the American Economic Association passed through the halls of the Social Science Research Building, where the Department of Economics and the Cowles Commission were located on the fourth floor.

The Cowles Commission had a different approach to economics than the preexisting Chicago view. The Cowles approach was severely mathematical, and it was in contrast to the Cowles Commission that much of the postwar Chicago emphasis on empirical research emerged. Neither Viner nor Knight was an econometrician; both emphasized the importance of real-world application of economic theory, and neither was statistical in method. Chicago became empirical and statistical largely through the work of Friedman, his colleagues, and students. When Viner and Knight led the department intellectually, there was not the great gulf between Chicago and the rest of the profession, methodologically as well as politically, as later characterized this relationship.

That there was nothing inevitable about the emergence of a libertarian Chicago school of economics during the 1950s through 1970s is indicated by the great changes in the Department of Economics in the late 1930s and first half of the 1940s. The Chicago economics department has never been especially large. It typically has had about 25 total members, including lesser positions. In the first half of the 1930s, the department was led and dominated by Viner, Knight, Paul Douglas, Harry Millis, Henry Schultz, Lloyd Mints, Simeon Leland, and John Nef. Henry Simons and Aaron Director were junior faculty.

By 1946, only Knight, Mints, and Douglas remained in the department, and Douglas had turned his attention to politics and would soon depart academia. Viner had left for Princeton. Knight was not the figure by the later 1940s that he was in the 1930s. Millis retired, Nef moved to the Committee on Social Thought, Schultz and Simons were dead. In addition, Leland left the department in 1946; yet another economist from the 1930s, Chester Wright, was approaching retirement; and Theodore Yntema left the business school in 1949. There were also the changes that always occur in lower-level positions.

In Henry Simons's papers, there is correspondence about a proposal for an "Institute of Political Economy" that would bring together a group of "traditional liberal" or "libertarian" economists. The institute would "afford a center to which economic liberals everywhere may look for intellectual leadership or support." Chicago would be an appropriate location because "Chicago economics still has some distinctively traditional-liberal connotations and some prestige." However, even at Chicago, traditional economic liberalism would "shortly be lost unless special measures are taken. . . . In the Department we are becoming a small minority."[1] This correspondence probably dates from 1945, so at least at this time there was no ideological "Chicago school."

George Stigler wrote in his memoirs:

There was no Chicago school of economics . . . at the end of World War II. In the 1930s economics appeared to be a little different at the University of Chicago than elsewhere, but the same statement could be made about most major universities . . .

By the 1960s, however, the profession had widely agreed that there was a Chicago school of economics. Edward Chamberlin had written a chapter on the Chicago school in . . . 1957 . . . He found the school to be distinguished "by the zeal with which the theory of monopolistic competition has been attacked" . . . H. Lawrence Miller wrote . . . on the school and its central views in 1962 . . . [B]y then the school was treated as well established and widely recognized—and widely denounced.[2]

Paul Samuelson held that there were two Chicago schools:

The first Chicago school was that of Knight, Viner, and Simons. It advocated use of the market, but recommended redistributive taxes and transfers to mitigate the worst inequalities of the *laissez faire* system . . .

The second Chicago school ought properly to be associated with the names of Milton Friedman, George Stigler, Aaron Director, and Gary Becker. Call it the Friedman Chicago school for short. It has lost the Simonsian imperative to use the tax system to modify economic inequality . . . [3]

Aaron Director, the older brother of Rose Friedman, may have been the first to refer to a Chicago "school" of economics in print. In

1946, he wrote of Simons after his death that "through his writings and more especially through his teaching at the University of Chicago, he was slowly establishing himself as the head of a 'school.'"[4] Martin Bronfenbrenner received his PhD in economics from Chicago in 1939. He remembered: "I never heard of any 'Chicago school' until I left Chicago." After service in World War II, Bronfenbrenner taught at the University of Wisconsin at Madison from 1947 to 1957, where he learned that "'the Chicago school'" meant "Pangloss plus Gradgrind, with touches of Peachum, Torquemada, and the Marquis de Sade thrown in as 'insulter's surplus.'"[5] Among the first published references to the "Chicago school" was in a valuable 8,000-word article, "The Economists," by *Fortune* editor and writer John McDonald in December 1950, which was a popular survey of contemporary economics.

At the same time as an explicit Chicago school of economics was forming, a battle raged between Friedman and the Cowles Commission. Two very different visions for the future of economics reigned between the emerging Chicago school—which included sympathetic adherents in the Department of Economics, business school, Department of Statistics, law school, and the Committee on Social Thought—and the Cowles Commission, which was located adjacent to and shared some appointments with the Department of Economics. There were at least two questions—a policy question and a methodological question. Since methodological questions are inherently so difficult, it is best to take the policy question first.

John Maynard Keynes was the dominant international economist during the second and third quarters of the twentieth century. He burst onto the scene with his dazzling *The Economic Consequences of the Peace* (1919), a blistering attack on the Versailles Peace Treaty after World War I and the makers of that treaty. Keynes predicted that excessive reparations demanded of Germany would prove impossible to be paid—and he was right. His next major work was *A Tract on Monetary Reform* (1923), a collection of articles from the previous three years. He was, in contemporary parlance, a "stabilizer"—one who sought stable domestic prices—in contrast to those, including Winston Churchill, who supported deflation in order to restore the pre–World War I British pound's international exchange rate. Keynes held that monetary policy should be determined primarily by national, rather than international, circumstances. Following the publication of *A Tract on Monetary Reform,* he waged an unsuccessful battle to prevent Great Britain from returning to the gold standard at prewar parity. In 1926, he wrote *The End of Laissez Faire.* He argued here that government should and must play a large role in macromanaging a modern society's economy.

His next work was his intended magnum opus when he wrote it, *A Treatise on Money* (1930). Through attacking it, Hayek achieved prominence at the London School of Economics. Keynes's focus remained monetary policy, but he was expanding his concept of appropriate government macro policy in managing a modern, developed economy to include fiscal policy. Britain never recovered from World War I. Between 1900 and 1920, British unemployment averaged 3.4 percent per year. Between 1921 and 1940, for a generation, unemployment averaged 13.7 percent per year. Something had gone awry. What?

Keynes's answer was that Britain had become an old, arthritic economy. "The forces of the nineteenth century have run their course and are exhausted,"[6] he maintained. The days of development uncoordinated by government to produce maximum production, such as characterized the nineteenth century, were over. His view became that large government budget deficits were required to absorb excess savings, but more than this, he came to emphasize that government must intervene in an advanced economy. He did not give credence to the idea of a free market in which government merely sets the rules for commercial engagement.

His next masterwork became the most influential economic treatise of the half-century, *The General Theory of Employment, Interest, and Money* (1936). Here, he continued to develop his thought and the future direction of economics. He emphasized the professional nature of economics—that it is not comprehensible to the average person.

Within this professional context, he largely bifurcated changes in the money supply from changes in aggregate prices. Fiscal policy became increasingly important. Monetary policy was now insignificant. He recommended large budget deficits and advocated high marginal income and estate tax rates to reduce excessive savings. There should be large and fluctuating government spending for its macroeconomic, as distinct from welfare state, purposes.

Moreover, as amended by Edward Chamberlin and Joan Robinson, the theory of imperfect competition added to Keynesian fiscal policy by incorporating a strong government regulatory component. The imperfect competition theorists believed that the competition presumed by free market theorists does not exist in practice. Therefore, government must regulate the private economy to a significant extent.

Keynes was not a socialist in the sense of favoring government ownership and management of the means of economic production. Once, attacking Marxism, he rhetorically asked: "How can I adopt a creed which, preferring the mud to the fish, exalts the boorish proletariat above the bourgeois and intelligentsia who, with whatever faults, are the quality of life and surely carry the seeds of all human advancement?"[7] He was, on a personal level, no egalitarian.

He wrote in the concluding pages of the *General Theory*:

> I see no reason to suppose the existing system seriously misemploys the factors of production which are in use. There are, of course, errors of foresight; but these would not be avoided by centralizing decisions. When 9,000,000 men are employed out of 10,000,000 willing and able to work, there is no evidence that the labour of these 9,000,000 men is misdirected. The complaint against the present system is not that these 9,000,000 men ought to be employed on different tasks, but that tasks should be available for the remaining 1,000,000 men. It is in determining the volume, not the direction, of actual employment that the existing system has broken down.

Thus I agree . . . that the result of filling in the gaps in the classical theory is not to dispose of the "Manchester System," but to indicate the nature of the environment which the free play of economic forces requires if it is to realize the full potentialities of production. The central controls necessary to ensure full employment will, of course, involve a large extension of the traditional functions of government. Furthermore, the modern classical theory has itself called attention to various conditions in which the free play of economic forces may need to be curbed or guided. But there will still remain a wide field for the exercise of private initiative and responsibility. Within this field the traditional advantages of individualism will still hold good.[8]

Keynes was a classical liberal. He sought government macromanagement of the economy through appropriate fiscal and monetary policies, not government ownership of business or excessive government regulation or management of economic decision making. He thus sought to save capitalism, not replace it.

Both Knight and Viner were known for their opposition to Keynes. As might be expected, Knight was much more strident in his criticism than Viner, who tended to present the facts rather than engage in virtual ad hominem attack, to which Knight was prone. Viner wrote in 1936 reviewing *The General Theory of Employment, Interest, and Money*: "The indebtedness of economists to Mr. Keynes has been greatly increased by this latest addition to his series of brilliant, original, and provocative books, whose contribution to our enlightenment will prove, I am sure, to have been even greater in the long run than in the short run."[9] He then proceeded to analyze aspects of Keynes's work in a balanced fashion.

Knight, on the other hand, responded harshly, as Don Patinkin narrated:

In his opening footnote Knight states that the article will be "primarily critical in nature," and he more than fulfills his promise. It is

Knight at his irascible and sarcastic best—or worst. I have had the opportunity of examining Knight's copy of the *General Theory*, the one which he presumably read in preparation for writing his review, and it is filled with pencilled marginal notes of vehement dissent. Thus on Keynes' statement . . . that "It is astonishing what foolish things one can temporarily believe if one thinks too long alone, particularly in economics," Knight commented "best statement in the book"—and we know of whom he was thinking. The expletive "Nonsense!"—replaced on occasion by even stronger terms—makes a frequent appearance in these margins.[10]

In his review, Knight wrote: "The next general comment which must be made on Mr. Keynes' book as a whole is that it is inordinately difficult to tell what the author means. This is true in particular because on general issues it appears certain that he does not mean what he says."[11]

The *Canadian Journal of Economic and Political Science*, in which Knight's review appeared, gave Keynes the opportunity to respond, but he declined, saying "with Professor Knight's two main conclusions, namely, that my book had caused him intense irritation, and that he had had great difficulty in understanding it, I am in agreement."[12] In 1940, Viner apparently proposed Keynes for an honorary doctorate in connection with the fiftieth anniversary of the University of Chicago. Knight shot the suggestion down: "I regard Mr. Keynes' neo-mercantilist positions in economics . . . as essentially taking the side of the man-in-the-street, against the effort of the economic thinker and analyst to get beyond and to dispel the short-sighted views and prejudices of the former. . . . His work and influence seem to me supremely 'anti-intellectual.'"[13]

Knight's intemperate reaction to Keynes coincided with the introduction of the Cowles Commission at Chicago. Members of the Cowles Commission ranged from Keynesians to socialists, politically and methodologically. They were imperfect competition theorists. Among their allies in the Department of Economics was the Polish socialist Oskar Lange, who, following the war, became a high-ranking official in the Polish Communist government. Lange was a leading figure at Chicago in the early 1940s.

The Cowles Commission brought tremendous intellectual vitality to campus. According to Lester Telser, who became a research assistant on the Cowles Commission in 1952 and remains a professor emeritus at Chicago to this day: "When Cowles was here, the economics of Chicago was unparalleled in the world. I would say it was the leading center in economics. No one else even came close."[14] Nobel economics laureate Lawrence Klein, also with the Cowles Commission, recalled that a "truly exceptional group of people was assembled in Chicago during the late 1940s. I doubt that such a group could ever be put together again in economics."[15]

That economics at Chicago did not move in a Keynesian and econometric direction following the war was largely the result of the return to the university in 1946 of three of the leading young economists and graduate students at Chicago in the 1930s—Aaron Director in the law school, Allen Wallis at first in the Department of Statistics and then as dean of the business school, and Milton Friedman in the Department of Economics. Friedman proved to be the main obstacle to the Cowles Commission's domination of economics at Chicago. The political differences between the Knight circle and the Cowles Commission were large. At a time when the bulk of economists moved in an interventionist direction, economists at Chicago—though not all of them, and perhaps not even most of them—became more free market–oriented and less supportive of government intervention and activity. The philosophical view of Chicago economics moved in a more libertarian direction as the larger economics and social science professions moved strongly in the direction of Keynesian and government action and intervention.

Thus, while it may be true, as Friedman maintained, that there was some philosophical continuity at Chicago almost from the beginning, and while, through Viner and Knight, a "Chicago view" was coming to be referred to as early as the 1930s, there was no "Chicago school" of economics until after World War II, consistent with what Stigler said. By the late 1950s, Friedman, Stigler, Director, and Wallis were at Chicago, together with Knight and Lloyd Mints in retirement, Hayek (by no means a Chicago economist, but perhaps the most prominent classical liberal in academia) on the Committee on Social Thought, and a host of lesser faculty and students. There were allied faculty at other institutions.

The methodological battles between the Cowles Commission and Friedman and his allies were perhaps even more intense than the political ones. With the shift from "political economy" to "economics" and the increasing mathematization and professionalization of the discipline, Chicago economists moved in a more empirical, historical, and statistical direction just as the rest of the profession moved the opposite way. Friedman and others were students of the Wesley Mitchell branch of Chicago economics at the National Bureau of Economic Research. Moreover, Viner was a methodological empiricist.

In a 1988 interview with economist J. Daniel Hammond, Friedman said that what made economics at Chicago different when he was a student was not political orientation, but

> treating economics as a serious subject versus treating it as a branch
> of mathematics, . . . treating it as a scientific subject as opposed to an
> aesthetic subject . . . The fundamental difference between Chicago
> at that time and let's say Harvard, was that at Chicago, economics
> was a serious subject to be used in discussing real problems, and you
> could get some knowledge and some answers from it. For Harvard,
> economics was an intellectual discipline on a par with mathematics,
> which was fascinating to explore, but you mustn't draw any conclu-
> sions from it. It wasn't going to enable you to solve any problems. . . .
> I think that's always been a fundamental difference between Chi-
> cago and other places. MIT more recently has been a better exem-
> plar than Harvard.[16]

Gary Becker said: "Friedman was not interested in theory for its own sake, but as a means of explaining behavior in . . . markets. So his theory was oriented toward explaining what happened in the real world. After all, he was a superb statistician . . . and an excellent analyzer of data, and he built on these skills in his . . . work on economic theory." Becker noted as well Friedman's "relentless pursuit of the connection between economic theory and empirical evidence."[17]

Friedman wrote that he, as well as the rest of the economics department, benefited from Cowles at Chicago—there was a "great deal of interaction between Cowles and the department."[18] He said in a 2004 interview that there was "no personal animosity"[19] between himself and members of the commission. He wrote in a February 1947 letter of recommendation for Tjalling Koopmans, who later became perceived as Friedman's chief adversary on Cowles, that Koopmans had a "real ability to get to the essentials of a problem and to expound these essentials simply and lucidly. He is one of the leading spirits in the development of the field of econometrics and is likely to do important work in that field. Koopmans is a very good teacher and has an extremely pleasant personality."[20]

There was a falling-out, or at least decline, in Friedman's relationship and that of his allies generally at Chicago with Koopmans and Cowles after Koopmans harshly criticized Arthur Burns and Wesley Mitchell's 1946 National Bureau of Economic Research volume, *Measuring Business Cycles,* in a prominent August 1947 article in the *Review of Economic Statistics,* "Measurement without Theory." This was six months after Friedman's letter of recommendation on Koopmans's behalf. Friedman was close to both Burns and Mitchell. In his review, Koopmans argued that, because Burns and Mitchell had no theory of a business cycle, they had no determinate idea of what data to gather or hypotheses to test. In a contemporaneous conference comment, Friedman made reference to "desultory skirmishing between what have been loosely designated as the National Bureau and the Cowles Commission techniques of investigating business cycles."[21]

Robert Solow, who received the Nobel Prize in Economics in 1987, told an amusing anecdote about the response to Lawrence Klein's *Economic Fluctuations in the United States* (1950) at a Cowles seminar: "There was formal discussion. Friedman concluded that the whole econometric model-building enterprise had been shown to be worthless and congratulated the Cowles Commission on its self immolation. Klein demonstrated the truth of the French doggerel:

Cet animal est très mechant.
Quand on l'attaque, il se defend.
[The animal is very bad.
When it is attacked, it defends itself.][22]

According to a number of historians of economic thought, relations between the Cowles Commission and Department of Economics at Chicago became less than harmonious. Melvin Reder wrote that, starting in the later 1940s, there was "struggle for intellectual preeminence and institutional control between Friedman, Wallis, and their adherents on one side, and the Cowles Commission and its supporters on the other. The struggle persisted into the early 1950s, ending only with . . . the departure of the Cowles Commission."[23] Historian of economic thought William Frazer writes that by the mid-1940s an "intense struggle in the economics department at Chicago was underway between Frank Knight and his former students on one side and the Cowles Commission and its adherents on the other."[24]

At the same time, they were not all bad times between the Department of Economics and the Cowles Commission. The following songs, written by graduate students and performed at an economics department party in about 1949, give an idea of the contrasting approaches of Cowles and the emerging Chicago school—and of interaction between the two. The first song, to the tune of "The American Patriot," presents the Cowles view:

We must be rigorous, we must be rigorous,

We must fulfill our role.

If we hesitate or equivocate

We won't achieve our goal.

We must make our systems complicate

To make our models whole.

Econometrics brings about

Statistical control!

Our esoteric seminars

Bring statisticians by the score.

But try to find economists

Who don't think algebra's a chore.

Oh we must urge you most emphatically

To become more inclined mathematically

So that all that we've developed

May some day be applied.[25]

The second song, about Milton Friedman, was sung to the tune of Gilbert and Sullivan's "When I Was a Lad":

When I was a lad I served a term

Under the tutelage of A. F. Burns.

I read my Marshall completely through

From beginning to end and backwards too.

I read my Marshall so carefully

That now I am Professor at the U of C

(Chorus) He read his Marshall so carefully

That now he is Professor at the U of C

Of Keynesians I make mincemeat

Their battered arguments now line the street

I get them in their weakest assumption:

"What do you mean by consumption function?"

They never gave an answer that satisfied me

So now I am Professor at the U of C

(Chorus) They never gave an answer that satisfied he

So now he is Professor at the U of C.[26]

It was not so much that there was, or was much, overt jockeying between Friedman and his allies and the Cowles Commission at Chicago. It was that the two groups had incompatible views of the future—of economics as a discipline, and of economics at the University of Chicago. Chicago economics could not sustain two such forceful, opposed, and dynamic entities as the Cowles Commission and Friedman and his allies.

Patinkin concluded a reminiscence of his years there: "That is the Chicago I remember from my student days. It is undoubtedly an idealization of the past to think of it as a time when giants walked the earth. There are always giants. But it is not an idealization to say that of the giants in economics who did then exist, an unusually large number were walking the corridors of the University of Chicago. And the fact that they were giants of different views, varieties, and vintages only increased their impact on us lesser beings."[27]

Jacob Marschak, the director and guiding spirit of the Cowles Commission during most of its years at Chicago, appears as a very appealing figure in his evaluation of Hayek's *The Road to Serfdom*. The work was proposed for publication to the University of Chicago Press largely through the efforts of Aaron Director (who had gotten to know Hayek during a year at the London School of Economics in the later 1930s). Marschak wrote in recommending Hayek's work for publication: "The current discussion between advocates and adversaries of free enterprise has not been conducted so far on a very high level. Hayek's book may start in this country a more scholarly kind of debate.... This book cannot be by-passed."[28]

By way of contrast, if it had been up to Knight, he would not have recommended publication. He wrote in his reviewer's report: "From the standpoint of desirability of publishing the book in this country,

I may note some grounds for doubt. . . . The author's treatment of the course of events leading to the Nazi dictatorship in Germany . . . strikes me as open to attack on the ground of over-simplification. . . . In sum, the book is an able piece of work, but limited in scope and somewhat one-sided in treatment. I doubt whether it would have a very wide market in this country, or would change the position of many readers."[29] Ironically, Jacob Marschak may well have been the decisive individual in recommending publication of *The Road to Serfdom* to the University of Chicago Press.

Keynesianism transformed the economics profession throughout England and the United States in the 1930s. Herb Stein, who was a graduate student at Chicago in the mid-1930s, remembered that after Keynes's *General Theory of Employment, Interest, and Money* was published, "Keynes's theory and prescription . . . swept through the profession like wildfire."[30] Milton Friedman, too, would later repeatedly draw attention to the Keynesian temper of the times in the late 1930s and through the 1940s and beyond.

Keynes changed the focus of modern economics from monetary to fiscal policy and from full employment equilibrium to less than full employment equilibrium. Friedman, by way of contrast, in the coming years would launch a broad attack on Keynesianism from the standpoint that monetary, not fiscal, policy is more important in influencing economic outcomes and inflation in the long and short runs than Keynes thought. Both Keynes and Friedman saw a significant positive role for government in macromanaging the economy—Keynes through fiscal policy and Friedman through monetary policy.

The econometric and Keynesian impulses are largely spent in contemporary economic theory. No one pretends to the ability to predict the future of the economy through finely equilibrated mathematical equations anymore. By way of contrast, the statistical presentation of economic activity remains robust. The later Keynesian emphasis on fiscal policy and related concepts, including a decisive investment multiplier, is now maintained by few. On the other hand, Friedman's monetarist approach in describing the causes and course of the Great Depression and of the greater impact of monetary than fiscal policy in macromanaging national economies is now accepted by many.

Hunter Crowther-Heyck writes in his biography of American social scientist and genius Herbert Simon, who was at Cowles in Chicago, that from its "creation in 1932 until its move to Yale in 1956, the Cowles Commission for Research in Economics was perhaps the single most important institution in the mathematical metamorphosis of modern economics."[31] That Friedman emerged as the leading economist at Chicago in the face of such competition speaks volumes.

7

THE CHICAGO SCHOOL
OF ECONOMICS

THE CRUCIAL DIVIDING YEAR in economics at Chicago was 1946. Viner left in March. Simons died in June. Friedman, Director, and Wallis arrived in September. There has been a tendency in recent histories of economics at Chicago to emphasize Hayek's role in the launch of the Chicago school after World War II. Robert Van Horn and Philip Mirowski wrote in 2009, for example, that their work "diminishes the importance of certain figures who have often loomed large in the folklore [of the rise of the Chicago school], such as Frank Knight or Jacob Viner; it reevaluates the role of others, such as Milton Friedman; and it elevates to prime positions some neglected figures such as Friedrich Hayek, Henry Simons, and Aaron Director." Regarding Simons in particular, Van Horn and Mirowski say: "From his marginal position at the Chicago Law School . . . Simons soon became the center of gravity for the group of Chicago economists Hayek had begun to imagine as a dedicated cadre . . . This was more than a pipe dream because Simons enjoyed close personal relations with President Robert Hutchins, who would help in multiple ways to facilitate what Simons had come to call 'the Hayek Project.'"[1]

Simons drifted away, to some extent, from the Department of Economics after his appointment to the law school. He maintained amicable relations with Hutchins, which others on campus, including Viner and Knight, did not. Simons noted Knight's tendency to move from economics to philosophy in the later 1930s and early 1940s. He wrote of Knight in the mid-1940s that he was "increasingly preoccupied with philosophy and philosophies, not to mention historians, theologians, and anthropologists, *et al.*, and is not deeply interested in concrete problems of economic policy."[2] Simons, however, held appointments in both the law school and economics department by the end of World War II, a year before his premature demise.

It is no doubt the case that after the war, Simons and Hayek sought to create at Chicago a center of classical liberal thinkers that would seek to keep these ideas alive and vibrant in academia. Moreover, Simons's death in 1946 inspired Aaron Director to return to Chicago, with Hayek's encouragement. Director, furthermore, played a significant practical role in the University of Chicago Press' publication of Hayek's *Road to Serfdom,* which was crucial in establishing Hayek's popular renown in the United States. But these are mostly circumstantial rather than intrinsic factors.

Milton Friedman was the heart and soul of the Chicago school of economics as it emerged and intellectually developed in the 1950s, 1960s, and 1970s. Indeed, were it not for him, there never would have been a Chicago school of economics in the popular mind, nor, probably, in the academic one. Whether he is appropriately considered the founder of the school or not, he was clearly its most recognized and influential member. More so than for any other individual, the Chicago school of economics was the Friedman school.

Born on July 31, 1912, in Brooklyn, New York, he was the fourth and last child and only son of Jeno Saul and Sarah Ethel Landau

Friedman. Both of Friedman's parents were born in the Austro-Hungarian Empire and immigrated to the United States at young ages, his father at sixteen in 1894 and his mother at fourteen in 1895. Milton liked to emphasize his parents' immigrant background. He was especially proud of his mother in this respect, who for a time worked as a seamstress in a sweatshop.

Secular in outlook from a young age, he rejected religious belief at about the time of his bar mitzvah. As a result of entering school a year early and skipping a grade, he was two years younger than the rest of his class. He was also very short, barely 5′2″. This never prevented him from dominating his surroundings as a result of his precociousness and ebullience. Following the death of his father when he was in high school, he entered Rutgers University at age sixteen in 1928.

Here Friedman blossomed. He took classes from two instructors in particular at Rutgers who would play a large role in his life and, later, the nation's economy—Arthur Burns and Homer Jones. Friedman considered Burns, who would serve on President Eisenhower's Council of Economic Advisers and was appointed chairman of the Federal Reserve Board by Richard Nixon, to have been almost a second father to him. Professionally, Burns led Friedman to the National Bureau of Economic Research, which was, after the University of Chicago, the second major institutional affiliation of Friedman's career. Homer Jones would become vice president of research at the St. Louis branch of the Federal Reserve. In this capacity, he generated much of the data on which Friedman's monetary theories were based. Jones led Friedman to Chicago, where Jones had been a dedicated graduate student of Frank Knight.

Friedman entered Chicago in September 1932 and received a master's degree in economics in one academic year. In September 1933, he went to Columbia (from which he ultimately received his PhD in 1946) for a year, and then returned to the University of Chicago as a researcher for the 1934–1935 academic year. His abilities were recognized and utilized at a young age by his teachers. He turned twenty-three just after his second year at Chicago.

For the next eleven years, he was away from Midway, showing that there truly was nothing foreordained about a free market school of economics at Chicago after World War II. During this period, Friedman taught at the University of Wisconsin at Madison and the University of Minnesota for one year each, and spent close to five years each in Washington, DC, and New York on two tours of duty in each—in Washington at a New Deal agency and with the Treasury Department, and in New York with the National Bureau of Economic Research and the Statistical Research Group during World War II. During the war, he helped to develop sequential analysis and visited Alamogordo, New Mexico, where the atom bomb was tested, on assignment. Both George Stigler and Allen Wallis also worked for the Statistical Research Group, which Wallis headed. Wallis also helped Friedman to secure his first position in Washington. Friedman and Stigler taught together and even shared the same office at the University of Minnesota during the year following World War II's close.

Paul Douglas, a rising political star, observed a real change in the climate of the faculty in the economics department and elsewhere at Chicago after World War II. "The university I had loved so much seemed to be a different place," he remembered. "Schultz was dead, Viner was gone, Knight was now openly hostile, and his disciples seemed to be everywhere."[3] The Chicago school of economics was born.

At first, there was intense doctrinal disagreement between Friedman and his emerging faction and the economists associated with the Cowles Commission. Friedman remembered the Cowles seminars as "exciting events in which I and other members of our department participated regularly and actively."[4] Cowles members took part in department seminars as well. Friedman remarked that the economics department in part benefited from Cowles because it had "very different views,"[5] both of economics as a discipline and ideologically than some in the department, including preeminently Friedman himself.

But there was a severe methodological dispute between the Cowles Commission and Friedman. Cowles emphasized complex econometric models with many mathematical equations to present economic theory. For Friedman, there was one and only one criterion for judging among models or theories of economic activity: their capacity to predict.[6] Friedman did not believe that the mathematical turn in economics during the twentieth century was a beneficial development. This was a crucial component of the Chicago view in economics. Though Friedman believed that proficiency in math was helpful in economics and cognition generally, he did not subscribe to an overemphasis on mathematical models for presenting economic theory. He wrote in a 1949 letter to C. W. Guillebaud at Cambridge: "Marshall was interested in constructing an 'engine for the discovery of concrete truth'; today, we seem to be interested in constructing a rigorous and abstract model for admiring contemplation—but definitely not for use."[7]

Friedman thought that the "relevant question to ask about the 'assumptions' of a theory is not whether they are descriptively 'realistic,' for they never are, but whether they are sufficiently good approximations for the purpose in hand. And this question can be answered only by seeing whether the theory works, which means whether it yields sufficiently accurate predictions."[8] He added: "The test of . . . theory is its value in explaining facts, in predicting the consequences of changes in the economic environment. Abstractness, generality, mathematical elegance—these are all secondary, themselves to be judged by the test of application." He decried that "abstractness, generality, and mathematical elegance have in some measure become ends in themselves"[9] in economic theory. Again, he had one—and only one—criterion for evaluating the effectiveness of theories: their capacity to predict.

Words have meaning. They can be used to describe events in the real world. Friedman's methodological view was that it is possible to make clear predictions about future economic activity, and if events do not follow the path one predicts, then one should change one's view— one's theory—of the world. Too many economists speak an irrelevant and esoteric mathematical language devoid of meaningful substantive content, he believed.

He maintained this position throughout his career. Intelligent individuals of good will often disagree. How should they resolve their differences? Make predictions and collect facts. He remarked in a 2003 letter that he believed mathematics was "overemphasized" and "carried too far" in contemporary economics, though it was a "useful tool."[10] According to Johan Van Overtveldt: "Friedman was highly critical of sophisticated mathematical modeling."[11]

Friedman made these comments on differences between writing for popular and scientific audiences in 1949: "It is perfectly understandable that there should be considerable reluctance in releasing figures for general public consumption that have a very large margin of error attached to them, and that accordingly lend themselves to misinterpretation. . . . Unfortunately, good public relations may be poor science. For the *analysis* of data, the fundamental point is that it is always better to have some data than none," noting that the "real problem of statistical analysis is to squeeze information from whatever data are available."[12]

There is a difference between statistical description of information and presenting economic theory, predictions of the future, in the form of mathematical equations. Friedman believed that statistical information is vital in theorizing of all sorts and in the description of real economic activity. Indeed, the precision of numbers is extremely helpful in making predictions and thereby in evaluating theories. He made these further comments:

> Of course, selection in publication is inevitable; no one can or should present every last figure he has collected . . . But at least in publications intended primarily for a scientific audience, it seems to me highly inappropriate for authors to suppress information because in their view it "may be misinterpreted" or "would do more harm than good." The fundamental premise of scientific work must

be that knowledge is better than ignorance; that appropriate use of published material will more than counterbalance inevitable misuse. The responsibility of scientific workers is to present their data accurately and precisely, and as fully as time, space, and resources will permit, not to set themselves up as censors. No one can predict in advance what uses—or misuses—will be made of any particular information. The history of science is studded with examples of the unexpected fruitfulness of material originally supposed of little or no value.[13]

Friedman considered the Cowles approach, and much of twentieth-century economic theory, to be excessively formal and mathematical—tautological in character rather than explanatory or predictive. He said of his interaction with the Cowles Commission that he was "anything but a devotee, or a disciple of their belief that the way to understand the working of the world was to construct big econometric models. In fact, I was a major critic of the kind of thing they were doing in Chicago. I introduced the idea of testing their work against naïve models, naïve hypotheses, and so on."[14] Don Patinkin, who was not always sympathetic to Friedman, told an anecdote about Friedman's participation in Cowles seminars. One of Patinkin's most distinct memories was a seminar in which Friedman advanced the "simple but powerful suggestion that a minimum test for the predictive efficacy of an econometric model is that it do better than a 'naïve model' which stated that the future would be like the past." Patinkin often wondered whether Friedman "thought that up on the spur of the moment, as well he might."[15]

People often differ about the way the world is. How should they determine whose views are more accurate? Friedman's argument was that prediction, and prediction alone, is the master-key. Scientific theories should be evaluated by the accuracy of their empirical predictions, accuracy both as to the number of correct predictions and their precision. If some theories provide more, and more accurate, predictions—which, of necessity, are of the physical world and are sensory—these are better theories.

Friedman's seminal work in method, "The Methodology of Positive Economics" (1953), originally titled "The Relevance of Economics to Prediction and Policy,"[16] is among the most-cited articles on method in economics. He gave an excellent encapsulation of his position as follows, in reply to the complaint that free market economic models are too far from reality to be useful:

> It is like saying that atomic physics does not attempt an empirical analysis of how things work in actuality but how they would work if things were really mostly empty space with atoms filling only a small part of it. Classical economics—at least in the hands of its masters—does attempt to explain how things work in actuality, not by describing them literally, but by the hypothesis that things work primarily as they would if men sought reasonably successfully and single-mindedly to pursue their own interests and as if their interests were predominantly to maximize the money income they could wring from a hostile environment. The test of the validity of this hypothesis—as of atomic physics—is not whether it describes faithfully the individual man—or individual table—but whether it yields correct predictions of mass phenomena.[17]

J. Daniel Hammond, who has written extensively on Friedman and his methodology, observes that Friedman was "considered throughout his career to be working outside standard econometrics."[18] Friedman's work in methodology was significant. He essentially announced to the economics profession that he was putting forward a single criterion for scientific relevance and accuracy—prediction.

Friedman's major field of focus during his years at Chicago was monetary theory and policy. His views evolved and developed substantially here. According to Wallis, Friedman started as a student at Chicago as a "Norman Thomas–type"[19] socialist, a mild socialist of the

American variety. Friedman did not recall his early political leanings especially well, and he does not appear to have thought much about politics when he was in his teens and early twenties. He originally intended to become an actuary. He recalled a few months before he died in 2006 that his interest in economics was fueled by the Great Depression:

> When I graduated from undergraduate college in 1932, I was baf-
> fled by the fact that there were idle machines and idle men and you
> couldn't get them together. . . . My self-interest to begin with was to
> understand the real mystery and puzzle that was the Great Depres-
> sion. My self-interest was to try to understand why that happened,
> and that's what I enjoyed doing. . . . Out of that I grew to learn some
> things—to have some knowledge. Following that, my self-interest
> was to see that other people understood the same things and took
> appropriate action.[20]

During the Great Depression and World War II, he adopted the conventional view, which was that fiscal policy trumps monetary policy and that there was little that could be done to right the Great Depression through monetary policy. After the war, he came to hold exactly the opposite opinion—that the Great Depression was a symptom of poor monetary policy; fiscal policy was almost impotent to remedy it. But this was in the future during the 1930s and early 1940s. He adopted the standpoint of the times, even testifying before Congress for the Treasury Department that wartime inflation could be controlled by increased taxes.[21]

Friedman's monetary work began as a project for the National Bureau of Economic Research in 1948 to investigate the "role of monetary and banking phenomena in producing cyclical fluctuations, intensifying or mitigating their severity, or determining their character,"[22] as he wrote in a memo at the time. He arrived at the view that there is no such thing as a business *cycle*—in the sense of regular, recurrent waves of economic activity: "I do believe that short-run fluctuations in the economy are simply the accumulation of random shocks. I don't believe there is such a thing as a business cycle."[23]

He had the following exchange with an interviewer in 1998:

Q: Ben Bernanke has said that business cycle models should explain both the post-war and the interwar eras and that we shouldn't have two sets of models to explain them both.

A: I agree with that, but I go further. I don't believe there is such a thing as a business cycle [i.e., a recurrent boom-bust cycle]. I believe there are economic fluctuations [i.e., occasional lapses from full employment].

Q: Oh, the plucking model, OK.

A: That's right. That is a single model which fits both the interwar and the postwar [periods].[24]

In addition to questioning an inevitable business cycle, Chicago economists were identified shortly after World War II with opposition to theories of monopolistic and imperfect competition. The essential Keynesian edifice was reinforced by the theory of monopolistic competition, for this explained why the classical liberal position of unbridled competition did not work in practice. Especially as a result of wasteful advertising—a thesis originally put forward by Thorstein Veblen and later by John Kenneth Galbraith—there was much consumption that was unrelated to utility maximization other than attempting to outdo one's neighbors.

In an inherently unproductive and unfair economy, most other economists thought that a large government role was especially desirable. The emerging Chicago school in the 1950s, in contrast, was known for its general anti-Keynesianism, particular opposition to imperfect competition models, and for its reliance upon free market and laissez-faire solutions at a time when most other economists adopted strongly pro-government views. The Chicago school's theoretical models and policy prescriptions differed from most of the rest of the profession. Chicago economists, preeminently Friedman, put forward new views on the Great Depression and the role of monetary policy.

It should be emphasized that "Chicago school" economists were not a majority in the economics department at Chicago and that they could also be found in the business and law schools and elsewhere. They nonetheless became the leading element in economics at Chicago. Hayek's role here should not be neglected. An important presence at Chicago on the Committee on Social Thought from 1950 to 1962, he never was a Chicago economist in matters of economic theory, where his Austrian perspective led him to different analyses of the economy than his economist colleagues. However, when it came to public policy and philosophy, there were great similarities between Hayek's and some Chicago economists' views. A number of economists at Chicago, including Friedman, Knight, Director, and Stigler, were initial members of Hayek's Mont Pelerin Society, which brought together leading classical liberals and libertarians from around the world for semiannual conferences.

That Chicago was a stronghold of anti-Keynesianism is attested by the aforementioned December 1950 *Fortune* article "The Economists." This article, by *Fortune* editor John McDonald, provides a fascinating look at the economics profession in the United States in the immediate postwar period. Frank Knight is pictured first— he is the "dean of anti-Keynesian, orthodox, classical economists" and the president of the American Economic Association that year. The profession was tiny compared to what it would become. There were about 5,000 economists with doctoral degrees in the United States, of whom more than 3,000 taught in colleges and universities. Knight was also described as the "great teacher and elder statesman of the orthodox classical school of economics in the U.S."[25]

"It is seventeen years," McDonald continued,

since the American economist, Edward Chamberlin, and the English economist, Joan Robinson, advanced the theory that started with the proposition that industrial markets are neither purely competitive nor purely monopolistic, but rather a hybrid containing elements of both competition and monopoly, and should be so regarded in economic analysis. It is fourteen years since the English economist, John Maynard Keynes, advanced the theory that the capitalist system could not automatically run itself and maintain full employment: that at times something had to be done to make it work.

McDonald said as well that the "effect of the 'Keynesian revolution' was to lend support to the increasing growth of the state in economic affairs,"[26] since emphasis on fiscal policy generally involves government spending.

McDonald provided among the first popular uses of the phrase "Chicago school" pertaining to economics:

The way things shaped up among U.S. economists in the 1930s one might have got the impression that this was a war between Harvard and the University of Chicago. While the fortress of orthodoxy was maintained at Chicago, Alvin Hansen at Harvard seized upon Keynesian theory and became its leading exponent in the U.S. Hansen and Knight have both been effective as teachers as well as producers of works on economics. From the *Chicago school* [emphasis added], which once included the witty philosopher of economics, Jacob Viner, have come such eminent younger classicists as Milton Friedman, George Stigler, and the late Henry Simons. Among those who emerged from Hansen's Harvard seminar was Paul Samuelson . . . The effect of Keynes, however, was not localized. He swept the profession, excepting Chicago.[27]

Many participants and authorities are clear that there was little or no reference to a Chicago school of economics before about 1950. D. Gale Johnson was a student at Chicago in economics from 1938 to 1940, and was a member of the economics faculty there from 1944 until his death in 2003. When asked in 2001 whether the appellation "Chicago school of economics" was used in the 1930s, he replied: "I don't think the reference came until the 1950s." Why? "Friedman had a lot to do with it."[28]

In his memoirs, Friedman provided an example that, prior to the 1950s, the appellation "Chicago school of economics" was not used. Writing about the first meeting of the Mont Pelerin Society in 1947, he quoted a later comment of the journalist John Davenport that the participants included a "'sprinkling of what became known as the Chicago School'"[29]—that is, they were not known as the Chicago school yet.

According to longtime Chicago economist Lester Telser, it is "fair to say the notion of the Chicago school came later," after World War II. It was "not from time immemorial—the notion really begins with Friedman and Stigler, not before."[30] Sam Peltzman, who came to Chicago as a graduate student in 1960 and has been on the faculty permanently since the early 1970s, shares this view. Gary Becker also believed that the phrase "Chicago school of economics" may not have been used before the postwar era.

Henry Spiegel, a judicious and well-read historian of economic thought, wrote: "At the time when Viner taught at Chicago, the designation 'Chicago School' was not yet a commonly used term."[31] There is apparently no reference to a "Chicago school" in histories of economic thought written before the 1960s, including Joseph Schumpeter's massive *History of Economic Analysis* (1954), Joseph Dorfman's multivolume *The Economic Mind in American Civilization* (1946–1959), and Paul Homan's *Contemporary Economic Thought* (1928). Similarly, there is apparently no reference to the "Chicago school" in the *American Economic Review* or *Journal of Political Economy* before the 1960s.

Stigler wrote in a contemporaneous comment on Lawrence Miller's 1962 article "On the 'Chicago School of Economics'" that Miller did not "really investigate the thesis that there is a 'Chicago' school. . . . Instead, he has merely sketched, less than completely, the views of my friend Milton Friedman."[32] When Friedman received the Nobel Prize in Economics in 1976, Paul Samuelson wrote that "every top-notch economics department would today feel deprived and one-sided if the fruitful Chicago viewpoint were not represented on its faculty. This new fact is a tribute to one great leader,"[33] Friedman.

Melvin Reder, who was a student at Chicago in the early 1940s, later a faculty member there, and wrote several articles on the history of economics at Chicago, said that after Friedman became a member of the faculty at Chicago in 1946, he "swiftly took over the intellectual leadership of one faction of the Department and energetically attacked the views and proposals of the others. His vigor in debate and the content of his arguments set the tone and public image of Chicago economics for at least a quarter century." Reder also wrote of a "Friedman Era" at Chicago in the 1950s and 1960s when a "steady stream of papers on money, methodology, price theory, the consumption function, public policy proposals, etc. kept economists at Chicago and elsewhere busy reacting to various Friedman initiatives. Outside Chicago—and in this period I was an outsider—the force of Friedman's ideas was very strong; at Chicago, it must have been even stronger."[34] According to Van Overtveldt, the thirty years between "Friedman's return in 1946 and departure in 1976 can be labeled the Friedman era without much exaggeration."[35]

David Rockefeller, grandson of John D. Rockefeller, studied at the University of Chicago in the late 1930s. His comments in his 2002 memoirs are of interest:

> The Chicago "school of economics" has gained a great deal of fame and not a little notoriety over the past fifty years for its unwavering advocacy of the market and strong support for monetarism. These ideas are intimately associated with Milton Friedman, whose views have now come to symbolize a Chicago school that is strongly doctrinaire in its insistence that government should not interfere at all with the market. . . . I have no doubt they [Viner and Knight] would

have resisted being categorized as members of the Chicago school in the narrow present-day meaning of the term.[36]

The postwar Chicago school of economics was the Friedman school—his positions were those associated with the school in both the popular and academic minds. These included a belief in the free market as the best productive institution for an economy at a time when most economists favored a larger and increasing government role, distrust of government, reliance on the quantity theory of money in explaining aggregate prices, and emphasis on monetary policy rather than fiscal policy to influence an economy's activity. He combined these more general positions with a dazzling array of specific public policy proposals throughout his career.

Gary Becker, Robert Lucas, Thomas Sowell, and many others remember Friedman as an outstanding teacher. Becker recalled that in his courses Friedman emphasized "careful formulation of the problem, concern about empirical implications, and testing these, when possible, with real data."[37] Empiricism was at the heart of Friedman's theoretical system.

Lucas has these recollections:

> The quality of discussions in Friedman's classes was unique in my experience. He did not call on students by name . . . permitting me and many other classmates to experience the intensity of engaging Friedman directly only vicariously. It was not dismissal that I feared no graduate student would have been dismissed . . . but the exposure of my confusion next to Friedman's quickness and clarity. He would engage a particular student in a dialogue, and once engaged no escape . . . was possible. Exit lines like "Well, I'll have to think about it" were no use: "Let's think about it now," Friedman would say.[38]

Friedman appeared on the front cover of *Time* magazine on December 19, 1969. *Fortune* magazine ran an article on him the same month, and he was featured on the front cover of the *New York Times Magazine* in January 1970. He became a media superstar, and this brought the Chicago school to the popular mind. This followed his prominent involvement with Barry Goldwater's campaign for president in 1964 and, significantly, his regular column in *Newsweek* starting in 1966. Daniel Patrick Moynihan said in 1971: "If you were to ask me to name the most creative social-political thinker of our age I would not hesitate to say Milton Friedman."[39]

There were really two aspects of Friedman's career, and it is important to be clear on this point. The first was as a professional and academic economist. Here he made great contributions in such areas as flexible international exchange rates, the consumption function, theory of money, monetary history, methodology, and the natural rate of unemployment. The second aspect of his career was as a public intellectual. He became perhaps the leading public intellectual in the world from the late 1960s to the early 1980s, and his political positions became those associated with the Chicago school in the public mind.

Following Friedman, the contemporaneous economist most associated with the postwar Chicago school was George Stigler. A tall, thin man with a keen sense of humor, Stigler did not return to Chicago to teach until 1958. He remained there for the rest of his life, until 1991, fifteen years after Friedman had left Chicago on retirement for San Francisco and the Hoover Institution. In a reminiscence of Stigler, Friedman speculated that he could have been a successful comedian, which was no mean compliment, as Friedman had a great sense of humor himself. Stigler stood a foot taller than Friedman, and when they were both at Chicago they were referred to as "Mr. Micro" (Stigler) and "Mr. Macro" (Friedman)—a reference to their respective emphases in microeconomics and macroeconomics, but also surely a play on their respective heights.

Stigler truly was a funny man. Former US Secretary of State, Treasury, and Labor George Shultz recalls Stigler's "rapier wit."[40] In a 1981 discussion of law and economics at the University of Chicago, Stigler kept throwing off one-liner after one-liner. Speaking of Henry Simons, he had this to say:

> It's true that he was the man that said that the Federal Trade Commission should be the most important agency in government, a phrase that surely should be on no one's tombstone. [laughter]

Commenting on the tenure controversy with respect to Simons in the economics department, he said:

> Knight was taking a wholly admirable view and saying, "Any discussion of his imperfections is a personal attack on me." [laughter] A level of discourse, thank God, I've never faced in a faculty meeting. [laughter]

Speaking of Friedman, he commented:

> Milton was teaching an enormously influential and powerful course in price theory, or at least so it is alleged by him. [laughter]

Another *bon mot* was:

> As Ronald [Coase] recounts his indebtedness I am reminded of the statement Leslie Stephen once made. He said he could never understand why a school was credited with producing those people it had not succeeded in repressing. [laughter][41]

Stigler first gained renown as a historian of economic thought. His dissertation was published in 1941 as *Production and Distribution Theories*. As his career progressed, he considered other subjects, including microeconomic theory and industrial organization. He wrote on the transmission of knowledge:

Great economists are those who influence the profession as a whole, and this they can do if their doctrines do not involve too great a change from the views and the knowledge of the rank and file of the science. It is simply impossible for men to apprehend and to adopt wholly unfamiliar ideas . . . It is possible by mere skill of presentation to create a fad, but a deep and lasting impression on the science will be achieved only if the idea meets the more durable standards of the science.[42]

He was an intellectual elitist. According to historian of economic thought Robert Leeson, who accords a high place in influence on economics to him: "Stigler concluded . . . that two-thirds of the articles surveyed were virtually worthless. There were commonly only about six really first-class scholars in any field . . . [A]cademic consensus (which could be unreliable) was achieved not by a professional 'plebiscite,' but only by an elite group within the profession."[43]

Edward Nik-Khah writes that during his years at Chicago, Stigler "trained relatively few students. Whereas one often encounters celebrations of Friedman's influence as a classroom teacher, the reviews of Stigler as a teacher are mixed at best. Suffice it to say that whatever Stigler's influence on events at Chicago, it could not have operated in precisely the same fashion."[44]

A work that sheds much light on Friedman and Stigler's early relationship is their correspondence on price theory edited by J. Daniel and Claire Hammond. The Hammonds clearly reveal here that there was nothing foreordained about the rise and reign of the Chicago-Friedman school of economics between about 1950 and 1980. They quote a November 1946 letter from Friedman to Stigler, a few months after Friedman had started to teach at Chicago, in which he said, commenting on the recent vote in the economics department to offer a position to Paul Samuelson: "We don't yet know the end of the story. But whatever it is, I am very much afraid that it means we're lost. The Keynesians have the votes & mean to use them. Knight is bitter & says he will withdraw from active participation in the dep't. [Lloyd] Mints, Gregg [Lewis] & I are very low about it."[45] The Hammonds write: "One can easily suppose today that when Milton Friedman joined the University of Chicago faculty in 1946 this was his dream job . . . But the letters reveal that during his first couple of years at Chicago he was uncertain that he was settled."[46]

In a letter on behalf of Friedman and Stigler in 1946 with respect to an article of theirs on rent control that was to be published by the Foundation for Economic Education (FEE), Stigler wrote: "We argue that inequality is bad."[47] Friedman wrote in opposition to FEE, concerning its proposal to delete "like us" from the following line that he and Stigler had written, "for those, like us, who would like even more equality": "If this phrase were omitted we would almost certainly be interpreted as opposed to more equality."[48] Friedman and Stigler also wrote in a draft of the paper that "the personal income tax . . . is admirably suited to reduce the inequality of income."[49]

The younger Stigler and Friedman, consistent with most economists and social scientists of their time, considered greater equality of income and wealth to be an important societal goal, though not an all-encompassing one. They believed that greater equality of income and wealth would accompany a properly functioning free market society.

Stigler gave several lectures at the London School of Economics after World War II in which he expressed some of his views on economic equality:

> The policy of ignoring inequalities of resources and battling vigorously against inequalities of income is a wanton subsidy to psychiatrists. Our concern should be much more with the ownership of resources that leads to the wide differences in income. We should seek to make labor incomes more equal by enlarged educational systems, improvements of labor mobility, elimination of labor monopolies, provision of medical care for poor children, and the like. We should

seek to make property incomes more equal (and smaller) by elimination of monopoly and by extremely heavy taxation of inheritance."[50]

At its best, the Chicago view in technical economic theory emphasizes empirical relevance and a strong concern with public policy. Stigler, like Friedman, was suspicious of the mathematical turn in economics: "We do not speak symbols at breakfast, or read them in the newspaper, or propose to the lady by formula. A few persons, by their specialization and aptitudes, secure that command over mathematics that makes it also a second nature—they hesitate only so long at a step in a proof as we in selecting a word. But they are mathematicians, not economists."[51] As with Friedman, the key for Stigler to using mathematics in economics was appropriateness and relevance to the task at hand, not argumentative sophistication. Stigler was for the market and government—consistent with the classical liberal view. He supported the wide use of the price and profit system in an economy and saw no inconsistency between this position and extensive government activity, including progressive income and estate taxation.

In their opposition to socialist ownership and government direction of the economy, the younger Friedman and Stigler were also in the classical liberal tradition. Unlike many of their contemporaries, they saw a continuing large role for private ownership, management, and control. Moreover, in part inspired by Hayek, they came to recognize the necessarily politically dictatorial nature of classical socialism, defined as government ownership and management of the means of economic production. At the same time, the younger Friedman, Stigler, and Hayek were also in the classical liberal tradition as they supported a potentially wide role for government activity. Ironically, all three were considered among the most conservative economists during the early as well as later stages of their careers, providing an idea of the larger perspectives of the times and the power of intellectual paradigms and frameworks.

For the young Friedman, the question with respect to greater equality in society was not of desirability but of practicality. He wrote Stigler in February 1948, concerning the latter's London lecture discussing equality: "I don't see where emphasis on income redistribution rather than resource distribution is a consequence of emphasis on equality. The argument is that proponents of equality would have done better to have concentrated on distribution of resources."[52] Stigler wisely observed: "Modern economic systems have made very aggressive levels of taxation feasible. The predominance of the corporate form, the decline of single proprietors, the proliferation of written records, make it possible to tax at rates John Stuart Mill considered wholly infeasible."[53]

Stigler was more pessimistic than Friedman on the possibility of reasoned discourse to change society, at least the sort of discourse the economist purveys. "The economist's influence upon the formulation of economic policy has usually been small. It has been small because he lacked special professional knowledge of the comparative competence of the state and of private enterprise. . . . Lacking real expertise, and lacking also evangelical ardor, the economist has had little influence upon the evolution of economic policy,"[54] he said in his 1964 presidential address to the American Economic Association.

Stigler stated the importance of Simons's views on more equal income and wealth distribution. Simons believed that there should be a "large movement toward income equality, achieved primarily by reliance upon a personal income tax . . . Income should include capital gains, inheritances, gifts—everything that increased a person's relative command over resources. This strong egalitarian element separated Simons from most conservatives, and indeed one could make a strong case that Simons was a modern liberal who understood price theory."[55]

In their positions after the 1950s, Friedman, Stigler, and others at Chicago moved away from emphasis on equality, as well as from theories of imperfect competition requiring government intervention, and toward focus on monetary rather than fiscal policy in influencing economic activity. To this, Friedman in particular would add criticism of government at almost all times and in almost all ways, with far less empirical support than his and other Chicagoans' work at other times in other areas. That is, in its reflexive antigovernment bias, the Friedman Chicago school of economics became more ideological than scientific, at least in addressing the general public.

8

CHICAGO ECONOMISTS
IN ACADEMIA

IN ACADEMIC ECONOMICS, Friedman and the other members of the Chicago school of economics during the 1950s, 1960s, and 1970s had great success and merited high approbation, which eventually came. Friedman's reconceptualization of the monetary source of the Great Depression was fundamental, and so was his continued advocacy of flexible international exchange rates. His depiction of the monetary source of inflation and his emphasis on the much greater influence of monetary policy than fiscal policy on national economic activity were accurate and wise. As an academic economist, Friedman's influence was highly salutary and first-rate.

The first apparent reference to a Chicago school of economics in an academic journal also came in 1950 when Martin Bronfenbrenner commented on the "so-called Chicago school of economic policy, whose intellectual parent is Frank H. Knight, but whose best-known publicist is Henry C. Simons, author of *Economic Policy for a Free Society*."[1]

In 1957, Edward Chamberlin attacked the "Chicago School of Anti-Monopolistic Competition."[2]

The place of the Chicago school of economics in academia at the beginning of the 1960s was well depicted by Laurence Miller's 1962 *Journal of Political Economy* article "On the 'Chicago School of Economics.'" Here, Miller said:

> To a great many economists, the phrase "the Chicago school of economics" is a recognizable and meaningful designation. Yet a number of people who would obviously be included in the school argue that this designation has no real content—that the Chicagoans do not constitute a school in any relevant sense and that there is no significant difference between a good Chicago economist and any other economist. This paper['s] . . . thesis is that the Chicagoans do in fact form an interconnected group with a set of common attitudes and interests which distinguishes them from the rest of the economics profession.[3]

This was essentially Friedman's view. Stigler, who was more likely to say that there was an inverse relationship between the Chicago school's content and reality, implying that the degree of commonality among economists from Chicago was overstated, nonetheless acceded to the position that a school came to exist after World War II and that Friedman was its dominating element. Stigler wrote in his memoirs:

> Professor Viner and his students . . . have testified that they had not encountered the name or the belief that there was a distinctive Chicago school during this early period (the 1930s and early '40s), and I have found no hints of such a belief in the economics profession before about 1950, and no widespread recognition of the school for another five years.
>
> By the 1960s, however, the profession had widely agreed that there was a Chicago school of economics. . . . The origins of the school can be identified only if the central theses of the school are

known. . . . The policy position was the more commonly recognized element of the school, and clearly Milton Friedman . . . was the primary architect.[4]

Ironically, Friedman barely made it onto the faculty at the University of Chicago in 1946. Rather, when Viner's position as the dominant price theorist became open, Stigler was selected. Friedman to this point had been largely a statistician, outside academia, and had fewer major publications than Stigler. However, the university administration, acting in the person of University President E. C. Colwell, intervened and vetoed Stigler's appointment. It was not unusual at Chicago for the central administration to turn down departments' recommendations for faculty appointments and promotions. In 1938, economist Harry Gideonese, a leading Hutchins opponent, was turned down for tenure by the central administration despite the unanimous support of the economics department.[5]

Stigler's position was then offered to Friedman, who began to teach at Chicago in the fall of 1946. Also in early 1946—before Friedman became a member of the Department of Economics at Chicago—Hayek was briefly suggested for a position in the department. However, this idea went nowhere because Hayek was not on the cutting edge of economic theory. When Hayek came to Chicago in 1950, it was as a member of the Committee on Social Thought and as a result of his protracted and difficult divorce.

Miller wrote in his 1962 piece: "The way in which Friedman and other modern Chicagoans concentrate their attack on government interference with the market represents a major departure from the earlier Chicago position."[6] Similarly, William Baumol said in 1983: "Chicago in the 1930s, 1940s, and 1950s . . . adhered to no party line in political philosophy or analytic approach. It welcomed pure theory, empirical analysis, literary writing, and mathematical economics; libertarians, neutrals, and socialists. . . . [I]t was hardly a piece with what has come to be called the Chicago School."[7]

One of the aspects of the Friedman Chicago school was the extent to which it for a time consisted of individuals who had been graduate students together and who then were colleagues and raised their families together. The University of Chicago is different than many other major institutions of higher education and research as many faculty live within walking distance of campus. Geographical proximity, together with the long and deep ties of those who came to be faculty members by the 1960s, contributed to Chicago's different view on economics.

With respect to public policy, it clearly was Friedman's views that became identified with the Chicago school of economics, starting with his participation in the Goldwater for President campaign in 1964 and continuing through his regular column in *Newsweek* starting in 1966 and his identification with Presidents Nixon and Reagan. An August 1964 *Newsweek* article, "Goldwater's Economists," had this to say about a meeting between the Republican presidential nominee and several economists: "Leading intellect of the group is Milton Friedman, . . . an articulate debater who is something of a maverick even in conservative circles. Master of the University of Chicago 'conservative school,' he is noted for his definitive research . . . and his highly controversial theories."[8] No other Chicagoan was present. That Friedman was mentioned as being part of the Chicago "conservative school" indicates that the term "Chicago school" of economics was not yet in popular parlance in 1964, though it was in academia.

Stigler wrote of his own arrival at Chicago to teach in 1958: "I was returning to an economics community in a stage of high prosperity. Friedman was an ascendant figure in world economics: his *Consumption Function* had revolutionized the statistical analysis of economic data, and his work on monetarism constituted the major attack on the ruling Keynesian doctrine."[9] Friedman was a leading figure in economics for more than seventy years after he, Homer Jones, Stigler, and Allen Wallis edited Knight's *The Ethics of Competition* in 1935. Among the other leaders in the profession with whom Friedman and Stigler interacted—those who were not at Chicago during their professional careers—were Paul Samuelson, John Kenneth Galbraith, and James Tobin. That such luminaries in the economics profession considered Friedman's work and that of other Chicagoans so significant indicates the high professional esteem in which it was held, irrespective of agreement.

Paul Samuelson received the first John Bates Clark Medal presented by the American Economic Association in 1947, and he received the Nobel Prize in Economics the second year it was awarded, in 1970—the first American to receive the award. Samuelson's *Foundations of Economic Analysis* (1948) and extremely successful textbook *Economics* (seventeen editions between 1948 and 2001, the last eight with William Nordhaus) greatly influenced the economics profession. In the 1976, tenth edition of *Economics,* Samuelson discussed Friedman, often in footnotes and focusing on his work on the consumption function. He presented Friedman as a contemporary libertarian: "People of all political persuasions should read Friedman's *Capitalism and Freedom.* It is a rigorously logical, careful, often persuasive elucidation of an important point of view. . . . Although one may, on reflection, agree with many or few of the positions advocated, it has been well said: 'If Milton Friedman had never existed, it would have been necessary to invent him.'"[10]

Over the course of the different editions of *Economics,* Samuelson's views on monetary and fiscal policies moved strongly in Friedman's direction. As Mark Skousen notes, Samuelson wrote in the 1955 edition: "Today few economists regard federal reserve monetary policy as a panacea for controlling the business cycle."[11] By 1973, Samuelson's view was that "both fiscal and monetary policies matter much."[12] In 1995, Samuelson and Nordhaus wrote: "Fiscal policy is no longer a major tool of stabilization policy in the United States. Over the foreseeable future, stabilization policy will be performed by Federal Reserve monetary policy."[13] Economist Todd Buchholz notes that in the 1985 edition of *Economics,* Samuelson and Nordhaus "conceded that 'early Keynesianism has benefited from "the rediscovery of money." Money definitely matters. In their early enthusiasm about the role of fiscal policy, many Keynesians unjustifiably downgraded the role of money.' Samuelson and Nordhaus did not mention the names of any perpetrators"![14]

John Kenneth Galbraith was, with Keynes and Friedman, perhaps one of the three most well-known economists in the twentieth century. Galbraith, who taught at Harvard, did not garner recognition from the economics profession commensurate with his popular renown. He never received the Nobel Prize in Economics.

Friedman discussed Galbraith in a 1976 lecture at the Institute of Economic Affairs in London; the institute's advocacy of freer markets, denationalization, and a generally lesser government role in Britain established it as the leading think tank advocating these ideas in Britain, and perhaps the world, from the 1960s through the 1980s.

Friedman subjected Galbraith to severe professional censure in the 1976 lecture: "The statistics on government spending made Galbraith's theme of private affluence versus public squalor an absurd claim. . . . [H]ow difficult it is to get testable hypotheses out of the Galbraithian canon. Galbraith speaks in broad general terms; he makes assertions about the world at large. But they are very seldom put in a form in which they yield testable hypotheses. . . . Instead of regarding him as a scientist seeking explanations, I think we shall get more understanding if we look at him as a missionary seeking converts."[15] Friedman and Galbraith occasionally visited each other in the summer in New England and also saw each other in India, when Galbraith was US ambassador there.

In his *The New Industrial State* (1967), Galbraith footnoted that "Professors Stigler and Friedman are, by wide agreement, the two ablest exponents of conservative economic attitudes in the United States."[16] In his history of economic thought, *Economics in Perspective* (1987), Galbraith wrote that Friedman was perhaps the most influential economic figure of the second half of the twentieth century. . . . A small, vigorously spoken man, uniquely determined in debate and discussion, entirely free of the doubt that on occasion assails intellectually more vulnerable scholars, Friedman was . . . the leading American exponent of the classical competitive market, which he held still to exist in substantially unimpaired form except as it had suffered from ill-advised government intrusion. . . . In the history of economics the age of John Maynard Keynes gave way to the age of Milton Friedman.[17]

James Tobin received the Nobel Prize in Economics in 1981. At Yale his entire career, he became the chair of the Cowles Foundation (formerly Cowles Commission) in 1955 when it moved to Yale. He was perhaps somewhat unsympathetic initially toward Friedman for this reason—there were some hard feelings as the Cowles Commission left Chicago, though Tobin had not been with Cowles at Chicago. Tobin engaged in considerable controversy with Friedman, particularly in the area of monetary theory and policy. In 1970 and 1971, Friedman and Tobin, together with others, had an exchange about monetary theory.

Tobin strongly criticized Friedman's views: "I have been very surprised to learn what Professor Friedman regards as his crucial theoretical differences from the neo-Keynesians. . . . Friedman's 'theoretical framework' does not provide monetarism, either its short-run or its long-run propositions, with strong theoretical support."[18] In his 1965 review of A Monetary History of the United States (1963), Tobin said, criticizing Friedman's theory: "We don't know what money is, but whatever it is, its stock should grow at 3 to 4 percent per year."[19] Friedman wrote in his 1971 response to Tobin that much of his criticism "leaves me utterly baffled. We seem to be talking at cross-purposes. I disagree far less with the substance of what he says than with the views he attributes to me,"[20] noting that Tobin did not provide empirical evidence for some of his positions.

A controversy over monetary history emerged from a 1969 article, "The Chicago Tradition, the Quantity Theory, and Friedman," in which Don Patinkin argued that Friedman's presentation of a Chicago quantity of money theory tradition was erroneous. Friedman was especially incensed by this suggestion because it was then used by Harry Johnson, in his Richard T. Ely Lecture before the American Economic Association in 1970, to charge Friedman with the

> invention of a University of Chicago oral tradition that was alleged to have preserved understanding of the fundamental truth among a small band of the initiated through the dark years of the Keynesian despotism. . . . Don Patinkin has very recently—and over-belatedly . . . —exploded these efforts to provide bridges between the pre-Keynesian orthodoxy and the monetarist counter-revolution. . . . There was no lonely light constantly burning in a secret shrine on the Midway, encouraging the faithful to assemble in waiting for the day when the truth could safely be revealed to the masses . . . Nevertheless, one should not be too fastidious in condemnation of the techniques of scholarly chicanery used to promote a revolution or a counter-revolution in economic theory.[21]

Friedman was, understandably, angered by Johnson's lecture. Leeson recapitulates the situation: "Tobin used his presidential prerogative to invite [Johnson] to deliver the 1970 Ely Lecture. Tobin chaired this eagerly anticipated session and remembers that Johnson's lecture 'created quite a stir.' It appeared to be a *deliberate* attempt to shoot Friedman down in flames."[22] In 1972, Friedman participated in a symposium on his monetary theory with several critics, including Patinkin and Tobin. In a preliminary draft of his article for that symposium, Friedman wrote that Patinkin was a "heartstruck swain" and attacked "the libels erected on that shaky foundation by Harry Johnson."[23] On the advice of a referee, Friedman deleted these references in the published version of the article.

In 2001, Friedman said with respect to this question of intellectual history that he was "baffled . . . at what all the fuss was about. . . . [V]ery little was at stake."[24]

George Shultz succeeded Allen Wallis as the dean of the business school when Wallis left Chicago to become the president of the University of Rochester in 1962. Shultz could not be as close personally or professionally to Friedman as Stigler and Wallis were, but Shultz and Friedman were affiliated at Chicago, on the larger national political stage, and at the Hoover Institution for more than forty years. Shultz was the member of the Chicago school who had the most direct practical influence, as secretary of Labor, director of the Office of Management and Budget, and secretary of the Treasury under President Richard Nixon and as secretary of State under President Ronald Reagan. Among Shultz's undersecretaries was Allen Wallis, who had a varied and distinguished career in government as well as academia. Shultz was instrumental in bringing William Simon into public service and advanced the career of Paul Volcker. Schultz was also a friend of Herb Stein.

Ted Schultz was president of the American Economic Association in 1960, Stigler in 1964, and Friedman in 1967. In 1976, Friedman was the first of this Chicago trio to receive the Nobel Prize in Economics; Schultz received his Nobel in 1979 for his contributions in agricultural economics; and Stigler received his in 1982. Hayek, who by this time was back in Europe, received the Nobel Prize in Economics in 1974.

Others affiliated with the University of Chicago as students, researchers, or teachers to receive the Nobel Prize in Economics include Paul Samuelson (1970), Kenneth Arrow (1972), Tjalling Koopmans (1975), Herbert Simon (1978), Lawrence Klein (1980), Gerard Debreu (1983), James Buchanan (1986), Trygve Haavelmo (1989), Merton Miller (1990), Harry Markowitz (1990), Ronald Coase (1991), Gary Becker (1992), Robert Fogel (1993), Robert Lucas (1995), Myron Scholes (1997), Robert Mundell (1999), James Heckman (2000),

Daniel McFadden (2000), Edward Prescott (2004), Roger Myerson (2007), Leonid Hurwicz (2007), Thomas Sargent (2011), Eugene Farma (2013), and Lars Peter Hansen (2013). To say that more great economists in the past century have, at some point, passed through the University of Chicago than through any other institution would be an understatement. Economics at Chicago has led the world.

9

LAW AND ECONOMICS, AND POLITICAL PHILOSOPHY

THE CONTRIBUTIONS OF ECONOMISTS at the University of Chicago extend beyond the realm of economics proper to the interrelationship between economics and other disciplines. Among the most important Chicago contributions have been those in the areas of law and economics and political philosophy. Signal in the movement establishing law and economics as a distinct field within economics was Aaron Director, the older brother of Rose Director Friedman.

In writing articles on the history of economics at Chicago, Melvin Reder was "struck by the many strong expressions of intellectual indebtedness both of Chicago economists and legal scholars (such as Edward Levi and Robert Bork) to Aaron Director. . . . Director appears to have exercised a great deal of influence upon the principal figures in Chicago economics from the 1930s to the present [1982]."[1] According to Ronald Coase: "Director was extremely effective as a teacher, and he had a profound influence on the views of some of his students and also on those of some of his colleagues . . . both in law and economics."[2] George Stigler wrote in 1974 that in "forming most present day policy views of Chicago economists, Director and Friedman have been the main intellectual forces" and that Director "played a major role in the Chicago school."[3]

Director was born in 1901 in Charterisk, Ukraine (then part of the Russian Empire). In 1914, his family immigrated to Portland, Oregon. In 1921, he went on a scholarship to Yale. In 1927, after working as a laborer, he went to the University of Chicago, subsequently bringing his younger sister, Rose, there to complete her undergraduate education. She then enrolled as a graduate student in the Department of Economics in 1932, where she met Milton.

Rose was a formidable presence in her own right. Tough and tenacious, she was a strong admirer of Frank Knight, more so than Milton was. She recalled years later: "It was a great privilege to work closely with Frank Knight. Some of my friends thought it would be a strain to work with so brilliant a man, but he was so modest about his own ability and, equally important, so very human that I never felt the slightest strain."[4]

Following his departure from the University of Chicago in 1934, Aaron Director worked for the Treasury Department in Washington, DC. In 1937, he went to England to work on his dissertation and became friends with Robbins and Hayek at the London School of Economics. During World War II, he worked in Washington in various government agencies. He remained connected with the University of Chicago and played a key role in the University of Chicago Press' publication of Hayek's *Road to Serfdom,* which became a huge success in the United States.

Hayek visited the United States in the spring of 1945 on a lecture tour sponsored by the University of Chicago Press. While in America, he was approached by Harold Luhnow of the conservative Volker Fund to write a *Road to Serfdom* directed specifically to the United

States. He declined because he intended to organize an international conference of classical liberal and libertarian scholars. (This conference did come to pass, paid for in large part by the Volker Fund—close to one-half the attendees at the 1947 gathering were Americans whose participation and travel the fund subsidized.)

Though Hayek would be unable to direct a classical liberal project in the United States himself, he encouraged the Volker Fund to support Henry Simons and Aaron Director in a similar pursuit at the University of Chicago. According to Ronald Coase, the project would have as its goal the "study of a suitable legal and institutional framework of an effective competitive system."[5] Following Simons's untimely death in 1946, Director agreed to come back to the University of Chicago to head the project. Hayek wrote Director in 1946 that this "seems to me the only chance that the tradition which Henry Simons created will be kept alive and continued in Chicago—and to me this seems tremendously important."[6]

Director returned to Chicago in 1946, just as Milton and Rose Friedman and Allen Wallis did. For a time, Aaron lived in an apartment attached to his sister and brother-in-law's home near the university. The project that Director led was the Free Market Study, whose members included Milton Friedman, Frank Knight, and Theodore Schultz.

Director's key insight was that monopolistic competition did not characterize the American economy—and that the law should not be based on the supposition it did. This was a vital contribution, for it helped pave the way for the free market revival in mainstream academic economics. Historian of economic thought Robert Van Horn writes:

> In a period of just ten years (1946–1956), the contents of liberalism at Chicago underwent a radical transformation. Director and other neoliberal advocates and converts no longer regarded monopoly as the great enemy of democracy, much less a force to be broken up by

the hammer of U.S. antitrust law. Rather, they argued that not only was monopoly not deleterious to the operation of the market, but also that it was a negligible symptom attributable to ill-functioning, ham-fisted activities of government.[7]

New academic views with respect to monopolistic competition and fiscal and monetary theory paved the way in the 1950s at Chicago for new positions in public policy.

Like some academic figures, Director communicated more through the spoken than the written word. His influence is therefore not as traceable as others'. He founded and—for its first five years—edited the *Journal of Law and Economics.* According to Richard Ebeling, Director's "greatest influence was through his teaching . . . during which he helped to change how an entire generation of economists and lawyers thought about government regulation and the impact of antitrust laws on market competition."[8]

Friedman commented on his brother-in-law:

> If you look at my price theory book, there is in the back a collection of problems which I gave to students. A large fraction of those . . . came out of Aaron . . . And that's the sense in which he was different from either Knight or Viner. He had, as it were, Viner's command of economic theory, and belief in economic theory as a real thing, but he had something that I think neither Knight nor Viner did have, which was this interest in solving . . . concrete problems—in particular, problems in the area of industrial organization. That's what led him to found the whole field of law and economics.[9]

Karl Brunner, who was at Chicago in the 1950s, recalled that Director "conveyed a remarkable insight how to use price theory to understand our world."[10] Stigler remarked that in Socratic discussion, Director's "influence has been magnitudes larger than almost anyone else I've ever met."[11] Friedman also said of Director that he did "not write much himself, but he had a tremendous influence on other people."[12] Wesley Liebeler, a student during the 1950s, remembers that Director was like the "character in the *Li'l Abner* comic strip, the 'bald iggle,' that has to be kept locked up . . . because whenever you . . . looked at him you were compelled to tell the truth."[13] Director was sometimes jokingly referred to at Chicago as "honest Aaron." Lionel Robbins called him a "perfectly civilized man."[14]

Paul Samuelson said: "Aaron Director was my first teacher, and it was he who seduced me into economics."[15] Samuelson also said of Director that he was "a person who has never published anything important, but he was very influential. He really was the one who converted the first Chicago school of Frank Knight, Jacob Viner, and Paul Douglas, which was pretty eclectic, into the second one, with Milton Friedman and so forth."[16] Milton and Rose Friedman dedicated their memoirs to Aaron, "brother and mentor."[17] He died at the age of 102 in 2004.

Ronald Coase, also important in the law and economics movement, was born in 1910 in England and attended the London School of Economics. He was best known for the "Coase Theorem," the proposition that the initial allocation of legal entitlements, or property rights, would not matter as long as transaction costs were nil. That is, a perfectly competitive market would allocate resources over time in the most efficient manner, for they would continually move to their highest and best uses. Also important in Coase's thought was the idea that the establishment of property rights, and their form, is an essential prelude to and shapes the content of market transactions. Following Director, Coase was editor of the *Journal of Law and Economics* for nineteen years. According to his student Steven Cheung: "Some of us feel that a genius in his prime should not have burdened himself with so time-consuming a task."[18] Coase was at the University of Chicago from 1964 until his death in 2013.

Friedrich Hayek, the most significant political philosopher at Chicago, was born in 1899 and died in 1992. His influence on some economists at Chicago was substantial, though he is not considered a member of the Chicago school because of his Austrian technical economic theory and methodology. When it came to the philosophy of a free market, it was an entirely different matter. Here, many acknowledged his influence.

With Milton Friedman, Hayek was one of the two great libertarian and classical liberal economists and political philosophers of the twentieth century. Born and raised in Vienna, he fought in World War I as a teenager for Austria. On returning home after the war, he studied at the University of Vienna, after which he came under the influence of Ludwig von Mises. In his seminal "Economic Planning in the Socialist Commonwealth" (1920), Mises asked how a socialist system would work. "There are many socialists who have never come to grips in any way with the problems of economics," he said, "and who have made no attempt at all to form for themselves any clear conception of the conditions which determine the character of free society. They have criticized freely enough the economic structure of 'free' society, but have consistently neglected to apply to the economics of the disputed socialist state the same caustic acumen."[19]

Mises stated his main point beautifully in an example he used to illustrate the importance of freely fluctuating prices to guide an economy. The socialist director, he said,

> wants to build a house. Now, there are many methods that can be resorted to. Each of them offers certain advantages and disadvantages with regard to the utilization of the future building, and results in a different duration of the building's serviceableness; each of them requires expenditures of building materials and labor. Which method should the director choose? He cannot reduce to a common denominator the items of various materials and various kinds of labor to be expended. Therefore, he cannot compare them.[20]

"Socialism," Mises concluded, is the "abolition of rational economy."[21]

Hayek was very impressed by Mises's argument and spent much of his career attempting to elucidate issues that Mises raised. Hayek's early work in economics followed Austrian business cycle theory, emphasizing the importance of changes in capital structure on economic activity—in particular the possibility of constructing incomplete capital structures as a result of inadequate savings and artificially low interest rates. Hayek's work in technical economic theory is not and has not generally been considered (other than by economists in the Austrian tradition) to be of much value or worth. Bruce Caldwell, general editor of Hayek's collected works, writes of Hayek's early work in business cycle theory that it "must now be viewed as chiefly of antiquarian interest."[22]

With respect to his writings in political and pure philosophy, it is a very different matter. Here, Hayek is considered to have made important contributions, and contributions that influenced individuals at Chicago—a number of whom became members of his international association of classical liberals and libertarians, the Mont Pelerin Society. Hayek was led to political philosophy through his participation in the socialist calculation debate. Prices, he believed, serve as guides to actions in the future. They are not determined by what has happened in the past.

Hayek conceived the political-economic problem differently than his socialist contemporaries. He did not consider society to be an "organization" but an "order." By this distinction, he meant that society is not, like an army, organized for a purpose; rather, it is an institution whose purpose is to fulfill the individual wills of its members. Society is an enabling institution rather than a purposeful one, intended to allow its members to pursue their individual good according to their own lights. The best society is not the one that gives the most direction; it is the one that enables each of its members to fulfill his or her individual dreams and aspirations to the greatest extent possible.

"There is," he wrote in his landmark 1936 essay, "Economics and Knowledge," a problem of the *division of knowledge* which is quite analogous to, and at least as important as, the problem of the division of labor. But, while the latter has been one of the main subjects of investigation ever since the beginning of our science, the former has been as completely neglected, although it seems to me to be the really central problem of economics as a social science. . . . Economics has come closer than any other social science to an answer to that central question of all social sciences: How can the combination of fragments of knowledge existing in different minds bring about results which, if they were to be brought about deliberately, would require a knowledge on the part of the directing mind which no single person can possess? The spontaneous actions of individuals will, under conditions which we can define, bring about a distribution of resources which can be understood as if it were made according to a single plan, although nobody has planned it.[23]

To the end of allowing prices to perform their magic, private property must be protected—for if there is no private property, then prices, in any meaningful sense, cannot exist. According to Mises student Bettina Bien Greaves, for Mises the "crucial factor with respect to economic calculation under socialism was not merely that economic agents cannot calculate without prices, but that without private property there can be no prices."[24] Completing the trinity of "p's," profits, in addition to prices and property, are necessary to direct resources to those who will use them more effectively than others. Though socialists may deride prices, profits, and property, they are the three essential knowledge-bestowing institutions that allow productive economic activity to occur.

Hayek first became involved with University of Chicago economists when he taught at the London School of Economics, or LSE. Frank Knight, in particular, was an influential figure for Hayek, together with Ludwig von Mises in Vienna and Edwin Cannan,[25] who had taught earlier at the LSE. As *The Road to Serfdom* was published in the United States by the University of Chicago Press and the press arranged Hayek's lecture tour in the United States in 1945, Hayek became increasingly close to individuals at Chicago. He visited Chicago several times before he came to the university to teach from 1950 to 1962.

His arrival in Chicago in the fall of 1950 to teach on the Committee on Social Thought was very closely connected with his divorce in the summer of that year. As he later recounted in an interview, he first married "on the rebound"[26]; his true love, a cousin, married someone else when, as a young man, Hayek went to America in 1923 for more than a year to study. Charlotte Cubitt—in whom Hayek and his second wife, Helene, confided—recalled, in her revealing memoir of him, Helene telling her that she "had never been in love with her first husband. She had married him solely to have children ... She had got to know him [her first husband] because he had frequently been admitted to their home, and she had been carried away by his ardent wooing. She should not have allowed him to do what he did, so she had to marry him, and while she was still suckling her first child Hayek had reproached her for marrying too quickly, and had urged her to seek a divorce."[27]

Hayek himself married in the summer of 1926, two years after he returned from America, and he and Helene did not see each other for a number of years until 1934. They then made the decision, again according to Cubitt recalling what the second Mrs. Hayek told her, that they must "be together one day no matter how unlikely it seemed at the moment."[28] In the years before and after World War II, Hayek and Helene carried on a long-standing affair that was interrupted by the war and his inability to travel to Vienna. After the war, they planned a double-divorce to be followed by marriage to one another. Helene's husband acceded to a divorce, though he died days before it was effected, but Hayek's first wife did not. Accordingly, in the spring of 1950, he spent a term at the University of Arkansas at Fayetteville en route to Chicago. Arkansas had at that time permissive divorce laws.

His divorce was granted on July 13, 1950. He married Helene in Vienna the next month.

It was difficult to travel to postwar Austria, and Hayek did not see Helene to resume their affair until the winter of 1946–1947. They then planned their simultaneous divorces and marriage, and he sought a position in the United States in large part to have the financial wherewithal to put their plan into effect. "What made me accept the offer from Chicago," he wrote later in his autobiographical notes, "was in the first instance solely that it offered the financial possibility of that divorce and remarriage which I had long desired and which the war had forced me to postpone for many years."[29]

The Committee on Social Thought at Chicago was an interdisciplinary group in the social sciences. Hayek's title on the committee was Professor of Social and Moral Science. A student of his in the early 1960s, Ronald Hamowy, recalled:

> He was an extremely distinguished-looking man with impeccable manners and a gentle scholarly way about him. I confess to having found him somewhat formal, and although I grew to become quite fond of him and saw him a number of times after having received my doctorate, there always existed a wall, however tenuous, that separated professor from student. Indeed, I never ceased to call him professor even though I last met him when I was in my forties and had been a professor myself for a number of years.[30]

The great work of Hayek's Chicago period was *The Constitution of Liberty* (1960), which when he wrote it was intended as his magnum opus. "There are but few individuals, in comparison with the whole of mankind, whose experiments, if adopted by others, would be any improvement on the existing practice," John Stuart Mill wrote in *On Liberty*, a century before *The Constitution of Liberty*. "But these few are the salt of the earth, without whom human life would become as a stagnant pool."[31] Hayek agreed with Mill. "The freedom that will be used by only one man in a million," he said in *The Constitution of Liberty,* "may be more important to society and more beneficial to the majority than any freedom that we all use."[32]

With this, Hayek turned hundreds of years of egalitarian thinking on its head. Far from inequality being detrimental to progress, the right kind of inequality—or diversity of social outcomes—emerging from a free market order is precisely what leads to and constitutes progress. His conception was that progress occurs in echelon fashion: First, some in a society obtain a new good or service, then others do, and finally the whole society does. Yesterday's luxuries become tomorrow's necessities. To prevent some from receiving new or more goods and services until all received them would bring human progress to an end.

Moreover, individuals are diverse. It was here that Hayek agreed with Mill the most, going as far as to end the text proper of *The Constitution of Liberty* with reference to Mill: "We cannot think of better words to conclude than those of Wilhelm von Humboldt which . . . John Stuart Mill put in the front of his essay *On Liberty:* 'The grand, the leading principle, towards which every argument unfolded in these pages directly converges, is the absolute and essential importance of human development in its richest diversity.'"[33] Hayek was emphatic that though it has been the "fashion in modern times to minimize the importance of congenital differences between men and to ascribe all the important differences to the environment," in fact

individuals are very different from the outset. The importance of individual differences would hardly be less if all people were brought up in very similar environments. As a statement of fact, it just is not true that "all men are born equal." We may continue to use this hallowed phrase to express the ideal that legally and morally all men ought to be treated alike. But if we want to understand what this ideal of equality can or should mean, the first requirement is that we free ourselves from the belief in factual equality.[34]

In Hayek's view, it was not merely that natural individual differences lead to a diverse social structure in a freedom-maximizing society, but that individuals have different tastes and preferences. Some prefer more income, some prefer more leisure. Earnings change over the life cycle and with education. The notion that uniformity should somehow dictate desired social outcomes is false.

The vital message of *The Constitution of Liberty* is that liberty is required in order to allow the new and unforeseen to emerge and develop. Hayek's concept of human nature was that the individual human mind is limited and puny. Advance is often the result of lucky accidents or breaks. The virtue of the market is not that it is always right or that the right outcomes always emerge from it, but that beneficial outcomes emerge from it more often than from any other system. The free market recognizes individual human weakness. Government and law are necessary, but are very likely to be misused. For this reason, the appropriate social goal is not the right direction of power, but the limitation of power—and in particular arbitrary power.

Property is an essential bulwark of liberty and a constituent of personal happiness. It helps to create an individual's private or protected sphere. Hayek here extended Mises's argument that freely floating prices are essential to a properly functioning economic order—and that private property is essential to prices—to the political argument that, without private property, human beings are little more than slaves. There is no "political" freedom separable from "economic" freedom. Economic freedom invariably has proved necessary to political freedom. Without the right to own a piece of land or a business, individuals have rarely had the right to vote. Economic and political freedom are inseparable.

Economists from Chicago have often made their mark at other institutions. James Buchanan, the 1986 recipient of the Nobel Prize in Economics, was a student at Chicago immediately following World War II. Buchanan was a thoughtful scholar, prescient, clear, and exact in his words. He was a student of Frank Knight, whom he revered and emulated. Of Knight, Buchanan said that he became the "role model who has never been replaced or even slightly dislodged over a long academic career. In trying to assess my own development, I find it impossible to imagine what I might have been and become without exposure to Frank Knight."[35]

Buchanan had a very successful career. In *The Calculus of Consent* (1962), with Gordon Tullock, he argued for limited government on the basis of human imperfection and the tendency of government bureaucrats to maximize their individual interests rather than the common interest. Buchanan thus shared the view of American founder James Madison, who wrote in *The Federalist*: "What is government itself, but the greatest of all reflections on human nature? . . . In framing a government which is to be administered by men over men, the great difficulty lies in this: you must first enable the government to control the governed; and in the next place oblige it to control itself."[36] Buchanan commented that, as a remedy for human imperfection, "widespread adoption of Judeo-Christian morality may be a necessary condition to the operation of a genuinely free society of individuals."[37]

The Virginia school of political economy that Buchanan headed was considered to be an offshoot of the Chicago school of economics. Buchanan, Tullock, Warren Nutter, and Routledge Vining—the Virginia school's principals—all graduated from the University of Chicago. Buchanan's importance stems from his role in developing the field of public choice. Essentially, his and others' idea is that public servants, whether elected or civil, should be considered to be as motivated by self-interest as others in an economy are. This approach emphasizes institutions. Buchanan stressed the tendency of government to grow. He long supported balanced budgets as a way to curtail the growth of government and to encourage the growth of the economy. Buchanan and Tullock also wrote: "Man's reason is the slave to his passions, and recognizing this about himself, man can organize his own association with his fellows in such a manner that the mutual benefits from social interdependence can be effectively maximized."[38] Like his mentor Frank Knight, Buchanan was a pure utilitarian.

There was substantial evolution in the ideas of Chicago economists over the years with respect to law and economics. In the 1930s, Viner was a major force, and he was greatly concerned about imperfect and monopolistic competition by large corporations, as was Henry Simons. As Director and others investigated the actual effects of bigness in business in the late 1940s and 1950s, they found that it hardly ever involved the loss of economic efficiency. Thus, in large part as a result of their efforts, the antimarket bias in much antitrust legislation was gradually reduced in law.

The accomplishments of Director and others at Chicago in reconceptualizing the factual nature of American business with respect to monopoly and oligopoly and their effects was fundamental in the transition of economic thinking to greater focus on free market policies in the 1950s, 1960s, and 1970s. Together with Friedman's reconceptualization of monetary policy, a lesser role for government was called for and enjoined.

10

HAYEK AT CHICAGO: PHILOSOPHER OF CLASSICAL LIBERALISM

IN HIS GREAT 1960 WORK, *The Constitution of Liberty,* written at the University of Chicago, Hayek advocated the ideas and policies of what is here called classical liberalism. It is important, again, to be clear on terminology. Historically, the word "libertarianism" has been used to denote the classical liberal position, and Hayek himself used "libertarian" at times to characterize his views in *The Constitution of Liberty.*

This is no longer correct usage of the term "libertarian." Rather, in contemporary discussion, "libertarian" has come to denote a neo-anarchist position in which government is "hated"[1] at virtually all times and in all ways; in which government can do almost no, if any, good—it can only do harm; and in which government is opposed rhetorically at almost every opportunity. In practice, contemporary American "libertarians," at least those elected to office espousing these views, irrespective of party label, advocate tax cuts for the wealthy, or, when that is not politically feasible, at least oppose tax increases, particularly on the rich.

In addition, contemporary American libertarians have formed strong, perhaps unbreakable, alliances with among the most backward-looking and irrational elements in contemporary society—fundamentalist religious believers who put forward as scientific fact such views as that the world was created 6,000 years ago, that God gave the current state of Israel to individuals who identify themselves as Jewish, and that the United States has a divinely appointed role to play in world history. The younger Hayek and younger Friedman would have had nothing to do with such beliefs. Moreover, they did not accept the socially conservative views of many, though not all, individuals espousing contemporary libertarianism.

The views of contemporary libertarians and social conservatives were not the views put forward by progressive, classical liberals. The views that Hayek and Friedman expressed during their mature, as well as younger, careers, when both taught at the University of Chicago in the 1950s, would now be best characterized as "classical liberal," especially in the case of Hayek. In *The Constitution of Liberty,* he enunciated the great positive statement of his thought that he had presented in a more negative form—against classical socialism—in *The Road to Serfdom.*

It is important to emphasize that Hayek's primary target of opposition was socialism in its classical form of government ownership and management of the means of economic production. He did not, for the most part, mean by "socialism" the institutions, programs, and policies of the welfare state. Indeed, throughout his career until old age, he endorsed many, perhaps most, of the aspects of the welfare state, which is why, during his younger career and in middle age, he is more appropriately considered to have been a classical liberal than a contemporary libertarian. Libertarians today deny almost any positive role for government. This was not the view of the younger and middle-aged Hayek at all.[2]

Starting from his arrival in England in 1931, Hayek made many statements that attest to his sentiments about the welfare state, and he recommended liberal public policies. In his inaugural address at the London School of Economics in 1933, he concluded on the thought of "the isolation of the contemporary economist and the refusal of modern progressivism to avail itself of the knowledge he can provide . . . The peculiar historical development which I have sketched has brought it about that the economist frequently finds himself in disagreement in regard to means with those with whom he is in agreement with regard to ends; and in agreement in regard to means with those whose views regarding ends are entirely antipathetic to him." He commented here as well on "the ends which they share in common"[3] of modern progressives and economists such as himself.

In *The Road to Serfdom,* he was emphatic that the tradition he followed was not what is here referred to as contemporary libertarianism, but classical liberalism. He saw and countenanced a large role for government:

> There is nothing in the basic principles of liberalism to make it a stationary creed, there are no hard-and-fast rules fixed once and for all. . . . There is, in particular, all the difference between deliberately creating a system within which competition will work as beneficially as possible, and passively accepting institutions as they are. Probably nothing has done so much harm to the liberal cause as the wooden insistence of some liberals on certain rough rules of thumb, above all the principle of *laissez faire.*
>
> It is important not to confuse opposition against . . . [socialist] planning with a dogmatic *laissez faire* attitude. . . . The successful use of competition . . . precludes certain types of coercive interference . . . , but it admits of others . . . and even requires certain kinds of government action. . . . To prohibit the use of certain poisonous

substances, or to require special precautions in their use, to limit working hours or to require certain sanitary arrangements, is fully compatible with the preservation of competition. . . . Nor is the preservation of competition incompatible with an extensive system of social services . . . The functioning of competition not only requires adequate organization of certain institutions like money, markets, and channels of information—some of which can never be adequately provided by private enterprise—but it depends above all on the existence of an appropriate legal system . . . Nor can certain harmful effects of deforestation, or of some methods of farming, or of the smoke and noise of factories, be confined to the owner of the property . . .

To create conditions in which competition will be as effective as possible, to supplement it where it cannot be made effective, to provide services which, in the words of Adam Smith, "though they may be in the highest degree advantageous to a great society are, however, of such a nature that the profit could never repay the expense to any individual. . . . ," these tasks provide indeed a wide and unquestioned field for state activity. In no system that could be rationally defended would the state just do nothing.[4]

In a 1945 interview, Hayek commented that The Road to Serfdom was "not really an attack on socialists; it is rather an attempt to persuade socialists . . . My main thesis is that they are mistaken in the methods for getting what they want to achieve." He also then said: "The fact that the government has important functions in providing conditions which will lead to a high and stable level of employment, nobody can doubt."[5] All the essentials of the classical liberal, as distinct from contemporary libertarian, position are present in Hayek's early and middle-aged work—an ample role for government in providing services, ensuring an economic minimum for all, and macromanaging the economy. To be sure, Hayek was on the side of less government rather than more, and emphasized better than anyone else the manifold economic benefits of a system largely based on private ownership and management of the means of economic production and the free exchange of goods and services. But the younger and middle-aged Hayek was no extreme antigovernmentalist.

George Nash, the great historian of modern American conservatism, provides perhaps the best description and characterization of the group and mind-set now dominating the thought of conservative, libertarian, and mainstream Republican political organizations: "radical libertarian anarchists." Nash traces the intellectual roots of this perspective to, among others, Ludwig von Mises and Murray Rothbard. The influence of the Mises-Rothbard point of view on contemporary politics should not be underestimated. Nash summarizes some of the slogans of the "anarcho-capitalists"—themes that have become mainstream in the Republican Party, Tea Party, conservative-libertarian think-tank world, and elsewhere: "Anarchy forever! Sock it to the State! MYOB (Mind Your Own Business)! Leave us alone! I am an enemy of the State! Taxation is theft!" Nash also says that, in the early 1970s, "The conservative accepted the State along with a 'presumption' against its expansion, said [William F.] Buckley. But a doctrinaire application of the capitalist paradigm to every sphere—no."[6]

Hayek, though a proponent of the welfare state for most of his career, distanced himself from this label. He emphasized possible beneficial government activities in *The Constitution of Liberty,* where he drew a distinction between coercion and taxation:

> Unlike socialism, the conception of the welfare state has no precise meaning. The phrase is sometimes used to describe any state that "concerns" itself in any manner with problems other than those of the maintenance of law and order. But, though a few theorists have demanded that the activities of government should be limited to the maintenance of law and order, such a stand cannot be justified by the principle of liberty. Only the coercive measures of government need be strictly limited. . . . [T]here is undeniably a wide field for

non-coercive activities of government and . . . there is a clear need for financing them by taxation.

He also said: "Let us consider . . . the distinction between the coercive measures of government and those pure service activities where coercion does not enter or does so only because of the need of financing them by taxation."[7]

He explicitly rejected the position that would be taken up by contemporary libertarians:

> No government in modern times has ever confined itself to the "individualist minimum" which has occasionally been described, nor has such confinement of governmental activity been advocated by the "orthodox" classical economists. All modern governments have made provision for the indigent, unfortunate, and disabled and have concerned themselves with questions of health and the dissemination of knowledge. There is no reason why the volume of these pure service activities should not increase with the general growth of wealth. . . . It can hardly be denied that, as we grow richer, that minimum of sustenance which the community has always provided for those not able to look after themselves . . . will gradually rise, or that government may, usefully and without doing any harm, assist or even lead in such endeavors. There is little reason why the government should not also play some role, or even take the initiative, in such areas as social insurance and education, or temporarily subsidize certain experimental developments.[8]

President Barack Obama could scarcely say it better himself. Indeed, the positions of the younger and middle-aged Hayek were closer to the positions of many Democrats today than to those of many contemporary Republicans. Those individuals who identify themselves as conservatives and libertarians today and who reject out of hand virtually any government intervention in or involvement with the economy (whatever that would mean); who oppose government aid to schools, families, unemployed people, the elderly, the sick, the disabled, and others; and who believe that government essentially can do no good—should remember that this position was explicitly rejected by the younger and middle-aged Hayek.

He also wrote in *The Constitution of Liberty*: "The case for natural parks, nature reservations, etc., is exactly of the same sort as that for similar amenities which municipalities provide on a smaller scale [including 'parks and museums, theaters, and facilities for sport'] . . . If the taxpayer knows the full extent of the bill he will have to foot and has the last word in the decision, there is nothing further to be said about these problems in general terms";[9] and: "The rigid position that government should not concern itself at all with such matters [including 'social insurance' and 'education'] . . . is defensible but has little to do with freedom."[10]

Statements from *The Constitution of Liberty* calling for a significant positive government role include:

sanitation or roads . . . The provision of such services has long been a recognized field of public effort.[11]

the non-coercive or purely service activities that government undertakes . . . such services as care for the disabled or infirm.[12]

activities which governments have universally undertaken . . . the provision of a reliable and efficient monetary system . . . the setting of standards of weights and measures; the providing of information gathered from surveying, land registration, statistics, etc.; and the support, if not also the organization, of some kind of education.[13]

services which are clearly desirable but which will not be provided by competitive enterprise because it would be either impossible or difficult to charge the individual beneficiary for them. Such are most . . . health services . . . and many of the amenities provided by municipalities for the inhabitants of cities.[14]

safety regulations in buildings . . . some regulation of buildings permitted in cities is unquestionably desirable.[15]

The effect which the use of any one piece of land often has on neighboring land clearly makes it undesirable to give the owner unlimited power to use or abuse his property as he likes.[16]

that the government may have to exercise the right of eminent domain for the compulsory purchase of land . . . can hardly be disputed.[17]

So far as the entry into different occupations is concerned, our principle does not exclude the possible advisability in some instances of permitting it only to those who possess certain ascertainable qualifications.[18]

A free system does not exclude on principle all . . . general regulations of economic activity . . . the appropriateness of such measures must be judged by comparing the over-all costs with the gain . . . This is true of most of the wide field of regulations known as "factory legislation."[19]

The range and variety of government action that is, at least in principle, reconcilable with a free system is thus considerable.[20]

Many others have noticed and commented on Hayek's support for classical liberal policies, including various conservatives and contemporary libertarians:

DAVID GLASNER: "The key distinction for Hayek was not big government versus small government, but between a government of laws in which all coercive action is constrained by general and impartial rules, and a government of men in which coercion may be arbitrarily exercised to achieve whatever ends the government, or even the majority on whose behalf it acts, wishes to accomplish. Though Hayek contemplated with little enthusiasm the absorption by the state of a third or more of national income, the amount and character of government spending were to him very much a secondary issue that directly involved no fundamental principle."[21]

ANTHONY DE JASAY: "Taxation as a proportion of national income is a rough measure of the domain of collective versus individual sovereignty over material resources. It sounds almost like deadpan black humor to state that 'except for raising the means,' government need not rely on coercion to render services. . . . There is an infinity of services to be rendered; they all satisfy some need. How much should be provided? We are in an ideological void in which minimal state, maximal state, and anything in between are equally admissible."[22]

GEOFFREY VICKERS: "For reasons which are not clear to me he allows as a proper exercise in government the grant of national minimum support to those who for any reason cannot support themselves; but he does not indicate what rule, if any, would regulate the level of this grant. He even gives the impression that in this, as in other matters, as long as the provision applies equally to the whole class the level is a matter for government discretion."[23]

HANS-HERMANN HOPPE: "Hayek's view regarding the role of market and state cannot systematically be distinguished from that of a modern Social Democrat."[24]

This perception of Hayek was shared by some of his old friends. Ludwig von Mises wrote in reviewing *The Constitution of Liberty:*

It was the great merit of Professor Friedrich von Hayek to have directed attention to the authoritarian character of socialist schemes. Now Professor Hayek has enlarged and substantiated his ideas in a comprehensive treatise, *The Constitution of Liberty*. In the first two parts of the book the author provides a brilliant exposition of the meaning of liberty and the creative powers of a free civilization.

Unfortunately, the third part of Professor Hayek's book is rather disappointing. Here the author tries to distinguish between socialism and the Welfare State. Socialism, he alleges, is on the decline; the Welfare State is supplanting it. And he thinks that the Welfare State is under certain conditions compatible with liberty.[25]

Hayek's old colleague at the London School of Economics, Lionel Robbins, wrote of *The Constitution of Liberty*:

The recognition of an order in society which has not been planned as a totality is clearly fundamental; and never has the pathbreaking significance of the great eighteenth century discoveries in this respect been better set forth than in Professor Hayek's luminous exposition, itself the source of many new insights. . . . [P]ropositions that have been repeated more or less parrot-wise for a hundred and fifty years acquire a meaning and depth seldom before realized.

Robbins also said:

Professor Hayek's attitude is not one of *laissez faire* in the sense of leaving nothing to government but the functions of the night watchman. Side by side with his critique of *etatiste* [statist] policies, there are developed a series of alternatives which, set out in a more systematic form, might well be regarded as a liberal agenda for state action. . . . Opinions may well differ, even among liberal thinkers, concerning the value or practicability of particular items of the Hayek agenda, and it is very easy to think of directions in which they might be extended. But, cumulatively, they form a program which those who have the cause of individual freedom at heart could do well to ponder seriously.[26]

Hayek sanctioned a substantial role for government throughout his earlier and middle-aged career. In addition to the views he put forward in *The Road to Serfdom* and *The Constitution of Liberty,* he approvingly concluded a lecture in 1963 on David Hume with the statement that Hume was

> far from denying that government had also positive tasks. Like Adam Smith later, he knew that it is only thanks to the discretionary powers granted to government that "bridges are built, harbors opened, ramparts raised, canals formed, fleets equipped, and armies disciplined; everywhere, by the care of government, which, though composed of men subject to all human infirmities, becomes, by one of the finest and most subtle inventions imaginable, a composition, which is, in some measure, exempted from all these infirmities."[27]

However, the classical liberal, as distinct from the contemporary libertarian, position extends beyond healthy support for significant positive and discretionary government programs and activities, as vital as these are for a decent, humane, democratic, just, and prosperous society. As Hayek also emphasized—and it is here that his long-lasting influence lies—a classical liberal order relies on a private market for the production of goods and services, in which private property, freely fluctuating prices, and profits are essential. Prices and profits, in Hayek's brilliant exposition, provide information and direct resources to those who use them best. Moreover, prices and profits depend on the existence of private property. But the younger and middle-aged Hayek was astute enough to recognize that prices, profits, and property are not merely not inconsistent with considerable government activity, but are strengthened by such activity.

Friedman, too, for many of his years at Chicago from 1946 to 1976 was closer to the classical liberal than contemporary libertarian position that he later adopted. His early work lacks the animus toward government that typifies most of his later writings. In his 1962 book *Capitalism and Freedom,* he noted that, in addition to its functions of preserving law and order and enforcing contracts: "Government may enable us at times to accomplish jointly what we would find it more difficult or expensive to accomplish severally." Though he immediately added that "any such use of government is fraught with danger," he also then said: "We should not and cannot avoid using government in this way."[28] He also then remarked: "The role of the state can never be spelled out once and for all in terms of specific functions."[29]

Friedman at this stage in his career recognized that "relying primarily on voluntary cooperation and private enterprise, in both economic and other activities,"[30] is not inconsistent with, and in fact requires, a substantial government role. He also embraced the freedom that classical liberals always support—of belief, thought, religion, and expression. He accepted all of the historical and contemporaneous elements of classical liberalism—democracy, individual rights, a large private-sector economy, and a significant role for government. He avoided the extremes of classical socialism (government ownership and management of the means of economic production) and contemporary libertarianism (virtually no government at all, extreme antigovernmentism).

It cannot be gainsaid, though, that even in *Capitalism and Freedom,* Friedman displayed a largely anarchist streak not seen in many of those who previously described themselves as classical liberals and libertarians, except—among major figures—Spencer, Mises, and Rand. At the same time, Friedman's list of specific government reform proposals contained some productive ideas. To the extent that Friedman—like

Knight, Viner, and Simons before him—advocated more freedom in economic interactions and transactions, there is much to what he said. The same cannot be said of his practical proposal in *Capitalism and Freedom* to eliminate, for example, national parks. This is a utopian idea. It may be good as a thought experiment, but it is not likely to be effectuated in public policy anytime soon. In general, a significant private-sector economy is not inconsistent with substantial government activity, at least in developed economies for most of the past century.

Embracing "smaller government" or "lower taxes" does not necessarily entail support for all of the radical libertarian and antigovernment proposals made by Friedman and Hayek later in their careers, as well as by libertarians today. It is possible to embrace smaller or more efficient government and some lower taxes without focusing on extreme proposals for limiting government or mostly advocating low taxes for the wealthy. It is possible to favor incremental and modest reform and to take transition issues seriously. It is possible to favor reform of society without favoring revolutionary change, whether in a Marxist or contemporary libertarian direction. Contemporary libertarianism receives its anarchist streak largely from Friedman, as well as from Rand and Mises—and not as much from Hayek, to Hayek's credit.

Perhaps the most well-known part of *The Constitution of Liberty* is its postscript, "Why I Am Not a Conservative." Here, Hayek forcefully argued that classical liberalism should not be conflated with conservatism, which is essentially a backward-looking doctrine, attitude, and belief. Rather, classical liberalism is a forward-looking creed and program—one that believes the future will be better than the present if humankind is able to learn the rules and practices of its teaching.[31]

Hayek reserved some of his harshest criticism for conservatism in his characterization of the too-prevalent conservative attitude toward scientific knowledge: "Personally, I find that the most objectionable feature of the conservative attitude is its propensity to reject well-substantiated new knowledge because it dislikes some of the consequences which seem to follow from it—or, to put it more bluntly, its obscurantism." In particular: "I can have little patience with those who oppose . . . the theory of evolution." For Hayek, and classical liberals generally, truth is among the highest values and goals toward which to strive and, imperfectly, attain. As he also held in concluding *The Constitution of Liberty,* the classical liberal considers the "advance of knowledge as one of the chief aims of human effort and expects from it the gradual solution of such problems and difficulties as we can hope to solve . . . [T]he liberal is aware that it is of the essence of human achievement that it produces something new; and he is prepared to come to terms with new knowledge." [31] Classical liberalism embraces the truth.

11

FRIEDMAN AS ECONOMIST
AND PUBLIC INTELLECTUAL

IN A TALK HE GAVE in 1962 on Hayek's departure from the University of Chicago for the University of Freiburg in what was then West Germany, Friedman said that the "thing that is interesting about Fritz Hayek . . . is the extent to which he has succeeded in straddling two kinds of worlds. The membership of this room consists of people who are here because of their interest in Fritz Hayek's work in science and also those who are here because of their interest in the enormous role he has played in spreading ideas among the public-at-large."[1] Much the same could be said of Friedman.

Friedman had at least two phases in his mature career, and it is important to be clear about them. From 1946 to 1976, he was a professor of economics in the Department of Economics at the University of Chicago. For about the first two decades of this period, he was predominantly an academic economist. Starting in 1964, however, with his participation as the lead economic adviser to Barry Goldwater, he became increasingly known outside academia to a general audience. Soon thereafter, he had a regular column in *Newsweek,* which was an important source of his growing popular prominence and influence.

Paul Krugman has remarked in a laudatory critique of Friedman after his death that his

> effectiveness as a popularizer and propagandist rested in part on his well-deserved reputation as a profound economic theorist, but there's an important difference between the rigor of his work as a professional economist and the looser, sometimes questionable logic of his pronouncements as a public intellectual. While Friedman's theoretical work is universally admired by professional economists, there's much more ambivalence about his policy pronouncements and especially his popularizing.[2]

Warren Samuels, a great historian of economic thought, similarly held that there was much difference between Friedman's professional work and his public policy advocacy. Samuels wrote in reviewing Milton and Rose Friedman's memoirs: "Friedman is a very rigorous economic theorist. His thinking on matters of political economy, however, is not as rigorous. . . . [These] memoirs reveal two very different Milton Friedmans: Friedman the rigorous economic scientist and Friedman the activist but nonrigorous ideological high priest of 'free markets,' 'limited government,' and 'free enterprise.'"[3]

Norwegian economist Agnar Sandmo shares this view: "It is tempting to draw a clear distinction between Friedman as a researcher and as an ideological spokesman." Sandmo adds that the "empirical foundations for his policy recommendations are much stronger" in areas of Friedman's expertise, such as monetary theory, "where they are backed up by theoretical models and empirical research, than in many of the other areas covered in his more popular writings."[4]

Friedman himself said in closing the preface to his memoirs: "My vocation has been professional economics. . . . My avocation has been public policy." He also said there: "The public-at-large knows me best for my involvement in public policy and for Rose's and my writings on public policy and political philosophy. However, these have been an avocation, not a vocation. . . . Public policy has always been a part-time activity."[5]

Friedman's first major foray as a public intellectual was in 1962, with the publication of *Capitalism and Freedom*. Based on lectures he gave at a series of Volker Fund conferences in the late 1950s, *Capitalism and Freedom* is the most likely of Friedman's works to enter the pantheon of great works in classical liberal philosophy. It is clearly a successor to John Stuart Mill's *On Liberty*. In *Capitalism and Freedom,* Friedman wrote that to the "free man, the country is the collection of the individuals who compose it, not something over and above them."[6] Jeremy Bentham, the founder of utilitarianism and Mill's intellectual godfather, said: "The interest of the community is one of the most general expressions that can occur in the phraseology of morals. . . . The community is a fictitious body, composed of the individual persons who are considered as constituting as it were its members. The interest of the community then is, what?—the sum of the interests of the several members who compose it."[7]

Individualism is at the heart of Mill's and Friedman's political and economic philosophy. "The heart of the liberal philosophy is a belief in the dignity of the individual,"[8] Friedman said. Mill wrote in *On Liberty:* "Over himself, over his own body and mind, the individual is sovereign."[9] Like Mill, Friedman emphasized the importance of genius and held that the great accomplishments in history were the "product of individual genius."[10] Mill said: "I insist thus emphatically on the importance of genius."[11]

Friedman correctly tied contemporary classical liberalism explicitly to the utilitarian tradition and to the Philosophical Radicals in England who were Bentham's followers: "Recognizing the implicit threat to individualism, the intellectual descendants of the Philosophical Radicals—Dicey, Mises, Hayek, and Simons, to mention only a few—feared that a continued movement toward centralized control of economic activity would prove *The Road to Serfdom,* as Hayek entitled his penetrating analysis of the process."[12]

Friedman's general classical liberal philosophy is a great statement of permanent issues. There is no problem at all with his general freedom philosophy, as his contributions in academic economics are significant and beneficial. The problem in Friedman's work arises concerning some of his later public policy recommendations, including his later abhorrence of government and his view that, with respect to federal government budgets, deficits do not matter.

He burst onto the national and international scene in the middle and late 1960s. He had been well known in academia, receiving the John Bates Clark Medal in 1951, which was then presented biennially by the American Economic Association to the top economist under the age of forty. He appeared on many University of Chicago Round Table national radio programs, increasingly wrote for popular audiences, and spoke to student and public audiences around the nation.

Nash writes that the "conservative case for the free society needed a fresh practical restatement in the 1960s. Fortunately for the movement, it was forthcoming—from the irrepressibly brilliant economist Milton Friedman and the rising Chicago School of economics." Nash also says: "The publication of *Capitalism and Freedom* and Friedman's emergence as a preeminent economist among conservatives constituted a major landmark in the evolution of the postwar Right . . . [B]y the end of the 1960s he was probably the most highly regarded and influential conservative scholar in the country, and one of the few with an international reputation." Among the merits of Friedman's work was that it "bristled with *specific, arguable* alternatives to liberal programs."[13] Melvin Reder wrote: "The remarkable success of the Chicago School during the third quarter of this century was due in large part to the fact that it was able to take a leading role both in scientific research and in providing a rationale for political conservatism."[14]

As discussed earlier, Friedman was a great opponent of government, which was not entirely to his credit. He, more than any other public intellectual, sustained and launched the international neoliberal movement that crested with the elections, administrations, and governments of Ronald Reagan in the United States and Margaret Thatcher in Great Britain during the 1980s. This period of domestic reform coincided with the collapse of Communism abroad.

The unexpected and sudden demise of the Soviet Union and of Communism in Eastern Europe appeared to validate the Chicago free market position. It is not that socialism would be desirable if it were possible—it is that socialism is not possible. It is not that humankind does not possess the goodness required to make socialism work. It is that humankind does not possess the knowledge. Prices, profits, and private property are necessary and essential institutions to overcome the division or fragmentation of knowledge that the specialization of labor brings. Friedman and Hayek turned the question of socialism from an ethical to a factual one.

Friedman considered the decisive test of Communism to be that in each of the cases of East and West Germany and North and South Korea, the capitalist portions of what previously had been single countries substantially outperformed the Communist parts. Institutions, and the ideas and beliefs on which they are built and rest, greatly matter.

Friedman was at or near the top of the international economics community during the 1960s and 1970s as his focus shifted from academic economics to public policy advocacy. In 1967, he was the president of the American Economic Association, and in 1976 he received the Nobel Prize in Economics. For this reason, he was especially pleased by the move of the economics profession in his direction on many issues, preeminently the relative importance of monetary and fiscal policy—and the influence of monetary policy.

His academic reconceptualization of the Great Depression was fundamental to public policy changes. Before Friedman's work, the standard explanation of the Great Depression was that it represented a crisis of capitalism. The stock market crash was seen as a vital point, when in fact it was of relatively minor significance. Friedman demonstrated that the source of the Great Depression was the collapse of the money supply, which the Federal Reserve System fostered. The Great Depression did not demonstrate the inefficacy of capitalism. It reflected the power of monetary policy.

Starting in the 1950s, he was the most vocal intellectual advocate for the reform of monetary institutions nationally and internationally. He supported floating international exchange rates. In this area, his intellectual and practical victories are so great that it is not too much to speak of the period since 1971 as the Friedman era in international trade. Yesterday's heresy became tomorrow's dogma.

With respect to national monetary policies, he hammered away on the essential point that "inflation is always and everywhere a monetary phenomenon."[15] Monetary policy is of great importance. It plays the key role in determining aggregate prices. Friedman presented the desirability of no or very limited inflation and the way to achieve this goal, with much influence on monetary policy around the world.

The monetary and economic arrangements recommended by Friedman—floating international exchange rates and free trade abroad, stable monetary policies and low inflation at home—have coincided with the greatest increase in economic growth and international trade in world history. His rethinking of the Great Depression was crucial. It refuted the notion that the free market had failed, and thereby influenced thought on the appropriate role of government, particularly in macroeconomic policy. Friedman's overarching concern from the late 1960s through early 1980s was inflation. He continually advocated monetary restraint to control inflation and said that fiscal remedies were useless to restrain inflation. These views, too, have become the new conventional wisdom.

Other areas in which he took a leading role included an all-volunteer army, a negative income tax, indexation of tax brackets to account for inflation, reduced government spending, lower taxation, school vouchers, and the legalization of drugs. He advocated the privatization of government services to the greatest extent possible, particularly as a way to reform education. Elsewhere around the world, he supported the denationalization of government-owned industries. Ultimately and late in his career, he came close to favoring a night watchman state, in which almost all relationships among individuals would be consensual and contractual, with a limited role for government in providing social welfare in the form of a "very low-level negative income tax"[16] combined with private charity.

At both the beginning and end of his career, Friedman was concerned with inequality. He said in a 1996 interview: "The greatest problem facing our country is the breaking down into two classes, those who have and those who have not. The growing differences between the incomes of the skilled and the less skilled, the educated and the uneducated, pose a very real danger. If that widening rift continues, we're going to be in terrible trouble. . . . We'll have a civil war. We really cannot remain a democratic, open society that is divided into two classes."[17]

Almost half a century earlier, he wrote with respect to the appropriate objectives of monetary and fiscal policy that the "basic long-run objectives, shared, I am sure, by most economists, are political freedom, economic efficiency, and substantial equality of economic power."[18] He affirmed economic equality as among the appropriate outcomes of a properly functioning political-economic order elsewhere early in his career, including in a work he co-authored with George Stigler, *Roofs or Ceilings? The Current Housing Problem* (1946), a tract against rent control. *Roofs or Ceilings?* includes the statement that Friedman and Stigler sought more efficient ways to achieve "even more equality than there is at present, not alone for housing but for all products."[19] At the initial meeting of the Mont Pelerin Society in 1947, Friedman stated that "liberalism has a humanitarian aim and is a progressive philosophy."[20]

He noted in *Capitalism and Freedom* that a "free society in fact tends toward greater material equality than any other yet tried," though he immediately went on to say that a libertarian regards economic equality as a "desirable by-product of a free society, not its major justification." He also said: "Another striking fact, contrary to popular conception, is that capitalism leads to less inequality than alternative systems of organization and that the development of capitalism has greatly lessened the extent of inequality. . . . Among the western countries alone, inequality appears to be less, in any meaningful sense, the more highly capitalist the country is."[21] Nash, commenting on this latter passage, says that, for Friedman: "The 'great achievement' of capitalism . . . was the increase of opportunities and the creation of less inequality than in any other economic system."[22]

Milton and Rose Friedman wrote in *Free to Choose* (1980):

Everywhere in the world there are gross inequities of income and wealth. They offend most of us. Few can fail to be moved by the contrast between the luxury enjoyed by some and the grinding poverty suffered by others.

In the past century a myth has grown up that free market capitalism—equality of opportunity as we have interpreted that term—increases such inequalities, that it is a system under which the rich exploit the poor.

Nothing could be further from the truth. Wherever the free market has been permitted to operate, wherever anything approaching equality of opportunity has existed, the ordinary man has been able to attain levels of living never dreamed of before. Nowhere is the gap between rich and poor wider, nowhere are the rich richer and the poor poorer, than in those societies that do not permit the free market to operate.[23]

Friedman's views on equality were complex and nuanced. He clearly favored a society in which there would not be gross inequalities in income and wealth. He was opposed to the unequal aspects of American society in 1996, and the United States has become substantially more unequal with respect to both income and wealth since that time. He did not believe that equality of result should be sought directly, but he believed that appropriate public policies lead to increasingly greater economic equality.

He was a close public policy adviser to Presidents Nixon and Reagan, though he served neither in a full-time or permanent capacity. Friedman's concept of a negative income tax dominated discussion of welfare reform during the first year of the Nixon administration, though Friedman opposed the final version of the legislation that emerged because it was not always the case that individuals would have been better off working than not working. The earned income tax credit is an important legislative descendant of the negative income tax debate.

Among the economists from Chicago who played leading roles in the Nixon and Ford administrations was Herb Stein, who was a graduate student at Chicago in the 1930s. Stein was chairman of the Council of Economic Advisers from 1972 to 1974, serving under Presidents Nixon and Ford. At one point, Chicagoans George Shultz and Stein were, respectively, secretary of the Treasury and chairman of the Council of Economic Advisers; another old friend of Friedman's— Arthur Burns—was chairman of the Federal Reserve Board; and many other Chicagoans and Friedman allies served elsewhere at high levels in government, academia, and business.

Stein concurred with the view of Adam Smith presented here. In a 1994 essay in the *Wall Street Journal,* he wrote of people who wore Adam Smith neckties that they did so in order to

> make a statement of their devotion to the idea of free markets and limited government. What stands out in *The Wealth of Nations,* however, is that their patron saint was not pure or doctrinaire about this idea. He viewed government intervention in the market with great skepticism. He regarded his exposition of the virtues of the free

market as his main contribution . . . Yet he was prepared to accept or propose qualifications to that policy in the specific cases where he judged that their net effect would be beneficial and would not undermine the basically free character of the system.[24]

Stein was a classical liberal, not a forerunner of today's contemporary libertarians. Like the younger Hayek and Friedman, he recognized and affirmed that government has a great positive role to play in contemporary society, and that to attempt to say otherwise is contrary to reality. He remarked:

> I would like to see the government do less in many dimensions. But I accept the fact that the federal government is going to be very big, and I would like to see it be better. . . .
>
> It is a basic premise . . . that current budget processes are not allocating the national output well. By that I do not mean simply that the national output is not being allocated according to my priorities. . . . I think we are devoting too little to . . . investment, education, and care for the very poor and too much to health care and the consumption of the nonpoor. But I would not regard my dissatisfaction as evidence that the process is not working. Different people have different priorities, not all of which can be satisfied. A compromise has to be reached, and we have a system for doing that.[25]

George Shultz gives Friedman much of the credit for the United States' implementation of flexible international exchange rates in 1971:

> Milton was a great teacher, and I found his ideas to be of tremendous applicability when I . . . [was] Secretary of the Treasury. . . . I argued vigorously in favor of closing the gold window, as that would lead us away from a system of quasi-fixed exchange rates and toward flexible exchange rates. Milton had convinced me that such a system

would be superior. . . . I had a long conversation with Milton. We could readily agree that the dollar should be allowed to float and that a system of flexible exchange rates should somehow be brought into being. Nevertheless, Milton and I both recognized how controversial that was. We looked for a plan that might bring the result we wanted, yet be reassuring. Milton produced a brilliant idea that would give us a system of flexible exchange rates in the clothing of a more familiar system of par values. . . .

I then took what amounted to Milton's plan to the president, who endorsed it. I encouraged him to present it to the upcoming meeting of the IMF and World Bank, the annual get-together of the world financial community. Instead, he announced that his Secretary of the Treasury [Shultz himself] would present the plan the following day.[26]

In a 2013 interview, Shultz commented on Nixon's intelligence and said that Nixon enjoyed Friedman intellectually.[27] In addition to his association with the idea of a negative income tax and floating exchange rates, Friedman was a key member of President Nixon's commission that recommended ending the draft.

As close as he was to Nixon, Friedman was even closer to Reagan. Friedman was the economist for whom Reagan had the most respect. Friedman's emphases on reducing inflation, on reducing the size of government, on lower and less taxation, and on reducing government regulation became Reagan's mantra and platform, as it became Margaret Thatcher's in Great Britain—another great Friedman admirer. Friedman and his wife, Rose's, *Free to Choose* became the bestselling nonfiction book in the United States in 1980, and through its accompanying PBS television series reached a large and influential international audience.

Among the most important chapters in *Free to Choose* is the first, "The Power of the Market." Here Friedman explained that a market is necessary in order to allow voluntary exchanges from which multiple parties benefit. Following Knight, he emphasized Smith's insight that when exchange occurs it leads both parties to be better off than they were before. Moreover, as Smith argued, "it is not from the benevolence of the butcher and the baker that we expect our evening meal, but from their regard to their self-interest."[28] As Friedman put it more than two centuries later, "Economic order can emerge as the unintended consequence of the actions of many people, each seeking his own interest."[29]

Self-interest is not the same thing as selfishness. An individual's self-interest is whatever he or she considers this to be, and very often, perhaps most often, includes the interests of others. The question is how to coordinate the actions of individuals, not to presume that they are perfectly altruistic—whatever that would be. Prices transmit vital information of supply and demand: Friedman completely followed Hayek in this respect. Profits direct resources to those who use them more effectively than others in a properly functioning market order. Private property is necessary for prices and profits. Government creates the structure within which economic and social activity takes place and provides vital and essential services, allowing society to exist. Friedman also emphasized that among the detrimental effects of inflation is that it distorts the information-bestowing character of prices. He held as well that inflation reduces the incentive to save over time, because funds will not be worth as much in the future.

As with Nixon, prior to Reagan's election Friedman served on a committee, the Coordinating Committee on Economic Policy, that prepared policy papers for implementation if Reagan were elected. "Once in office," Friedman remembered, "Reagan acted very much along the lines that we recommended."[30] George Shultz chaired the Reagan economic policy committee, whose report was titled "Economic Strategy for the Reagan Administration" and dated November 16, 1980—twelve days after Reagan's election as president.[31]

Here, Friedman and others stressed the importance of government and of government policy. Current economic problems, "having been produced by government policy . . . can be redressed by a change in policy."[32] The top problem at the time was considered to be inflation, which had reached double-digit levels in the 1970s. The program that Shultz, Friedman, and others put forward included these Friedmanian points, which were incorporated into Reaganism whole:

> Restrain government spending.
>
> Reduce the burden of taxation and regulation.
>
> Conduct monetary policy in a steady manner, directed toward eliminating inflation.[33]

With respect to eliminating inflation and encouraging economic activity, the report recommended Friedman's approach that a consistent and "moderate rate of monetary growth is an essential requirement both to control inflation and to provide a healthy environment for economic growth."[34]

It is interesting to observe that in this foundation document of Reaganomics, Reagan's economic advisers and intellectual inspirers advocated "widely shared prosperity"[35] through 1980, Friedman's emphasis on greater economic equality as an appropriate goal of government policy was not entirely lost. It is also interesting to observe that the key element of Reaganomics—sharply lower marginal personal income tax rates—was downplayed in the report prepared by Shultz and Friedman. By way of contrast, the leading inspiration for sharply lower marginal personal income tax rates was the effusive Arthur Laffer, who, as a result of his success in promoting the idea that lower personal income tax rates increase total tax revenue, should be ranked as one of the most influential, if not also most detrimental, economists in history.

It bears emphasizing that Friedman, Shultz, and other Chicago "Old Guarders" were not initially inclined toward sharply lower marginal personal and corporate tax rates, other than, in Friedman's case, mostly as a way to reduce government expenditures—the so-called starve the beast strategy. They did not embrace the "Laffer curve" of increased tax revenue through cutting tax rates. In addition, Friedman did not believe that changes in fiscal policy, as desirable or undesirable as they might be for other reasons, had much impact on national economic performance. By way of contrast, it was Laffer, together with Robert Mundell, Robert Bartley, Jude Wanniski, and Jack Kemp, who launched the supply-side revolution in economic policy. Both Laffer and Mundell spent considerable time at the University of Chicago. The phrase "supply-side" economics was coined by Stein, in a slightly pejorative manner.

President-elect Reagan provided the first, one-word endorsement for the paperback edition of Friedman's *Free to Choose* in January 1981: "Superb." Friedman wrote later: "No other president in my lifetime comes close to Reagan in adherence to clearly specified principles dedicated to promoting and maintaining a free society."[36]

As Friedman's prominence skyrocketed from the late 1960s through the early 1980s, so did that of the Chicago school of economics. He was seen as the most influential representative of an important perspective. Martin Anderson, who served as a leading domestic policy adviser to Presidents Nixon and Reagan, said:

> Of the thousands of people who have helped shape the new intellectual forces sweeping around the world, Milton Friedman probably has had the greatest influence. By his articles, lectures, books . . . , and television series, Friedman has had an enormous impact on the . . . changing view of the nature of a free society. The breadth and depth of this influence cannot be explained by just the words he wrote and spoke. A lot of it can only be explained by his extraordinary personality.[37]

Chicago economists and Friedman reached the peak of their influence during the Reagan administration. George Shultz became secretary of state. Allen Wallis was undersecretary of state for economic affairs. Beryl Sprinkel, a former Friedman student, was a chairman of the Council of Economic Advisers. William Niskanen, another Chicago student, served on the Council of Economic Advisers. Dozens of individuals in the Reagan administration were either directly or at a remove students, or colleagues, of Milton Friedman.

According to Ed Meese, attorney general and perhaps Reagan's closest adviser, Friedman was the "guru"[38] of the Reagan administration. Meese writes: "Of special importance among the academic advisors was Professor Milton Friedman . . . [who] was a particular favorite of the President. His staunch advocacy of private enterprise, the free market, and tax limitation (dating back to California), and his extensive knowledge of monetary matters were invaluable to the administration."[39]

According to Shultz, Friedman was "by far" a more influential thinker for the Nixon and Reagan administrations than Hayek. In the cases of both Nixon and Reagan, but especially Reagan, Friedman was "known personally" by the president. "Milton was a presence" in the Reagan administration, Shultz says, and was literally present. Hayek, by way of contrast, was a "mythical figure."[40] Hayek had little to no influence on Nixon, and Nixon's presidency from 1969 to 1974 preceded Hayek's return to popular prominence through receiving the Nobel Prize in December 1974. Niskanen remembered that Reagan was "influenced by people like Milton Friedman and understood that inflation was always a monetary phenomenon."[41] David Stockman, the early director of the Office of Management and Budget for Reagan, recalls that Friedman had a "big role"[42] in the Reagan administration.

Friedman's and Chicago economists' influence extended beyond the United States. It was particularly strong in the English-speaking world. One of the avid watchers of *Free to Choose* in Great Britain was Prime Minister Thatcher, who came to office in 1979. In February 1980, just before the series was to run in England and while Reagan was campaigning for president of the United States, Thatcher met with Friedman in England. *Punch* magazine ran a cartoon of her bowing reverently before a television set playing Friedman when the series aired.

Rich Thomas, *Newsweek*'s chief economic correspondent, wrote in a summary of Reagan's economic program in 1988 upon his departure from office:

> Before there was Reaganomics, there was Milton Friedman. . . . Friedman became Reagan's tutor on economics. . . . Friedman's gospel stresses the paramount importance of money—the absolute necessity of stable growth in the supply of cash and credit circulating in the economy at any one time. But Friedman also has a little-known theory about budget policy that Reagan absorbed and practiced from Day One in the White House.
>
> In Friedman's view, the most important thing about budgets is the level and direction of spending—not the size of the deficit. . . . Guided by Friedman's theory, Reagan set aside the deficit problem when he came to Washington . . . [43]

Friedman was emphatic that the size of deficits mattered little compared to the amount of government spending, but with very little empirical evidence for this position. He did not consider at all the influence of substantially lower marginal income and estate tax rates on income and wealth concentration in the top one-tenth of 1 percent and 1 percent, nor other deleterious consequences of severely inegalitarian tax policies and continuous deficit spending.[44]

12

THE 1980s CRESCENDO
AND CONTEMPORARY
LIBERTARIANISM

AS THE 1980S BEGAN, it appeared that the two former University of Chicago professors Milton Friedman and Friedrich Hayek were on top of the world intellectually and politically. With Ronald Reagan the president of the United States and Margaret Thatcher—whose high opinion of Hayek was similar to Reagan's of Friedman—the prime minister of Great Britain, two acolytes of Friedman and Hayek occupied the ultimate positions of power in the English-speaking world. As change spread across Eastern Europe and the Soviet Union in the late 1980s and early 1990s, Hayek appeared to be a prophet.

Friedman was the more popular and prominent of the two, particularly during the 1960s and the first part of the 1970s. Hayek was practically a forgotten figure during this time. His great popular work,

The Road to Serfdom, was published in 1944. Friedman became a media superstar during the 1960s. He was everywhere, particularly in the United States but also internationally.

Then, in 1974, Hayek received the Nobel Prize in Economics, making him the first economist from a classical liberal/libertarian perspective to be selected. The award rejuvenated him. After Thatcher became prime minister of Great Britain in 1979, his star rose again.

Friedman was more focused on the United States than Hayek, though Hayek saw the United States as the leader of world civilization during his lifetime. In general, Hayek became more of a European than American figure in the last three decades of his life, from his departure from Chicago to West Germany in 1962 until his death in 1992. Both Friedman and Hayek were read in Eastern Europe in the years preceding the collapse of Communism. Friedman is perhaps more read in Asia; his influence has been particularly strong in Hong Kong.

It is hard today to remember how pervasive the opinion was that the Soviet Union possessed a powerful economy almost until it fell. In the 1973 edition of his famous textbook, *Economics,* Paul Samuelson predicted that although the Soviet Union had a per capita income roughly half that of the United States at the time, it would catch up by 1990. Arnold Beichman collected a number of examples from *Economics* of Samuelson's misunderstanding of global macroeconomics. Beichman noted that in the 1976 edition of the work, which is among the bestselling economics texts of all time, Samuelson called it a "vulgar mistake to think that most people in Eastern Europe are miserable."[1] In the next edition, four years later, he merely removed the word "vulgar."[2]

As Beichman points out, in the 1985 edition of *Economics,* that "entire passage had disappeared. Instead, he . . . substituted a sentence asking whether Soviet political repression was 'worth the economic gains.' This non-question Samuelson . . . identified as 'one of the most profound dilemmas of human society.' In the face of looming Soviet economic disaster the 1985 Samuelson text offered these paragraphs: 'But it would be misleading to dwell on the shortcomings. Every economy has its contradictions . . . What counts is results, and there can be no doubt that the Soviet planning system has been a powerful engine for economic growth.'[3] There may have been no doubt, but Samuelson's certainty was utterly misplaced.

In the 1989 edition of *Economics*—as Soviet-style Communism was collapsing around the world, and as Eastern Europe was aflame in revolution that would spread to the Soviet Union two years later— Samuelson opined that "contrary to what many skeptics had earlier believed," the "Soviet economy is proof that . . . a socialist command economy can function and even thrive."[4] Skeptics, indeed! Those nuts, Ludwig von Mises and Friedrich Hayek!

Samuelson was not alone in his miscomprehension of the Soviet economy until the end. Historian of conservatism Lee Edwards writes that Arthur Schlesinger, Jr., "after a 1982 visit to Moscow, said that he found more goods in the shops, more food in the markets, more cars on the street, 'more of almost everything, except, for some reason, caviar.' Clearly referring to the Reagan administration, Schlesinger said that those in the United States 'who think the Soviet Union is on the verge of economic and social collapse, ready with one small push to go over the brink, are . . . only kidding themselves.'"[5]

John Kenneth Galbraith opined in 1973, after visiting the People's Republic of China: "There can be no serious doubt that China is devising a highly effective economic system."[6] This was as China was emerging from the Cultural Revolution that almost destroyed its society and economy. Galbraith visited the Soviet Union for two months in 1984. His view at that time, shortly before the rapid decline of the country, was: "Since the Russian system functions less than perfectly, some Americans have gone on to suggest that it is in crisis—in danger of collapse. This I strongly doubt; nor, I think, is it the view of competent observers generally."[7] As with Samuelson's certainty, Galbraith's "competent observers" were wholly in error. In

1989, MIT economist Lester Thurow praised the "remarkable performance" of the Soviet economy, and said: "Today it is a country whose economic achievements bear comparison with those of the United States."[8]

Yale historian Paul Kennedy wrote in his acclaimed *The Rise and Fall of the Great Powers* (1987) of "the quite impressive economic progress which was made in the USSR—and throughout the Soviet-dominated bloc—since Stalin's final years. In many respects, the region was even more transformed than western Europe during those few decades."[9] Though Kennedy also stated and even emphasized economic deficiencies in the Soviet Union, his comprehensive analysis was not what would become standard even a few years later.

Samuelson, Schlesinger, Galbraith, Thurow, Kennedy: all were and have been vitally involved in economic and political discussion, particularly at the intellectual level, for decades. They all were wrong with respect to the development and operation of Communism in the Soviet Union, Eastern Europe, China, and elsewhere in the decades following World War II. Hayek and Friedman were right: A system that relies largely on a private economy to produce most personal consumption goods and services is more efficient and effective—more productive—than a command or dictatorial economy.

That Hayek and Friedman were so fundamentally and transparently right on the crucial global macroeconomic public policy issue of the second half of the twentieth century—the inefficiency of command economies—does not, however, mean that they were right in the virtual neoanarchism that both preached later in their careers. Indeed, in their calls for radical and revolutionary change in contemporary Western developed societies, they were outside the classical liberal tradition, which generally counsels incremental and gradual change. Revolution is sometimes called for, but generally not against the most productive and freest economic and social system in history—classical liberalism, or democratic welfare state capitalism. The move from classical liberalism to contemporary libertarianism by Friedman and Hayek was new.

Keynes expressed criticism of what would become the contemporary libertarian position as well as anyone in his reaction to *The Road to Serfdom*. He wrote Hayek in 1944 after reading the book on one of his wartime trips to the United States:

My dear Hayek, The voyage has given me the chance to read your book properly. In my opinion it is a grand book. We all have the greatest reason to be grateful to you for saying so well what needs so much to be said. . . . [M]orally and philosophically I find myself in agreement with virtually the whole of it; and not only in agreement with it, but in a deeply moved agreement. . . .

I come to what is really my only serious criticism of the book. You admit here and there that it is a question of knowing where to draw the line. You agree that the line has to be drawn somewhere, and the logical extreme is not possible. But you give us no guidance whatever as to where to draw it. It is true that you and I would probably draw it in different places. I should guess that according to my ideas you greatly underestimate the practicability of the middle course. But as soon as you admit that the extreme is not possible, and that a line has to be drawn, you are, on your own argument, done for, since you are trying to persuade us that so soon as one moves an inch in the planned direction you are necessarily launched on the slippery path which will lead you in due course over the precipice.[10]

Classical liberalism is not the "road to serfdom," as so many contemporary libertarians, social conservatives, neoconservatives, and others appear to believe. Just because it is ineffective for government to run all of an economy does not mean that it is effective for there to be no government. Opposition to Communism is not support for virtual anarchism and revolutionary changes to existing society. Robert Skidelsky, the great biographer of Keynes, speculates that, had he lived longer, Keynes might have written a work in political philosophy.

"Capitalism," Skidelsky writes, "may have vanquished socialism, but the debate between *laissez faire* and Keynes' philosophy of the Middle Way is still fiercely joined."[11] Skidelsky also believes that the discussion between Hayek and Keynes on "how much government intervention is compatible with a free society was never properly joined."[12]

Friedman truly moved in a progressively more radical direction over the course of his long life. According to his biographer William Ruger:

> Friedman grew more radical as he got older. In the 1940s and early 1950s . . . Friedman's rhetoric was much less positive about *laissez faire* and much friendlier toward state action . . . At that time, Friedman was also more vocal about the importance of equality of economic power and the role of the state in reducing inequality. As time went on . . . Friedman saw greater and greater problems with government action. . . . [He] became more radical in education policy (more favorable to complete privatization), social welfare policy (questioning whether even a negative income tax was justified in principle), and monetary policy (more friendly to free banking/competitive currencies). By the 1990s, he was arguing that government had become "a self-generating monstrosity."[13]

Scholars of classical liberalism and libertarianism Brian Doherty, Angus Burgin, and J. Daniel Hammond share this view of Friedman's development.[14]

In contrast to his late views, the Friedman of *Capitalism and Freedom* was closer to the classical liberal position. As quoted earlier, he wrote there that the "role of the state can never be spelled out once and for all in terms of specific functions." He also observed:

> The paternalistic ground for governmental activity is in many ways the most troublesome to a liberal . . . Yet there is no use pretending that problems are simpler than in fact they are. There is no avoiding

the need for some measure of paternalism. . . . There is no formula that can tell us where to stop. We must rely on our fallible judgment and, having reached a judgment, on our ability to persuade our fellow men that it is a correct judgment, or their ability to persuade us to modify our views.

He said further that neighborhood effects justify "governmental action to alleviate poverty; to set . . . a floor under the standard of life of every person in the community."[15]

With respect to education, he said in *Capitalism and Freedom*: "The school system, with all its defects and problems, with all the possibility of improvement through bringing into more effective play the forces of the market, has widened the opportunities available to American youth and contributed to the extension of freedom." He also wrote then that "government intervention into education can be rationalized on two grounds. The first is the existence of substantial 'neighborhood effects' . . . The second is the paternalistic concern for children." He then noted: "I am by no means sure that the [voucher] arrangements I now propose would . . . have been desirable a century ago."[16]

In his long retirement in San Francisco beginning in 1976, however, he came to favor almost the complete discontinuation of government involvement in and with education, and denounced the public education system. "A monopoly is a monopoly is a monopoly," he thundered at an education conference in 1992. "A socialist institution is a socialist institution is a socialist institution, and the school system in the United States next to the military is by far and away the most socialized industry in the country."[17] In their memoirs, he and Rose wrote: "While a case can be made for both compulsory schooling and financing, it is by no means a conclusive case. Indeed, we have since [publication of *Capitalism and Freedom*] been persuaded by the empirical evidence . . . that neither is justified."[18] In late correspondence, he remarked on higher education: "I am much more dubious than I was when I wrote *Capitalism and Freedom* that there is any justification at all for government subsidy of higher education."[19] He noted late in life that his views on education had "become more extreme"[20] over his career.

In his long old age in San Francisco as a public intellectual, Friedman enjoyed making strongly antigovernment pronouncements—he became against government at almost any time, for any reason, in almost every area. Whereas in his active career as an academic economist at Chicago, he took pains to provide detailed empirical, often statistical, support for his positions, his form of argument now shifted toward broad and radical pronouncements with little empirical back-up. Essentially, Friedman the academic economist became Friedman the antigovernment celebrity.

He acknowledged that his later work and opinions were not of the same caliber as his earlier work: "I don't regard what I've done in the field of monetary policy as on the same level as what I've done about trying to get rid of the draft or legalizing drugs."[21] He often said that he wished to be remembered primarily for his academic work. He wrote in a 2001 letter: "My contribution to the libertarian cause has not come on the level of values . . . but rather by empirical demonstration, . . . by advancing the science of economics and showing the relevance of those advances to the policy of economics."[22] He remarked in an interview shortly before he died: "I really had two lives. One was as a scientist—as an economist—and one was as a public intellectual."[23] Burgin notes that as Friedman "matured as an economist, he gradually began shifting his focus away from his technical work and toward his pursuits as a popular proselytizer."[24]

Hayek, too, shifted from a classical liberal to a contemporary libertarian position late in his career—notwithstanding that he specifically rejected this position earlier. In about 1977, in a section entitled "The abolition of the government monopoly of services," he wrote in concluding the third volume of *Law, Legislation and Liberty* (1973–1979):

Any governmental agency allowed to use its taxing power to finance such services ought to be required to refund any taxes raised for these purposes to all those who prefer to get the services in some other way. This applies without exception to all those services of which today government possesses or aspires to a legal monopoly, with the only exception of maintaining and enforcing the law and maintaining for this purpose (including defense against external enemies) an armed force, *i.e.,* all those from education to transport and communications, including post, telegraph, telephone and broadcasting services, all the so-called "public utilities," the various "social" insurances and, above all, the issue of money.[25]

The late, popular Friedman and Hayek should be abandoned for their earlier, scholarly selves.

Perhaps the economist at the University of Chicago today who is doing the most important work in the classical liberal tradition is James Heckman, who received the Nobel Prize in Economics in 2000. Heckman originally enrolled in graduate school in economics at the University of Chicago in 1965. He was vitally influenced by the civil rights movement and other issues of the day. He retains an empirical emphasis and public policy focus that is absent in some of his colleagues' work. His encompassing position on the appropriate role of government is an antidote to others' views. He remarked in an autobiographical talk: "People sometimes forget that Chicago has a strong empirical tradition and think of the Chicago School as a body of scholars who embrace particular ideas about free markets. In fact, a central feature of the Chicago approach has been that it values careful empirical analysis and generally demands empirical justification for policy proposals."[26]

He made these important comments on the significance of clearly understandable public policy recommendations:

Chicago . . . had an aversion to the technocratic vision of economic policy . . . favored by many leading schools. Rather than endorsing the concept that a brilliant elite should make policy for the masses,

Chicago believed in the innate common sense of the common man if an argument were presented clearly. There was the belief that anything really important could be conveyed in a simple, effective manner. Friedman's steady stream of clearly written *Newsweek* policy columns was the best demonstration of this approach to public policy. People should be educated to make informed choices, not managed by technocrats who know more than they do.[27]

Heckman's writings have spanned many areas across his career. Among his most important recent work is his call for expanded preschool opportunities. True to the classical liberal and historical Chicago free market tradition, he sees government neither as a universal panacea nor a universal bane. Rather, good public policy is mostly a matter of empirical observation, what Friedman called "positive economics."[28] Heckman writes in *Giving Kids a Fair Chance* (2013): "Gaps in both cognitive and non-cognitive skills between the advantaged and the disadvantaged emerge early and can be traced in part to adverse early environments, in which a growing proportion of children are now raised. . . . Social policy should, then, be directed toward the malleable early years."[29] Adam Smith, Jeremy Bentham, John Stuart Mill, Jacob Viner, Frank Knight, Henry Simons, and the younger Hayek and Friedman would all have agreed.

CONCLUSION

CURRENT APPLICATIONS OF CHICAGONOMICS

"VARIED ITERATION," Frank Knight reportedly said, is "required to impress new truths on reluctant minds."[1] I hope through the varied iteration in this book to have led readers who were not already inclined in this direction to the following views in particular:

1. There is a great difference between "classical liberalism" and "contemporary libertarianism." Classical liberalism is the tradition of Locke, Hume, Smith, Bentham, Mill, Marshall, Cannan, Keynes, Viner, Knight, Simons, Robbins, and the younger and middle-aged Hayek and Friedman. It is a view that emphasizes private property and free exchange in the production of most goods and services and embraces a healthy but not all-encompassing role for government. From the classical liberal outlook, the appropriate role of government includes the provision of social services and

activity in many other areas, including macromanagement of the economy through monetary and fiscal policies and the use of progressive taxation to equalize economic outcomes. The classical liberal approach supports gradual and incremental change, when conditions in a society are at all tolerable.

Contemporary libertarianism, by way of contrast, is the tradition of Spencer, Mises, Rand, Rothbard, and the older Hayek and Friedman. It is a doctrine that advocates revolutionary changes from the status quo in the United States and elsewhere. Government functions and spending would be greatly reduced in virtually all areas at all levels of government, leaving a "night watchman" state essentially protecting private property rights. Gradualism is rejected by contemporary libertarians other than as a political expedient. Contemporary libertarians genuinely believe that their plans for radical economic reform and governmental transformation could be accomplished easily, with immediate benefits to almost all, were it not for the opposition of special interests. Contemporary libertarianism favors profound inequality in society—progressive taxation, in particular, is rejected.

Both classical liberalism and contemporary libertarianism oppose classical socialism, that is, government ownership and management of the means of economic production. Both are committed to democratic forms of government—classical liberalism robustly so, and contemporary libertarianism increasingly tepidly so. Both have strong concepts of individual rights in expression and belief. Classical liberalism is more likely to see individual rights in the area of property as occurring within a societal context; contemporary libertarians are more likely to consider individual property rights as natural and indefeasible. Classical liberalism provides healthy support for government, while recognizing its drawbacks and inefficiencies. Contemporary libertarianism is more inclined toward hatred of government and opposition to it at almost every turn.

2. Friedrich Hayek and Milton Friedman embraced versions of classical liberalism for much or even most of their younger and middle-aged careers; both supported some variant of contemporary libertarianism later in life. Particularly in the case of Friedman, his support for contemporary libertarianism increased as he shifted from being primarily an academic economist to being primarily a public intellectual. Throughout his career, Friedman was interested in and supported greater economic equality. Through the early 1950s, he supported progressive income and estate taxation to achieve greater economic equality. Even later in his career, he considered increasing equality to be one of the defining features of a properly functioning free market order.

3. Adam Smith is properly considered a "classical liberal," as here defined, not a "contemporary libertarian." Smith supported nascent welfare state activities of government and progressive taxation in some areas.

4. As an organized and recognized entity in academia and among the general public, the "Chicago school of economics" was an almost exclusively post–World War II phenomenon. It was inextricably tied to the academic success and popular renown of Milton Friedman.

The greatest problem facing the United States today is the substantial inequality, especially on the basis of age and family structure, that increasingly characterizes American society and the economy. America is increasingly unequal, particularly with respect to the share of income and wealth that families with children have and possess. There have been other greatly unequal societies, but among the unusual features of inequality in the United States at this time is that families with children receive such a small share of income and possess such a small share of wealth.

Families with children under age eighteen are almost unrepresented in the top strata of income and wealth. Many, perhaps almost half of, children in the United States now experience poverty during some portion, if not much or even most, of their childhood. Nearly one-quarter of all American children under the age of eighteen live in poverty right now.[2] Families with children under age eighteen are overwhelmingly poor, working class, and lower middle class. Moreover, those with more education tend to have fewer children and delay having them. If current trends continue in the United States, only about one child in three will be raised by her or his biological father until the age of eighteen. Biological fathers and males generally are becoming largely irrelevant in the raising of children. The relatively small proportion of males who raise their children combined with males who do not have children at all means that, in the coming decades, only about one in four men in the United States will raise biological children until age eighteen.

The general inequality of current American society is well portrayed—though inadvertently so—by former *Wall Street Journal* editor Stephen Moore, who reveres the later and popular Friedman. In a remarkable August 2012 analysis for the Manhattan Institute, Moore provides data that show that in 2007, the top 1 percent of earners in the United States received 22 percent of national income, the top 5 percent received 37 percent, and the top 10 percent of earners received 48 percent of national income.[3] Concerning the top 0.1 percent of earners (one-in-a-thousand earners), they received about 10 percent of national income.[4] The bottom half of earners in the United States received about 12 percent of national income.[5]

This means that the top 0.1 percent of earners in the United States in 2007 received almost as much national income as the bottom 50 percent of earners, and the top 1 percent received almost twice as much national income as the bottom 50 percent.[6] There is no getting around it: the contemporary United States is very unequal.

This is especially so because accumulated wealth is even more dis-proportionately concentrated than income. According to the Federal Reserve Survey of Consumer Finances, the top 1 percent of Americans possessed about 35.4 percent of national wealth in 2010.[7] In 2007, the top 20 percent of Americans owned about 84 percent of wealth, and the bottom 40 percent held about 0.3 percent of national wealth.[8] Since children are so disproportionately located in the bottom half of income earners, it truly is the case that American families with chil-dren receive a very small proportion of national income and hold a very small proportion of national wealth, indeed. All should be able to agree on these facts.

The current inequality that confronts America was not always so. Historically, the United States was known for equality: The founda-tion document of the United States, the Declaration of Independence, affirms that "all men are created equal," which is one of the most in-spiring passages in world history. Amazingly, Moore and other con-temporary libertarians and conservatives have attempted to use the data presented here to demonstrate that the rich pay too much in taxes and that their taxes should be reduced! This is an excellent example of what the Chicago economist Harry Johnson meant when he said that the "most helpful circumstance for the rapid propagation of a new and revolutionary theory is the existence of an established orthodoxy which is clearly inconsistent with the most salient facts . . . , and yet is sufficiently confident of its intellectual power to attempt to explain those facts, and in its efforts to do so exposes its incompetence in a ludicrous fashion."[9] Somehow—what can only be called, incredibly—Moore and others believe that the data he provides substantiate the position that tax rates on the rich are too high.

Moore remarks, for example, that "since the late 1970s, even as tax rates fell by half, the amount of taxes paid by the wealthy, and their percentage of total income taxes paid, increased vastly."[10] There are several points of importance here. First (as Moore acknowledges), as a result of increases in Social Security and Medicare tax rates—which affect most Americans more than the personal income tax—the top 1 percent of income earners paid 22.9 percent of all US federal taxes in 2009 (as opposed to personal income taxes alone).[11] Yet their share of national income, as noted above, was 22 percent in 2007.

Moore opposes the rough proportionality of taxation to income that has characterized comprehensive taxation at the federal level, including both the personal income and payroll taxes, in the recent past. In calling for lower personal income taxes on the wealthy, he comes perilously close to advocating regressive taxation—that the rich should pay a lower proportion of their income in taxes of all sorts than those who receive less income. Moreover, and what could only be called hypocritical (though perhaps and even probably unknowingly on his part), he finds it very unjust that the top 1 percent of earners paid 22.9 percent of all federal taxes in 2009, but he says absolutely nothing with respect to the justice of the top 1 percent receiving 22 percent of national income. In other words, it is perfectly appropriate for the top 1 percent to receive 22 percent of national income, but it is completely inappropriate for the top 1 percent of earners to pay 22.9 percent of all federal taxes. Moore considers it to be a "misconception" and "myth" that "when all other [including payroll as well as personal income] taxes are counted, the rich get off easy."[12]

Even more extreme is Professor Walter Williams of George Mason University, who is also a devotee of the later Friedman. So pernicious and despicable does Williams consider the contemporary United States to be that he comes close to sanctioning—if in fact he does not—the violent overthrow of the existing government of the United States: "I believe our nation is at a point where there are enough irreconcilable differences between those Americans who want to control other Americans and those Americans who want to be left alone" that national dissolution may be the best course. "Americans have several options," Williams continues. "We can like sheep submit to those who have contempt for liberty and our Constitution. We can resist, fight and risk bloodshed and death in an attempt to force America's tyrants to respect our liberties and Constitution." Though he goes on to say that his "personal preference"[13] would be a peaceful resolution, his perspective—as that of many other contemporary libertarians—is clear: so tyrannical and unjust is the government of the United States at this time, so despotic are its elected and appointed officials and system, that armed insurrection is a course to consider, if not, in the final analysis, to pursue.

This is an utterly nonsensical view. From this writer's perspective, the inequality that exists in the United States today is egregious and deplorable but does not justify armed revolt. For Williams to believe that the current policies as a whole of the United States and its system—including with respect to income and wealth distribution—merit the use of such words and phrases as "fight and risk bloodshed and death" to indicate possible societal direction, "sheep" to describe the people of the United States, and "America's tyrants" to characterize elected officials and government administrators is very much in error. Professor Williams should recant these words.[14]

Another contemporary libertarian who advocates severe inequality is television journalist and columnist John Stossel. He writes: "It's true that today, the richest 1 percent of Americans own a third of America's wealth. One percent owns 35 percent! But I say, so what?"[15] The possibility that the top 1 percent owning 35 percent of America's wealth might indicate something is wrong in American public policy is a thought that never enters his mind. He also writes that the top 1 percent owning a third of wealth is "what happens" when "people are free."[16]

Moore, Williams, Stossel, and other contemporary libertarians and conservatives are committed to the welfare of the top few and to maximizing their share of national income and wealth almost exclusively. Though they may to some extent cloak their arguments in the form of "a rising tide lifts all boats," this is really a secondary aspect of their argument. Their primary practical concern is to lower the tax rates of all sorts on the wealthy. Almost all contemporary libertarians and conservatives support a policy that the rich should pay proportionately less in taxes than individuals with less income, at least concerning certain forms of income including dividends and capital gains, and oppose an inheritance tax (the "death" tax).

Beyond federal taxation, state and local taxes have also become more regressive in recent years. According to Matthew Gardner of the Institute on Taxation and Economic Policy: "Nationwide, the poorest 20 percent of taxpayers pay 11.1 percent of their income in sales, property, and [state] income taxes—while the best-off 1 percent pay just 5.6 percent. . . . Middle income families pay more too—9.4 percent on average nationwide."[17] In addition, the comprehensive tax system benefits affluent Americans more than those with less income through such provisions as deductions for mortgage interest and retirement savings and the cap on payments into Social Security and Medicare.[18] It has been widely reported that the top 400 income earners in the United States have paid average federal tax rates of less than 20 percent in recent years.[19]

For millions of Americans, merely a move to comprehensive taxation proportional to income at the federal, state, and local levels would be a step in the direction of tax fairness, as so many higher-income—especially the highest-income—Americans pay a smaller share of their income in federal, state, and local taxes than those who have lower incomes and much less wealth. Contemporary libertarians and conservatives, in their concern that existing comprehensive tax and government spending policies are redistributing income and wealth from the rich to the poor, are not it touch with reality.[20] Compared to historical American society, redistribution of income and wealth *is* occurring—but from the middle and working classes to the rich, particularly the ultrarich; from the young to the old; and from families to the elderly.

The tax policies of the Reagan administration were very detrimental for the United States. Slashing personal income tax rates and increasing payroll taxes were exactly the opposite of optimal public policy and are largely what have caused the current growing inequality in American society, contributing to the weakening of families.[21] It should be noted that many Democrats supported the economic recovery and tax reform acts of 1981 and 1986 that lowered personal income taxes and the Social Security reform act of 1983 that raised payroll taxes.

The increase in economic inequality in the United States in recent decades has been fueled by the lower taxes on the wealthy. Of course the rich have more income and wealth than they used to have—their income and wealth are taxed much less than they were before 1981. It is not that taxes on the rich have dropped, and now the rich are more productive. It is that because taxes on their income and wealth have dropped, now the rich have much more money in the forms of both income and wealth. As Henry Simons emphasized eighty years ago, unless there are high progressive income and estate taxes, income and wealth will concentrate. That is how money works in an advanced economy.

Low marginal tax rates on the wealthy and a greatly unequal society are inextricably tied together. Free market capitalism requires substantial progressive income and estate taxation. The notion that the great classical liberals—Locke, Smith, Bentham, Mill, and the others—were fighting for a greatly unequal society is completely false. Their recommended public policies were intended to lead in exactly the opposite direction. Moreover, they were exponents of democracy and extolled middle class societies.

The very unequal nature of current American society is borne out by the fact that, pursuant to Moore's data, the top 0.1 percent of earners receive something like 400 times as much personal income per capita as the bottom 50 percent of earners.[22] Also troubling is that even those who are in relatively high percentiles as earners receive relatively modest amounts of personal income. Consider, for example, the 75th to 90th percentiles of earners in the United States—those who receive more income than about three-quarters to nine-tenths of the population. This 15 percent of the population near the top of the income pyramid receives merely 20 percent of national income.[23] That is barely more than average. About 80 percent of Americans now receive less than average income, and 90 percent have less than average wealth.

America's current, radically inegalitarian distribution of income and wealth, especially on the bases of age and family structure, was not always so. In 1950, the bottom 50 percent of earners in the United States received about 22 percent of national income,[24] not, as at present and noted above, 12 percent. Moreover, the elderly were more likely to be in poverty than children.

It is hard to imagine a better life for America's children and families when working families with children receive and possess such a small share of national income and wealth. Social conservatives, particularly, would do well to consider that there are policy alternatives to cutting taxes on the wealthy and reducing social services for the poor that might benefit America's children and families. Contemporary libertarians and conservatives should avoid economic policies that merely give more money to the rich.

Moreover, this writer believes that were he alive today, Milton Friedman would be receptive to and partially endorse some of these sentiments and recommended public policies. Perhaps his last sustained thoughts on appropriate social welfare policy were contained in a 2005 letter, slightly more than a year before he died:

> Re paternalism, you raise a very difficult question that I cannot answer to my satisfaction. A great deal depends on how many would fail to use the money [provided by a negative income tax] responsibly. However, the number in that category is in part a consequence of the welfare institutions available. I agree with you that if "not 1 to 2 percent but 10 to 15 percent of people in modern industrial society require strong support" it becomes very difficult if not impossible to maintain a free society. . . .
>
> I believe you are factually right we [are] switching away from cash payments to payments in kind. The closest example of that is in

San Francisco where the mayor's pet program of Care Not Cash for the homeless is one in which, instead of providing a monthly stipend as we did before, the city now provides shelter and a much smaller stipend. . . .

Any welfare scheme whatsoever will involve a disincentive to work, and that is certainly true of the negative income tax as well as of the various current bevy of welfare programs . . . The question is what is the incentive at the margin . . .

These are not very satisfactory random comments on the subject of paternalism. I recognize that paternalism has to play a role. The question is how much and in what way, and I am not sure that there is much you can say about that on a general level. I guess what has impressed me most about welfare in kind is that the actual effects are in practice usually very different from the intended effects. The law of unintended effects works here. . . .

I remain persuaded that repeal of all of the specific welfare measures and their replacement by a very low level negative income tax would be an improvement. As you suggest, there would be some people who would fall between the cracks and for whom this would not be an adequate degree of charity. However, I believe it would reduce the number of such people to a level at which private organizations and private individuals would more than make up the difference . . . I realize that it is utopian to suppose that we could get such a change right now. We can only go at it incrementally . . . [25]

This was a reasonably moderate final statement on welfare, close to, if not in, the classical liberal tradition. Friedman was, ultimately, a man of the left. He believed that the facts—positive economics— should dictate public policy. He was a pure utilitarian who favored the greatest good for the greatest number. He was a rationalist. His views were wholly secular and of this world. In addition to his final, reasonably moderate views in 2005 as to appropriate social welfare policy, he responded to a question at the same time about gay marriage: "I do not believe there should be any discrimination against gays. They should be subject to the same laws as everyone else."[26] He also did "not agree with . . . moral condemnation of stem cell research" and "would oppose legislative limits on such research"[27] at a time when embryonic stem cells were used in research and therapy. He was pro choice on abortion.[28] In the area of foreign policy, he was noninterventionist as well as opposed to the draft. With respect to immigration, in the absence of welfare benefits, he supported open borders. He advocated the legalization of drugs, marijuana in particular. Milton Friedman was no contemporary conservative.

According to the 2014 *Forbes* edition on the richest 400 people in America: "The 400 wealthiest Americans are now worth $2.3 trillion, up 13 percent from a year ago."[29] By way of contrast, the poorest 130 million Americans, including about 50 million of America's 75 million children under the age of eighteen, are worth less than $350 billion, less than one-sixth as much as the top 400.[30]

There are better societies than the hereditary and gerentocratic plutocracy advocated by proponents of contemporary libertarianism and conservatism. This writer's father, William Ebenstein, was a noted political scientist who lectured at the University of Chicago in the 1930s and was a colleague of Friedman at the University of Wisconsin at Madison in 1940–41. My father wrote in an essay on capitalism in 1954:

> Legislative action cannot equalize the I.Q. of the population, and there will always be differences of ability, drive, and motivation, but laws can make equality of opportunity more real by trying to equalize conditions before the race starts: increased inheritance taxes lessen the impact of inherited wealth, progressive income taxes favor the lower-income groups, and free education (from nursery school to university) benefits the indigent more than the affluent. In other words, equality of opportunity, if it allows ability alone to operate,

quickly establishes and perpetuates inequality. *Need,* too, must be considered; it adds to the principle of efficiency that of happiness.[31]

Public policies that should be implemented in the United States at this time include:

1. Restore the marginal federal income tax rate on the top 1 percent of earners to 50 percent, and the rate on the top 0.1 percent to 70 percent
2. Restore the top marginal federal estate tax rate on estates above $100 million to 77 percent
3. Reduce general sales taxes and increase other taxes at state and local levels to provide local government revenue
4. Forgive and provide better ways to work off student loan debt; reduce college, university, and technical school tuition
5. Raise the federal minimum wage for able-bodied adults to $12 per hour, index the minimum wage to growth in gross domestic product
6. Expand the earned income tax credit, especially for working families
7. Limit public employee unions, particularly public employee pensions, but encourage private employee unions
8. Increase domestic production of energy, especially natural gas
9. Reduce regulation to stimulate economic growth
10. Maintain a permanent low-interest rate monetary policy consistent with low inflation
11. Retain free trade policies
12. Increase high-skilled immigration
13. Reduce Social Security and Medicare taxes, particularly on working families

These policies would largely, though not entirely, be a return to the economic policies of the 1950s, 1960s, and 1970s—when growth in the United States was faster, debt was lower, national income and wealth were more equally distributed, and families were stronger. The goal is not to increase total taxation,[32] but to redistribute taxation back from the middle and working classes to the wealthy and super-rich with the goal of creating a more just and prosperous, as well as equal, society.

Perhaps the ultimate irony in the movement to lower marginal income tax rates sharply is that it was intended to lead to greater economic growth than had existed when marginal income and estate taxes were higher. But economic growth has been lower during the period of reduced top marginal rates than when top rates were higher, as political economists across the political spectrum agree. David Boaz, the conscience of the Cato Institute, writes in The Libertarian Mind (2015): "Our economy is growing at barely half the annual rate it did in the 1950s and 1960s (even before the slowdown that began in 2008)."[33] Herb Stein wrote in 1989 after the Reagan administration left office: "It is worth comparing the behavior of the economy under the system we are now celebrating with the behavior of the economy under the New Economics of Kennedy and Johnson. From 1980 to 1988, real GNP rose by 26 percent; from 1960 to 1968, real GNP rose by 42 percent. . . . The proportion of the population living in poverty declined during the earlier period, while it did not in the later period. Also more progress seems to have been made in reducing inequality between the wages of whites and blacks in the earlier period than in the later one."[34] Joseph Stiglitz, who received the Nobel Prize in Economics in 2001 and was chairman of the Council of Economic Advisers under President Bill Clinton, writes that US gross domestic product growth was "not as strong in the past thirty years (1981–2011) as the previous thirty years (an average annual growth of 2.8 percent versus 3.6 percent)."[35]

It is surprising that so many contemporary conservatives have embraced the tenets of radical anarchistic libertarianism that, in Boaz's words, would restrict the functions of government to "police, courts, and national defense"[36]—perhaps a 90 percent diminution in government at all levels. In no way could this be considered a conservative, reasonable, or realistic approach to issues of government and policy in contemporary society. It is not really a very practical system that only works for the top few.

The goal of progressive taxation is not to create a society in which equality of result is the outcome or paradigm, but one in which the current vast and growing inequalities that typify the United States do not continue—and are reversed. It is time to reaffirm the cardinal American belief that all people are created equal.

In closing *The Constitution of Liberty,* Hayek quoted Lord Acton: "At all times sincere friends of freedom have been rare, and its triumphs have been due to minorities, that have prevailed by associating themselves with auxiliaries whose objects often differed from their own; and this association, which is always dangerous, has sometimes been disastrous."[37] It is time to restore the heritage of classical liberalism to the political, economic, and social left; and it is time for true classical liberals to work for fundamental change and reform in the political, economic, and social right. It is time to tax the rich more through restored progressive taxation—the tax policies that prevailed when the United States was at its greatest. The evolution of free market economics at the University of Chicago has much to contribute to this end.

PHOTOGRAPHS OF CHICAGO ECONOMISTS

James Laurence Laughlin was the first chair of the Department of Political Economy (University of Chicago Photographic Archive, [apf1-03687], Special Collections Research Center, University of Chicago Library)

Frank Knight, progenitor of the Chicago school of economics (University of Chicago Photographic Archive, [apf1-03515], Special Collections Research Center, University of Chicago Library)

Henry Simons, advocate of progressive taxation (University of Chicago Photographic Archive, [apf1-07613], Special Collections Research Center, University of Chicago Library)

Jacob Viner and Theodore Schultz (r), two key Chicago economists (University of Chicago Photographic Archive, [apf1-07483], Special Collections Research Center, University of Chicago Library)

Milton Friedman taught at Chicago from 1946 to 1976 (University of Chicago Photographic Archive, [apf1-06231], Special Collections Research Center, University of Chicago Library)

Friedrich Hayek wrote The Constitution of Liberty *at Chicago (University of Chicago Photographic Archive, [apf1-08493], Special Collections Research Center, University of Chicago Library)*

George Stigler was a close Friedman ally and friend (University of Chicago Photographic Archive, [apf1-07966], Special Collections Research Center, University of Chicago Library)

James Heckman, contemporary Chicago economist (Damien Rodriguez)

APPENDIX 1

INTERVIEW WITH MILTON FRIEDMAN ON FRIEDRICH HAYEK

(THE FOLLOWING INTERVIEW of Milton Friedman by the author took place on October 9, 1995.)

Q: How would you describe Hayek personally?

A: In terms of his personal characteristics, Hayek was a very complicated personality. He was by no means a simple person. He was very outgoing in one sense but at the same time very private. He did not like criticism, but he never showed that he didn't like criticism. His attitude under criticism, as I found, was to say: "Well, that's a very interesting thing. At the moment, I'm busy, but I'll write to you about it more later." And then he never would!

On the other hand, he wasn't like von Mises. He wasn't intolerant at all. You cannot conceive of Hayek doing the kind of thing that Mises did, when, for example, he wouldn't talk to Machlup for three years because Machlup had come out for floating exchange rates at a Mont Pelerin meeting. Hayek did not do that. That was, I believe, because of the influence of the London School on him. He was very much tempered by the London School.

On the other hand, Lionel Robbins was enormously upset with the way in which Hayek treated his first wife. He resigned from the Mont Pelerin Society on that ground, and he wouldn't talk to Hayek. It was years before they were reconciled, primarily, I believe, by the acts of Hayek's children. And that is highly relevant to his personality, I think.

Q: Would you say that he was a proud man?

A: Oh yes, no question that he was a proud man. But I never have been able to absorb—I never have been able to integrate into my own view—because I never had any experiences remotely like this—the kind of thing that happened with respect to his first wife. The big dilemma is the way Hayek treated his first wife. I find that very hard to reconcile with his personality as I knew him, as I experienced him. He was usually very thoughtful of others. He was very sure of his own ideas.

He changed greatly over time in that respect. One of the things I'm sure you've read are the letters in *The Collected Writings of John Maynard Keynes* between Hayek and Keynes. Hayek comes out very badly in those letters, in my opinion. Keynes comes out like the kindly, generous uncle, and Hayek comes out like a very arrogant, self-centered young man, which he was.

. . .

[re: *Prices and Production*] I must say, I think that's one of the worst of Hayek's books.

Let me emphasize. I am an enormous admirer of Hayek, but not for his economics. That, again, is subject to misunderstanding. It depends on what you mean by economics. I'm not talking about his understanding of economics, his application of economics to the real world, or anything like that, but his contributions to the science of economics, not to economic practice, not to anything else. I think *Prices and Production* was a very flawed book. I think his capital theory book is unreadable. I cannot say I've read it. [laughter] It's very unreadable.

On the other hand, *The Road to Serfdom* is one of the great books of our time. His writings in [political theory] are magnificent, and I have nothing but great admiration for them. I really believe that he found his right vocation—his right specialization—with *The Road to Serfdom*. His earlier works were intended to be part of the literature of technical economics as a science, and, indeed, it was that characteristic of them that impressed Lionel Robbins and led Lionel to bring him from Austria to London.

I never could understand why they were so impressed [at the London School of Economics] with the lectures that ended up as *Prices and Production,* and I still can't. . . . these very confused notions of periods of production, different orders of products, and so on.

The interesting thing about that has something to do—as of that point, he had not freed himself from the methodological views of von Mises. And those methodological views have at their center that facts are not really relevant in determining, in testing, theories. They are relevant to illustrate theories but not to test them, because we base economics on propositions that are self-evident. And they are self-evident because they are about human beings, and we're human beings. So, we have an internal source of final knowledge, and no tests can overrule that . . . Praxeology.

That methodological approach has very negative influences. It makes it very hard to build a cumulative discipline of any kind. If you're always going back to your internal, self-evident truths, how do people stand on one another's shoulders? And the fact is that fifty, sixty years after von Mises issued his capital theory—which is what's involved in Hayek's capital theory—so-called Austrian economists still stick by it. There hasn't been an iota of progress.[1]

It also tends to make people intolerant. If you and I are both praxeologists, and we disagree about whether some proposition or statement is correct, how do we resolve that disagreement? We can yell, we can argue, we can try to find a logical flaw in one another's [argument], but in the end we have no way to resolve it except by fighting—by saying you're wrong and I'm right.

On the other hand, if you take . . . an approach which says what we do in science is to offer hypotheses about the consequences of certain events and, if we disagree, we test those by trying to seek empirical evidence that contradicts our predictions—if you and I disagree, we have another way to solve our problems, resolve our differences. I say to you, what facts can I find that will convince you I was right and you were wrong? You say to me, what facts can I find that will do the opposite? Then we go out and observe the facts. That's how science progresses.

Now, as I said, I believe that Hayek started out as a strict Misesian, but he changed. Robbins also at one point was a strict Misesian. But the more tolerant atmosphere of Britain, then subsequently of the U.S., and his exposure to a wider range of scholars, led him to alter that position. And as I say, he was never as intolerant personally as Mises was. . . .

[Re Ludwig von Mises:] He's always fascinated me . . . I agree with so much of what he says, and yet I disagree absolutely with his methodology and his intolerance. As I say, I don't believe Hayek shared that at all.

Now, I first met Hayek, I believe, in 1946 or 1947, when he was coming through Chicago on one of his lecture tours or doing something about the Mont Pelerin Society, but I really first met him at the first Mont Pelerin Society meeting. That's where I first got to know him in a more serious way. And then, of course, during the ten years he was at the University of Chicago. We saw him on and off. Hayek's second wife, Helene, and Rose were great walkers. I attended Hayek's seminar.

Q: How often did you attend his seminar?

A: I attended his seminar regularly whenever I was in town. They were wonderful seminars primarily because of the range of people he brought in as speakers. They were very broad-ranging in conception. The seminar I remember best is one on methodology in which Enrico Fermi talked. That had a very great influence on my own work. He talked about the concept of measurement, and I will never forget the statement that impressed me most . . . Measurement is the making of distinctions, . . . and the finer the distinctions, the finer the measurement. It's a marvelously productive idea. In fact, it's the only one of Hayek's seminars I remember as an individual seminar. I cannot tell you who else he had there, but the main appeal of it was that they attracted people from a number of different departments. He was not in the economics department but on the Committee on Social Thought.

Q: In Richard Cockett's *Thinking the Unthinkable,* there's a quote that Lionel Robbins drafted the first statement of aims of the Mont Pelerin Society. Is that correct?

A: Oh, of course. There's no doubt about it. . . . Lionel was a wonderful human being, but also had an unrivaled capacity for the use of language. I've never known anybody who could stand up and speak off-hand in beautiful, grammatically perfect sentences. At any rate, there was nobody else at the meeting who could have reconciled the differences in politics among the participants in that statement as well as Robbins. After we had spent days discussing these issues and tried to draft a statement, Lionel finally took it over and drafted the one we all signed.

Q: Do you think he's an underappreciated figure?

A: He's a fascinating figure and an underappreciated figure, in one sense and not in another. He was not a deeply original thinker, but he was an extraordinarily insightful analyst of literature who wrote extremely well. He was two people. He was one person before World War II, before he was corrupted by Keynes, and another person after World War II, when he became a man of the world—trustee of the art institute and so on. As a human being, I had a great deal of contact with Robbins, more than I had with Hayek, and as a human being you would find it hard to find a more decent, more honorable, more delightful human being. And that shows up in his reaction to Hayek's treatment of his first wife.

. . .

He [Hayek] brought her to Great Britain when he was called to the London School, but she never got as involved. He got very involved in the British scene, but his first wife was more or less left on her own to take care of the kids in Golder's Green, where they had a house of some kind. She was not very much involved, as I understand, but I don't know very much about this. . . . At any rate, my feeling is she was not very happy. She did not really feel part of it. . . . As I gathered from Robbins at the time, he sort of left her in the lurch in London, never having really struck down real roots. . . . All I know is that Robbins thought he had treated her in an absolutely unacceptable manner. . . . It is a different era and the standards of that time are not the standards of today. But by the standards of that time, and, more importantly—it isn't the standards of that time, it's the standards of Lionel Robbins . . . I believe that he would think that a provocation would have to be very,

very great indeed to justify such behavior. And I share his view. Look, I recognize the change of circumstances. We have two children, both of whom have been divorced and are on second marriages. At the same time, Rose and I have been married for fifty-seven years, so you have both sides of that picture.

   . . .

Q: Was the second Mrs. Hayek an intelligent woman?

A: Oh yes, a very intelligent woman. I only met the first Mrs. Hayek once. I don't really remember how. I don't know if it was at Robbins's or what.

     Aaron [Director] was largely responsible for getting the University of Chicago Press to publish *The Road to Serfdom*. He played a very significant role in that and he served for many years as the representative for the Mont Pelerin Society—the Mont Pelerin Society was incorporated in Illinois, and Aaron was the secretary of it for the books for many years.

Q: There is some indication in the 1956 introduction to *The Road to Serfdom* that it was to some extent suppressed—

A: Now, what he says there is that publishers refused to publish it because of what they thought of its content.

Q: Do you think there's much to that?

A: I don't have the slightest doubt. There's no doubt about that, no doubt. There isn't. You know, you're a young man, and you have no idea of the climate of opinion in 1945 to 1960 or 1970. I really have a hard time knowing how to tell you about that, because it really is unbelievable. We had the same experience. I published *Capitalism and Freedom* in 1962. That's seventeen years later. It's a book that's now sold close to a million copies. It was not reviewed by any American publications, other than the *American Economic Review*. It's inconceivable that at that time—I was a full professor at the University of Chicago; I was very well known in the academic world—it is inconceivable that a book on the other side by someone in that same position would not have been reviewed in every publication—the *New York Times*, the *Chicago Tribune*—

   . . .

     And the only reason Hayek received the Nobel Prize—you know why Hayek received the Nobel Prize. The rules of the Nobel, when the Nobel Prize was set up in economics were that it could not be given for five years to a Swede. This was the sixth year. They wanted very badly to give the prize to Myrdal. But Myrdal was way over on the left of the spectrum, and they thought they would be subject—this is my reconstruction; I cannot give you documentary evidence—they thought they would be subject to great criticism, so they decided to link Myrdal with Hayek, left with right, and off-set the criticism. [laughter]

Q: It seemed to make a really significant—

A: It had tremendous influence on Hayek. No question. It rejuvenated him. The recognition—I never understood this personally, from a personal point of view. What difference does it make? As I used to say when I was asked the question, I'm much more interested in what economists fifty years from now will think about my work than I am in what seven people in Sweden happen to decide right now.

. . .

Q: In *Hayek on Hayek,* there is a passage where Hayek discusses his relations with the Chicago school and he calls your *Essays in Positive Economics* "as dangerous as Keynes'" work—

A: He's right! [laughter] There was that big methodological difference. As I say, he had bridged it to some extent. Mises could never have written *The Constitution of Liberty. The Constitution of Liberty* is Hayek's descent into the Chicago school. It's the only one of his works that makes extensive reference to absolute experience. If you look at the range of topics that he covers in *The Constitution of Liberty* and the way he goes about it, it's a different style altogether than most of his books. . . .

So far as what Hayek says about his influence on the Chicago school, that's a more complicated question. He has had no direct influence so far on the Chicago school; he was not a member of the department. You know the story about Luhnow and his offer to finance Hayek a professorship at Chicago for ten years, I think that's what it was, and the administration asked the economics department whether they would be willing to offer a post to Hayek, and they refused. I was there at the time, but in a very junior capacity. I was not involved in that decision in any way. But in retrospect, I think they were right.

Q: Nef says in his autobiography that the economics department didn't want Hayek because of *The Road to Serfdom.*

A: That had nothing to do with it, nothing to do with it. They didn't want him, there are two things—number one, they had a very strong feeling that they should choose their own members and not have members appointed from the outside. Independent of the name, they would have reacted negatively to any suggestion from the administration. But number two, they didn't agree with his economics. *Prices and Production,* his capital theory—if they had been looking around the world for an economist to add to their staff, their prescription would not have been the author of *Prices and Production.* So far as *The Road to Serfdom* was concerned, it played no role at all. The fact of the matter is, in terms of ideology, the majority of that department was on Hayek's side. The University of Chicago Department of Economics was known countrywide in the profession to be distinctive because it was so relatively free market. So, *Road to Serfdom* would have been a plus, not a minus. No, I am sure that the fundamental reason they rejected him was a combination of they would have had to assume responsibility after ten years from their funds—he was not a person they would have chosen to add—and they didn't want their membership dictated by the administration. . . . The fact that Hayek was free market would never have been a disqualification. There were people, don't misunderstand me—there were probably more Keynesians than free market people in the department. But at that time, there weren't, no. No, there weren't. I don't think so, at that time.

Q: Earlier, there would have been?

A: Later, later. Let me tell you what the real problem is there. We went looking for the best Keynesian we could find because we thought we didn't have enough. We hired Harry Johnson, and after a year or so he became a Chicago [economist]. [laughter] The truth of the matter is, he was converted, and that's what tended to happen to the people of the opposite view who came to Chicago. Now, but in my opinion, Hayek could never have written *The Constitution of Liberty* if he had not come to Chicago. Now, if you look at those footnotes, now, of course, it depends on what chapter. I'm trying to find a typical example of his discussion on rent control, or public housing, and so on.

　. . . So, as far as Hayek's influence on Chicago is concerned, it was not through the economics department, except as he influenced individuals like myself who went to his seminar and so forth and interacted with him. Hayek's influence on Chicago was much more through the students he brought, through the group that established the *New Individualist Review*—his influence there was very strong and very great.

Q: Did he ever participate in the Money and Banking Workshop?

A: No. . . . It is true that he and I differed very sharply on monetary policy. This is really the Austrian-von Misesian—

Q: Was he a monetarist?

A: No, he was not a monetarist. The truth of the matter is, he really got out of that side of the business. . . . Don't misunderstand me. He was not a monetarist in the sense in which that term has come to be understood, but he understood, he really knew a great deal about the monetary system. He understood perfectly well the role of money in the society. He was perfectly aware that you couldn't have inflation without excessive printing of money. The problem was the manner in which it operated. He and his followers—like all of von Mises's followers—believed fundamentally that it operated by changing the structure of production through the period of production concept. That there were higher order goods, lower order goods—that was the way it operated. Therefore, it mattered a great deal how money got into the system. Where it came in, where it did not. Now, our view was not in contradiction to that in one sense. But that wasn't what was really important. What was really important about money was simply that it leads people to spend more money and that spending more money tended to lead in the first instance to more employment and output, but then it converted into pressure on prices and that what was important was these lags in the process.

　Mises was for a gold standard. Hayek went around and around the bush on that. He at one point came out for a commodity standard. . . . He later came out for free banking in which he thought banks would establish a commodity or gold standard. But he was not a gold nut like von Mises was. But he was strongly opposed to the use of aggregative concepts like the quantity of money or national income. He said you can't get anywhere with those aggregative concepts without breaking them down and looking at their components and processes. And there's some truth to that. I don't doubt for a moment that the aggregate concepts conceal as well as reveal. But they do reveal a good deal. And so far as what he was referring to was monetary policy in Britain, I was urging on the British, so far as I had any influence at all, that they establish monetary goals in terms of the quantity of money. And that's what he objected to. He didn't like the concept of the quantity of money because it was one of these aggregative things.

Q: What's your view of Keynes's *Treatise?*

A: . . . The *Treatise* is an enormous book. It's two volumes and a lot of it is very good, and just as good today as when it was written. But Keynes did no longer believe that the particular mechanism he described in there . . . He rejected that. The fundamental concept underlying the *Treatise* is one which the fundamental fluctuation is in prices, not output. The real shift between it and the *General Theory* is to make the action go into output, not prices. That's an oversimplification, but I think it's a correct statement.

. . .

Don't misunderstand me. Keynes was a great economist, one of the greatest economists of all time. I just happen to believe—the *General Theory* offered a hypothesis about the way the world worked. Now, like every scientific hypothesis, it may be a very imaginative and thoughtful hypothesis, but it may be wrong. And I don't object to the hypothesis on theoretical grounds. I object because I think its predictions were not confirmed by reality, and that the evidence rejects it. It's a very appealing and very subtle hypothesis that turned out to be wrong. It was the right kind of hypothesis which tries to have a very simple explanation for very complicated phenomena. It's just wrong. It doesn't work. I want to emphasize I'm a great admirer of Keynes in general. I disagree with him very strongly so far as that particular hypothesis is concerned. And I also disagree very strongly with his approach to public policy. . . .

Q: There's a quote from *Hayek on Hayek* to the effect that in 1946 when Keynes died, he and Hayek were the best-known economists.

A: I can't judge it, because he's writing that from Britain. And it certainly would not have been true in the United States. At no time in the United States that I can remember would Keynes's name have been linked with Hayek as of the same eminence in economics. In fact, I would say Robbins would have been more likely to have been linked with Keynes in the American world. I'm speaking about the University of Chicago, of course. I don't have all the reading lists.

When did I read *Prices and Production?* It must have been in connection with one of my courses. So it must have been on the reading list. On Mints's reading list. He had everything.

I would say in the United States he was not a well-known economist. But certainly he was not on a level with Keynes. Now, I'm not saying that wasn't true in Britain. Britain was a different story.

. . . .

Q: On the *Fatal Conceit,* there's sort of two schools of thought as to the extent to which Hayek pulled that together. What's your view?

A: I've always been troubled by what role he played in that. I don't have enough knowledge to give you an answer. I don't think it's one of Hayek's better works. It's awfully forced. It's put into this form of, "I'm going to show you once and for all, by God, and after you hear this you'll have no answer to me whatsoever." It's not up to Hayek at his best.

APPENDIX 2

LETTER FROM PAUL SAMUELSON ABOUT MILTON FRIEDMAN

(THE FOLLOWING LETTER from Paul Samuelson to the author is dated June 30, 2005.)

Research deadlines force me to be ultra-brief in my reactions to your letter about Milton Friedman.

1. Having known him for more than 70 years and been on civil terms with him despite many fundamental differences in our views, I must declare him to have been the single most important academic economist pushing the modern generation rightward—rightward to a libertarian position that extols economic efficiency even at the cost of much enhanced personal inequalities.

2. Hayek or Ludwig von Mises had little influence on worldwide economist academics. (The same holds, from the left, for Galbraith's small influence on academics.) Hayek's stock as a theoretical economist was overpriced for a short period after his *Prices and Production* (1931). For students at Harvard, Stanford, MIT, Chicago, LSE, Stockholm, Rotterdam, or Tokyo, Hayek's name dropped into a black hole in the 1932–1975 period. His *The Road to Serfdom* had a better vogue with lay readers antagonistic to the Mixed Economy. However, its thesis that modest social reforms are the gateway to the cruel totalitarian state was poorly confirmed by the economic and political history of

1939–2005 and few ever cracked the pages of his disappointing tome on capital theory.

3. Friedman's *Capitalism and Freedom* is his most influential legacy. It adds little to 1920 economic theory but it spells out what to non-economists is an extremist version of libertarianism. (No driver's licenses, no surgeon's licenses, . . .) A careless reader would think he has proved the deadweight losses involved in traffic lights.

4. Friedman's "permanent income" hypothesis has rightfully commanded widespread respect among modern economists. His 1950–1990 MV = PQ monetarism has been thriving less well. On his own "positivism" credo, its predictive usefulness has been eclipsed both from the right and the left by a Lucas-Sargeant-Prescott rational expectationism and also by Eckstein-Greenspan-Modigliani macro models. Where econometric techniques are concerned, since the exodus from Chicago of the Cowles group, . . . the action has been elsewhere: co-integration, unit roots, and numerous Nobel awards.

5. As a teacher, Milton Friedman achieves an A+ grade. (Typical reaction: At Princeton in 1951 an undergraduate star in economics was somewhat burned out. After Milton's first Chicago class the star was reborn. He literally "couldn't wait for each successive class." You can guess who is speaking [Gary Becker]. He speaks for many.) It did not matter that the syllabus Friedman taught from was the Marshallian partial equilibrium paradigm abandoned elsewhere all over the world. The National Bureau of Burns and Mitchell, which Friedman defended in its dying days, was pretty widely despised and bears small relation to the modern thriving [Martin] Feldstein era.

6. Aaron Director was my first teacher, and it was he who seduced me into economics. I recognized early his brother-in-law's high IQ. By Friedman's own choice he opted away from intricate unsolved problems at the frontier of our subject. That was a loss to the rest of us.

7. All of his writings I've read with care. Why? Because I can learn more from scholars I disagree with. On one vital point, I've altered my view in favor of *flexible* rather than *fixed* exchange rates. On fundamental macro, I grade a two-prong Taylor's Rule as winning hands down against a Friedman-Schwartz rule of pre-set growth in one or another of the . . . definitions of "the *money* supply." . . .

Sincerely yours,
Paul A. Samuelson

BIBLIOGRAPHICAL ESSAY

A VERITABLE BEVY of excellent works on the history of economics at the University of Chicago has appeared in recent years, drawing on extensive archival research and not necessarily predisposed to the ideological perspectives of leading Chicago figures. These works include Angus Burgin, *The Great Persuasion: Reinventing Free Markets since the Depression* (Cambridge, MA: Harvard University Press, 2012); Robert Van Horn, Philip Mirowski, and Thomas A. Stapleford (eds.), *Building Chicago Economics: New Perspectives on the History of America's Most Powerful Economics Program* (Cambridge: Cambridge University Press, 2011); Ross B. Emmett (ed.), *The Elgar Companion to the Chicago School of Economics* (Cheltenham, UK: Edward Elgar, 2010); Philip Mirowski and Dieter Plehwe (eds.), *The Road from Mont Pelerin: The Making of the Neoliberal Thought Collective* (Cambridge, MA: Harvard University Press, 2009); and Johan Van Overtveldt, *The Chicago School: How the University of Chicago Assembled the Thinkers Who Revolutionized Economics and Business* (Chicago: Agate, 2007).

The most celebrated of these works is Burgin's *Great Persuasion,* which is essential reading for anyone interested in unraveling the relationships among Jacob Viner, Frank Knight, and Henry Simons. This writer shares Burgin's thesis of the increasingly radical libertarianism of Milton Friedman over the course of his career, as well as Burgin's emphasis on Friedman's unique, important, and radicalizing role in the international neoliberal movement. With respect to Hayek, Burgin states that he "explicitly condoned a vigorous role for the state" (p. 90). Concerning Friedman, Burgin says: "During the 1960s Friedman became a forceful advocate for *laissez faire* on the public stage, developing an argumentative framework that would provide the foundation for much of the Republican Party's policy platform in the decades that followed" (p. 187). Drawing heavily on archival research from around the world, the *Great Persuasion* is a landmark work.

Van Horn, Mirowski, and Stapleford's *Building Chicago Economics* is an important contribution to understanding free market economics at Chicago, featuring articles by many scholars. The editors note that during "the 'Reagan revolution' of the 1980s, the doctrinal principles and policy prescriptions of the Chicago school had their heyday in American politics" (p. xx). Jamie Peck notes that of Reagan's outside Economic Advisory Board: "Fully half of the members . . . had substantial Chicago connections" (p. xliv). Edward Nik-Khah considers the controversy surrounding the aborted Milton Friedman Institute at the University of Chicago following his death. Van Horn, Mirowki, and Stapleford write: "The founders of the postwar Chicago School (including Friedman, Stigler, and Aaron Director) departed quite sharply from the classical liberalism that had animated their mentors at the university, such as Frank Knight and Henry Simons" (p. xix).

Emmett's *Elgar Companion to the Chicago School of Economics* also features many fine articles, including in its second part discussions of nineteen Chicago economists. This work provides much information on many lesser figures among Chicago economists, as well as on the principal ones. Emmett's conception of the Chicago school is broad. In particular, see the essay on Henry Simons by Sherryl D. Kasper: Simons "suggested a radical alteration of the federal tax structure to make it more progressive so as to lessen the concentration of income and wealth that gave certain members of society more economic and political power" (p. 333).

Mirowski and Plehwe's *The Road from Mont Pelerin* is a work of broad scope, considering neoliberalism around the world but placing too much emphasis on the Mont Pelerin Society. The society did not have the influence that is here presented. Moreover, the society was more philosophically diverse in its early years than indicated. See the review of this work by Brian Doherty in the *Freeman* (September 21, 2011).

Perhaps the most focused work to discuss economics at the University of Chicago is Van Overtveldt's *The Chicago School: How the University of Chicago Assembled the Thinkers Who Revolutionized Economics and Business.* Van Overtveldt worked on this volume for many years and conducted more than one hundred interviews. It offers both source material on and descriptions of almost everyone of note who passed through Chicago in economics and business from the opening of the university in 1892 through 2005. Van Overtveldt emphasizes the role of Laughlin: "Economics at the University of Chicago was different from that which was practiced at other centers of economic research in the last decade of the 19th century. It was James L. Laughlin . . . who created this difference" (p. 3).

Van Overtveldt notes that "Knight consistently argued that economic freedom is essential to the existence of all other forms of freedom, including religious, political, and intellectual freedom" (p. 61). Following Knight, Friedman sought to maximize freedom as the outcome of a social order above any other good. Van Overtveldt also says that "Knight never engaged in a blind defense of capitalism and the free market system" (Ibid.). Van Overtveldt presents his subject thematically as well as chronologically and provides much information on many figures. He notes that through 2004, twenty-four of fifty-seven individuals to receive the Nobel Prize in Economics were either primarily affiliated with the University of Chicago or had been affiliated with it for some important part of their careers. In addition, of the twenty-nine economists to receive the John Bates Clark Medal between 1951 and 2005, ten have had an important association or primary affiliation with Chicago. Also, between 1947 and 1977, the American Economic Association presented the Francis A. Walker Medal every five years to a living American economist who had made the greatest contribution to economics. Five of the seven recipients, including the first four—Wesley Mitchell, John M. Clark, Frank Knight, and Jacob Viner—had strong Chicago roots and affiliation, as did the sixth recipient, Theodore Schultz.

Van Overtveldt mentions that the "list of schools developed at the University of Chicago is long. A few in the social sciences include: the pragmatic philosophy of John Dewey at the beginning of the twentieth century; the urban sociology of William Thomas, Robert Park, and Ernest Burgess that flourished during the period 1920–1950; the political science approach inspired by Charles E. Merriam that flowered over the years 1910–1940; the school of theology following Charles H. Arnold's work; and the approach of the English department led by Ronald Crane in the 1950s (pp. 43–44). He praises Laughlin, whose "major criterion in attracting people for his new department was scientific excellence, not conformity" (p. 49). Van Overtveldt quotes Emmett: Laughlin "assembled around him many of the best economists of his day regardless of their political or theoretical leanings" (Ibid.). Van Overtveldt appropriately calls attention to the role of William Rainey Harper, the first president of the University of Chicago, in establishing the traditions at the university that found expression in the Department of Political Economy and then in the Department of Economics. For reviews of the *Chicago School,* see Warren J. Samuels, Jeff E. Biddle, and Ross B. Emmett (eds.), *Research in the History of Economic Thought and Methodology,* vol. 26-A (Bingley, UK: JAI Press, 2008), which includes three reviews. A fourth review is provided in the 2009 edition of *Research in the History of Economic Thought and Methodology,* vol. 27-A.

Warren J. Samuels, *The Chicago School of Political Economy* (New Brunswick, NJ: Transaction Publishers, 1993), is a collection of articles that originally appeared in the December 1975 and March 1976 editions of the *Journal of Economic Issues.* Samuels wrote: "Whether the success of the School is due to the merit of its ideas, the hard work . . . or personality of its members, or the spirit of the age . . . , the School is arguably the most successful in economics since World War II" (p. xi). He included James Buchanan and Ronald Coase, as well as Friedman, Stigler, and Gary Becker, in the Chicago school. Several of the contributors emphasize Knight's role in the creation of the school.

Joseph Dorfman, *The Economic Mind in American Civilization,* vol. v (New York: Viking Press, 1959), a general history of economics in the United States, provides much information on economists at Chicago. No Chicago school is identified at this time, but Knight and Viner are identified as two leading "traditionalists." Dorfman had this to say about Viner: He "resembled the classical masters in his ability to make contributions to a large number of different areas of economics—especially to the history of economic doctrine, value theory, international trade, money and banking, and public finance. His adherence to the classical and neoclassical tradition did not mean slavish acceptance" (p. 488).

Malcolm Rutherford, *The Institutionalist Movement in American Economics, 1918–1947: Science and Social Control* (Cambridge: Cambridge University Press, 2011), is the leading work in the field. The chapter "Institutionalism at Chicago and Beyond" is particularly valuable. Also see David Seckler, *Thorstein Veblen and the Institutionalists: A Study in the Social Philosophy of Economics* (Boulder: Colorado Associated University Press, 1975), which includes an informative foreword by Lionel

Robbins; and Joseph Dorfman et al., *Institutional Economics: Veblen, Commons, and Mitchell Reconsidered* (Berkeley and Los Angeles: University of California Press, 1964).

Among Viner's more important and accessible works are the collection *The Long View and the Short* (Glencoe, IL: Free Press, 1958) and *Religious Thought and Economic Society* (Durham, NC: Duke University Press, 1978). Among the gems in the former are "Adam Smith and *Laissez Faire*" and "Bentham and J. S. Mill: The Utilitarian Background." Also see the posthumous collection, Jacob Viner (Douglas A. Irwin, ed.), *Essays on the Intellectual History of Economics* (Princeton, NJ: Princeton University Press, 1991). In his introduction, Irwin notes that the "major aim" of Viner's essay on Smith was "to correct the view that Adam Smith was a doctrinaire proponent of *laissez faire*" (p. 17). Lionel Robbins, *Jacob Viner: 1892–1970* (Princeton, NJ: Princeton University Press, 1970), is a brief reminiscence. Noting Viner's individualism and idiosyncrasy, Robbins commented: "He belonged to no school and he repudiated any intention of founding one" (p. 10).

Kenneth R. Hoover—who played the key role in securing Hayek's files from his former secretary, Charlotte Cubitt, for the Hoover Institution—noted in *Economics as Ideology: Keynes, Laski, Hayek, and the Creation of Contemporary Politics* (Lanham, MD: Rowman & Littlefield, 2003) that in the summer of 1947, Viner "refused an invitation to join the Mont Pelerin Society, disdaining activity for 'political purposes'" (p. 190). Hoover also notes that, after Hayek secured funding from the Volker Fund for a position in the United States, Viner wrote him on July 30, 1948, that, despite Hayek's wish to come to Princeton, "the authorities found the arrangements 'impossible to accept.' Viner suggested that 'any of the respectable institutions' would have the same objection and that some sort of independence as 'guest professor' . . . might be less controversial," as a result of the outside funding issue. According to Hoover, Aaron Director wrote Hayek, also in July 1948, that "an appointment to the faculty of the Committee on Social Thought, chaired by Professor John U. Nef, might meet with the support of Hutchins . . . Hayek wrote back that he would be delighted at the prospect. Matters moved along. Nef wrote that Hayek's appointment was approved by his colleagues" (p. 191). Hoover's discussion of Hayek's divorce (pp. 190–195) is the best to have appeared.

The January-February 1972 edition of the *Journal of Political Economy* features memorial articles on Viner by Fritz Machlup, Paul Samuelson, and William Baumol. Also see Henry W. Spiegel, "Jacob Viner," in John Eatwell, Murray Milgate, and Peter Newman (eds.), *The New Palgrave: A Dictionary of Economics*, vol. 4 (London: Macmillan, 1991). Eugene Rotwein, "Jacob Viner and the Chicago Tradition," *History of Political Economy* (Summer 1983), calls attention to many of Viner's statements on his thought and philosophy, a number of which are included here. Rotwein notes that Viner "characterizes 'public goods' as 'an increasingly important element in welfare'" (p. 269) and that he was, reluctantly, inclined to a greater measure of paternalism than some of his Chicago libertarian successors. As opposed exclusively to cash payments to the poor, Viner did "not share such an abiding belief in man's rationality, and he argues . . . that habits and customs may lead to patterns of consumption behavior that are injurious to the individual" (p. 271). Also see Paul Oslington, "Jacob Viner on Religion and Intellectual History," an informative and undated Internet article.

Luca Fiorito and Sebastiano Nerozzi, "Jacob Viner's Reminiscences from the New Deal," in Warren J. Samuels, Jeff E. Biddle, and Ross B. Emmett (eds.), *Research in the History of Economic Thought and Methodology: A Research Annual* (Bingley, UK: JAI Press, 2009), provides valuable information on Viner's service in government, which was more influential than often recognized. Fiorito and Nerozzi note: "Viner's activity as economic adviser has received only a minor and fragmentary attention by both historians of economic thought and general historians of the Roosevelt and Truman administrations" (p. 81).

No full-length biography has been written on Viner, Knight, or Simons, though each would be a worthy subject. More has been written on Knight than on Viner, including by Ross Emmett, the leading Knight scholar. Among Emmett's works are *Frank Knight and the Chicago School in American Economics* (Oxfordshire, UK: Routledge, 2009) and, as editor, *The Chicago Tradition in Economics 1892–1945*, 8 vols. (London: Routledge, 2002) and *Selected Essays by Frank H. Knight* (Chicago: University of Chicago Press, 1999). Also see Emmett's work as editor, *Frank H. Knight in Iowa City, 1919–1928, Research in the History of Economic Thought and Methodology*, vol. 29-B (Bingley, UK: Emerald Group Publishing, 2011) and *Documents Related to John Maynard Keynes, Institutionalism at Chicago & Frank H. Knight, Research in the History of Economic Thought and Methodology*, vol. 31-B (Bingley, UK: Emerald Group Publishing, 2013), the latter of which focuses on Knight's relationship with Frederick Kershner.

The eight-volume *Chicago Tradition in Economics 1892–1945* includes much information in the introductory essays by Emmett as well as the republication of leading articles and chapters by many Chicago economists. Gordon Tullock's foreword to "The Simons Syllabus" in vol. VIII is a valuable historical document. Emmett's introduction to *Selected Essays by Frank H. Knight* is informative. He notes: "Given the large task Knight gave himself, it is not surprising that he was generally a better critic than he was a systematic social theorist" (vol. I, p. x). Warren Samuels writes in the foreword to *Frank Knight and the Chicago School in American Economics* of the earlier Chicago economists that they "did not play games with policy. They did not oversimplify and exaggerate" (p. xxi).The second volume of the *Selected Essays* includes Knight's critical, indeed almost hostile, review of Hayek's *The Constitution of Liberty*.

The 1973 edition of the *Journal of Political Economy* includes papers delivered by Warner Wick, T. W. Schultz, and George Stigler at a memorial service in Knight's memory. Also see George Stigler, "In Memoriam: F. H. Knight," *American Economic Review* (December 1973); James Buchanan, "Frank Knight," in Edward Shils (ed.), *Remembering the University of Chicago* (University of Chicago Press, 1991); and Richard S. Howey, "Frank Hyneman Knight and the History of Economic Thought," in Warren J. Samuels (ed.), *Research in the History of Economic Thought and Methodology*, vol. I (Greenwich, CT: JAI Press, 1983)—the last of which includes significant biographical information.

William S. Kern, "Frank Knight's Three Commandments," *History of Political Economy* (Winter 1987), is a good article on Knight's ethical thought. Edward Shils, *Portraits: A Gallery of Intellectuals* (Chicago: University of Chicago Press, 1997), contains an excellent essay on Knight and essays on Robert Maynard Hutchins and John Nef. Robert H. Nelson, *Economics as Religion: From Samuelson to Chicago and*

Beyond (University Park: Pennsylvania State University Press, 2001), presents a very positive estimate of Knight's influence (p. 114).

Of Knight's own work, see the collection of essays *Freedom and Reform: Essays in Economics and Social Philosophy* (Indianapolis, IN: LibertyPress, 1982 [1947]). There, he makes this comment on the liberal tradition: "The core of liberalism—what most distinguishes it from other views of life—is a manifold revolution in the conception of truth. We need not attempt to answer Pilate's famous question, 'What is truth,' as we need not give a formal definition of freedom in any metaphysical sense. We assume that there is an intelligible difference between believing, on the basis of facts, reasoning and the critical evaluation of evidence, and 'prejudice,' or believing by choosing to have faith in some traditional dogma or myth or authoritative pronouncement" (p. 468). James Buchanan commented in introducing the work on Knight's "intellectual-moral courage to treat nothing as sacred" (p. x).

J. Bradford DeLong, "In Defense of Henry Simons' Standing as a Classical Liberal," *Cato Journal* (Winter 1990), maintains that Simons was a classical liberal and that the Chicago school of economics of the 1950s through 1970s moved to a more doctrinaire libertarian position that led it to misevaluate Simons's view. This is an exceptional work in historical recovery. DeLong writes: "I claim that Henry Simons indeed was a pure, consistent, and thoughtful classical liberal. The policy prescriptions Coase identifies as 'interventionist' are in fact derived from sound libertarian principles. And they do not indicate any lack of faith in markets or any falling away from a pro-free market orientation" (p. 603). DeLong presents essentially the distinction between classical liberalism and contemporary libertarianism made here. Also see DeLong's weblog for June 1, 2011, "The Intellectual Collapse of the Chicago School of Economics Continues . . ."

Robert L. Bartley, "Jack Kemp vs. Henry Simons," *Wall Street Journal* (January 18, 1996), held: "Simons was an economist at the University of Chicago from 1927 to . . . 1946. A stalwart of *laissez faire* Chicago school economics, he was at the same time godfather of the notion that the tax system should be used to redistribute income." Bartley also called Simons a "world-class economist," while disagreeing strongly with his call for progressive taxation. Herb Stein, in a follow-up piece, wrote: "What Simons would think today is the proper degree of progression, I don't know. I will, however, offer one law derived from sixty years of observation since I took his course: Whatever is the existing degree of progression, people who pay the top rate will think it is too much" ("Regarding Henry Simons," *Wall Street Journal* [January 30, 1996]).

George J. Stigler, *Memoirs of an Unregulated Economist* (Chicago: University of Chicago Press, 1988), provides background on Chicago and expresses Stigler's own views. Stigler, *The Economist as Preacher and Other Essays* (Chicago: University of Chicago Press, 1982), contains a number of helpful essays, including one on Simons. Stigler had much to say with respect to Mill, Smith, Bentham, and the evolution of economics. He correctly traced this evolution to the philosophical utilitarianism of Bentham's school.

James M. Buchanan, *Better than Plowing and Other Personal Essays* (Chicago: University of Chicago Press, 1992) includes remembrances of his time studying at Chicago, from 1945 to 1948, emphasizing Knight. Thomas Sowell's autobiography, *A Personal Odyssey* (New York: Free Press, 2000), includes recollections of his time as a student at Chicago. Like Friedman, Sowell's scholarly work is more valuable than his popular work. In particular, see Sowell's *A Conflict of Visions: Ideological Origins of Political Struggles* (New York: William Morrow, 1987), *Conquests and Cultures: An International History* (New York: Basic Books, 1998), and *On Classical Economics* (New Haven, CT: Yale University Press, 2006). Chicago economists of an earlier generation to write autobiographies included Paul H. Douglas, *In the Fullness of Time* (New York, 1971), and John U. Nef, *Search for Meaning: The Autobiography of a Noncomformist* (Washington, DC, 1973).

Another partly autobiographical work to see, for enlightenment and entertainment, is Herbert Stein, *On the Other Hand . . . Essays on Economics, Economists, and Politics* (Washington, DC: American Enterprise Institute, 1995). Stein notes: "If we look around the world today and say that capitalism has survived and succeeded, we have to recognize it as the capitalism as altered by the New Deal, not the capitalism of 1929" (p. 37). He said in another work, *Governing the $5 Trillion Economy* (New York: Oxford University Press, 1989): The "influence of the federal government is going to continue. How influential it should be is a matter of controversy. Many people would like to see it reduced, although a significant decrease is extremely unlikely. After all, the Reagan administration was more devoted to reducing the federal influence than any other administration in this century, and its net effect was small if not zero. The federal influence will not be reduced to unimportance" (p. 6).

William Breit and Roger L. Ransom, *The Academic Scribblers,* 3rd ed. (Princeton, NJ: Princeton University Press, 1998), includes chapters on Knight, Simons, and Friedman. Breit and Barry T. Hirsch (eds.), *Lives of the Laureates,* 5th ed. (Cambridge, MA: MIT Press, 2009), is an outstanding collection of autobiographical lectures by Nobel laureates in economics, including Friedman, Stigler, Buchanan, Coase, Becker, Robert Lucas, and James Heckman. Heckman provides excellent observations on economics at Chicago in the 1970s.

H. Laurence Miller, "On the 'Chicago School of Economics,'" *Journal of Political Economy* (February 1962), sees a major division between Friedman and earlier Chicago economists in their approach to government. Also see, in the same issue, Stigler's "Comment" and Martin Bronfenbrenner, "Observations on the 'Chicago School(s).'" A later contribution in this series was A. W. Coats, "The Origins of the 'Chicago School(s)'?" *Journal of Political Economy* (October 1963), which held, commenting on the possibility of a link between Chicago positions over time: "As far as I am aware, there is no doctrinal continuity between the initial period—which, at the very latest, terminates with J. L. Laughlin's retirement as head of the department in 1916—and more recent circumstances" (p. 487).

J. Ronnie Davis, *The New Economics and the Old Economists* (Iowa City: Iowa State University Press, 1971), is an informative presentation of largely Chicago economists' views during the Great Depression. Gordon Tullock wrote in the foreword that Davis "ably demonstrates that the point of view held by almost all leading economists in the United States during . . . the Great Depression was a view which most modern laymen would denominate 'Keynesian'" (p. x). The economists at Chicago and elsewhere in the United States were for more government activity during the depression—particularly in the United States, where the worldwide slump was the most severe. Also see Davis, "Three Days with Knight: A Personal Reminiscence," *Nebraska Journal of Economics and Business* (Winter 1974).

Don Patinkin, *Essays On and In the Chicago Tradition* (Durham, NC: Duke University Press, 1981), is a noteworthy and provocative collection of articles. Patinkin was a student at Chicago from 1941 to 1947. This work contains a great deal of information on the history of economics at Chicago. Patinkin commences with personal reminiscences and continues with essays on Knight. After chapters presenting his own work, Patinkin returns to historical topics in "The Chicago Tradition, the Quantity Theory, and Friedman," originally published in 1969.

Melvin Reder wrote two valuable articles on the history of the Chicago school: "Chicago Economics: Permanence and Change," *Journal of Economic Literature* (March 1982), and the entry on "Chicago School" in Eatwell, Milgate, and Newman (eds.), *The New Palgrave: A Dictionary of Economics,* vol. 1. He wrote in the former: "In retrospect, the Chicago economics of the 1930s may appear as the precursor of what it was to become in the 1960s and 1970s. But in prospect this did not seem the only possible course of development, or even the most likely" (p. 2). In the latter, he divided the school's history into three periods: "(1) a founding period, in the 1930s; (2) an interregnum, from the early 1940s to the early 1950s; and (3) a modern period, from the 1950s to the present" (p. 413).

Milton Friedman, "Schools at Chicago," in Lanny Ebenstein (ed.), *The Indispensable Milton Friedman: Essays on Politics and Economics* (Washington, DC: Regnery, 2012), provides Friedman's views in a 1974 talk before the University of Chicago's board of trustees. Also see here Friedman's 1951 essay "Neo-Liberalism and Its Prospects" for how far his views traveled over the years: "By the standards of nineteenth century individualism, we are all of us collectivists in smaller or greater measure" (p. 4).

Works on Friedman include William Ruger, *Milton Friedman* (New York: Continuum, 2011), an elegantly written and insightful summary of Friedman's life and thought. Abraham Hirsch and Neil de Marchi, *Milton Friedman: Economics in Theory and Practice* (New York: Harvester Wheatsheaf, 1990), focuses on Friedman's methodology and contains an excellent bibliography of works on Friedman. Eamonn Butler, *Milton Friedman: A Guide to His Economic Thought* (New York: Universe Books, 1985), is an introduction to his work in technical economics.

William Frazer, *Milton Friedman and the Big U-Turn* (Gainesville, FL: Gulf/Atlantic Publishing, 1988), is a two-volume work about Friedman's life, career, and influence. Frazer calls attention to ties between British and American policies in the 1980s during the Thatcher and Reagan governments, reflecting Friedman's influence. He quotes Milton Viorst: "'Milton Friedman is . . . the quintessence of the intellectual as a political power. He holds no office and his hands are on none of the levers of influence in Washington. He conquers by the force of his ideas'" (vol. 1, p. 21).

J. Daniel Hammond, *Theory and Measurement: Causality Issues in Milton Friedman's Monetary Economics* (Cambridge: Cambridge University Press, 1996), provides an excellent summary of *A Monetary History*'s development and a description of reaction to it, including in Great Britain. J. Daniel Hammond and Claire H.

Hammond (eds.), *Chicago Price Theory: Friedman-Stigler Correspondence, 1945–1957* (London: Routledge, 2006), is a fascinating look at, and presentation reflecting deep knowledge of, Friedman and Chicago economics.

Richard Cockett, *Thinking the Unthinkable: Think-Tanks and the Economic Counter-Revolution, 1931–1983* (London: Fontana, 1995), is an excellent presentation of the development of conservative-libertarian think tanks in Great Britain, emphasizing Hayek and Friedman. According to Cockett, when *Free to Choose* appeared on British television, it had an "enormous impact on British public opinion" (p. 154). Arthur Seldon, the long-time editorial director of the Institute of Economic Affairs, referred to the "Friedmanite counter-revolution against Keynes 'sponsored' at the IEA" (Arthur Seldon [ed.], *Hayek's 'Serfdom' Revisited* [London: Institute of Economic Affairs, 1984], p. xxii).

Richard M. Ebeling, "Milton Friedman and the Chicago School of Economics," *Freeman* (December 2006), contains these observations:

> The Chicago school blossomed into one of the most influential schools of thought after Friedman joined the economics faculty in 1946 and then was joined by . . . George J. Stigler in 1958.
>
> Friedman revolutionized macroeconomics, while Stigler helped to do the same in microeconomics. Friedman challenged the dominance of Keynesian economics in the postwar period, and Stigler's writings undermined many of the rationales for government regulation of business.
>
> Their common method of analysis, which became a near hallmark of the Chicago school, was rigorous mathematical modeling combined with statistical research to demonstrate the empirical validity or falsity of an economic theory or policy prescription. [p. 2]

Also see Ebeling, "The Limits of Economic Policy: The Austrian Economists and the German ORDO Liberals," in Ebeling (ed.), *The Age of Economists: From Adam Smith to Milton Friedman* (Hillsdale, MI: Hillsdale College Press, 1999), for a discussion of the German ORDO school, which flourished after World War II and recommended many of the policies of classical liberalism, including "redistribution of income through the tax system to modify unacceptable or socially destabilizing inequalities of wealth," "a series of social insurance programs to meet certain minimal requirements for some segments of the society," and "urban and rural planning" (p. 154). Hayek was a great admirer of the ORDO liberals.

The fall 2006 edition of the *Hoover Digest* contains a number of tributes to Friedman, by George Shultz, Gary Becker, Thomas Sowell, and William F. Buckley, among others. Robert Barro writes in his contribution that "in the mid-1960s, when I started as a graduate student in economics at Harvard, my professors viewed Milton as a right-wing, midwestern crank" (p. 25).

Robert Leeson, *The Eclipse of Keynesianism: The Political Economy of the Chicago Counter-Revolution* (New York: Palgrave, 2000), is a provocative work, containing mostly previously published articles. Leeson, *Keynes, Chicago and Friedman* (London: Pickering & Chatto, 2003), is a collection of materials on whether there was a quantity theory of money tradition at Chicago before Friedman began teaching there. This work consists of two volumes with a total of about 900 pages, including more than 150 pages by Leeson. Friedman contributed the preface.

Craig Freedman, "The Chicago School of Anti-Monopolistic Competition—Stigler's Scorched Earth Campaign against Chamberlin," and David Colander and Freedman, "The Chicago Counter-Revolution and the Loss of the Classical Liberal Tradition," are both undated Internet articles based in large part on interviews with Chicago figures. The former quotes Friedman in 1997: "Beginning with the 1930s, there was a period of very active work on economic theory, macro and micro, in both areas. What became prestigious was work in a kind of economic theory, namely pure and largely mathematical oriented. And it did not really have any considerable history. Now that period of change and development, that excitement, has disappeared. We are now in, what I would say is, a relatively flat period of additions to the structure" (p. 6). Also see Freedman, *Chicago Fundamentalism: Ideology and Method in Economics* (Singapore and Hackensack, NJ: World Scientific Publishing, 2008), which focuses on Stigler and Friedman.

Among the best collections of essays on Friedman and his work is Mark A. Wynne, Harvey Rosenblum, and Robert L. Formaini (eds.), *The Legacy of Milton and Rose Friedman's* Free to Choose: *Economic Liberalism at the Turn of the 21st Century* (Dallas, TX: Federal Reserve Bank of Dallas, 2004). James Gwartney and Robert Lawson make good observations on the value of numerical data. According to contemporary Austrian economist Peter Boettke, on the basis of a citation analysis: "Comparison of the scientific impact of Hayek and Friedman . . . weights strongly in favor of Friedman. . . . Friedman dominates over all the classical liberal economists who have won the Nobel Prize (Buchanan, Coase, and Stigler) and the older generation of Mises and Knight" (p. 148). J. Daniel Hammond (ed.), *The Legacy of Milton Friedman as Teacher,* 2 vols. (Cheltenham, UK: Edward Elgar, 1999), is a collection of articles by Friedman's students, preceded by descriptions of Friedman as a teacher. Hammond's introduction provides a good description of Friedman's role as a professor at the University of Chicago.

Juan Gabriel Valdés, *Pinochet's Economists: The Chicago School in Chile* (Cambridge: Cambridge University Press, 1995), is an even-handed account of its subject. Valdés provides no evidence for Friedman's involvement in the Chilean regime of Augusto Pinochet, other than his and Arnold Harberger's 1975 trip to Chile, but notes that during the second half of the 1970s, when much of the rest of academia condemned Chile for its political abuses, Friedman and other free market economists praised it for its economic reforms. Bret Stephens, "How Milton Friedman Saved Chile," *Hoover Digest* (Summer 2010), is a positive presentation of Friedman's influence on Chile. Also see J. Daniel Hammond, "Markets, Politics, and Democracy at Chicago: Taking Economics Seriously," in Van Horn, Mirowski, and Stapleford's *Building Chicago Economics* for a discussion of Friedman's trip to Chile.

Naomi Klein, *The Shock Doctrine: The Rise of Disaster Capitalism* (New York: Metropolitan Books, 2007), is a crackpot work that attempts to tie brief passages by Friedman that ideas often have to wait until the time is right for their implementation to a "shock" economic doctrine in Chile, China, Russia, and the United States. Klein does not really make an argument—she has, rather, written a polemic. For a response to Klein, see Johan Norberg, "The Klein Doctrine: The Rise of Disaster Polemics" (Cato Institute, Briefing Papers, May 14, 2008).

Paul Krugman, "Who Was Milton Friedman?" *New York Review of Books* (February 15, 2007), is an excellent critique after his death: "The world has moved a long way in Friedman's direction. And even more striking than his achievement in terms of actual policy changes has been the transformation of the conventional wisdom." Also see Krugman, "How Did Economists Get It So Wrong?" *New York Times Magazine* (September 2, 2009), for discussion and criticism of Chicago economic positions.

Among the most positive tributes to Friedman following his death was Lawrence H. Summers's "The Great Liberator," in the *New York Times* (November 19, 2006). Summers, a nephew of Paul Samuelson and Kenneth Arrow, wrote that Friedman was "the most influential economist of the second half" of the twentieth century. "Any honest Democrat will admit that we are now all Friedmanites. Mr. Friedman never held elected office but he has had more influence in economic policy as it is practiced around the world today than any other modern figure. . . . I have lost a hero—a man whose success demonstrates that great ideas convincingly advanced can change the lives of people around the world."

The October 1993 edition of the *Journal of Political Economy* is a memorial issue containing ten articles on Stigler, by Friedman, Wallis, Becker, and Sowell, among others. In a longer memorial essay on Stigler for the National Academy of Sciences, Friedman wrote: "I never knew him to do a mean or hurtful or unworthy thing to anyone," and "George was an extremely valuable colleague. He provided much of the energy and drive to the interaction among members of the Chicago economics department, business school and law school that came to be known as the Chicago School" (in Ebenstein, *The Indispensable Milton Friedman*, pp. 217–218)—indicating that even Friedman on occasion expressed the opinion that there was not a strongly identified Chicago school before the late 1950s or so and Stigler's return to Chicago.

Edmund W. Kitch (ed.), "The Fire of Truth: A Remembrance of Law and Economics at Chicago, 1932–1970," *Journal of Law and Economics* (April 1983), is the transcript of an exceptional gathering of thirty former University of Chicago students and former and current faculty focusing on the contributions of Aaron Director and Ronald Coase to the field of law and economics. Among the participants were Milton and Rose Friedman, Stigler, Wallis, Becker, and Robert Bork, in addition to Director and Coase. Friedman said: "The real tradition of Marshallian as opposed to Walrasian analysis of economic problems at Chicago began with Jacob Viner. It was Viner's teaching of economic theory at Chicago for many years which made that a basic tradition there. George [Stigler] and Allen Wallis and I, Aaron [Director] himself, were all influenced by that as students at Chicago" (p. 211). Friedman also said that he had forgotten the full details of Simons's early work, suggesting that some of his statements of continuity in the ideology of Chicago economists may have been a result of misrecollection.

A number of obituaries were written on Director's death in September 2004. These include Richard M. Ebeling, "Aaron Director on the Market for Goods and Ideas," *Freeman* (November 2004), and Adam Bernstein, "Aaron Director Dies at 102; Helped Fuse Economics, Law," *Washington Post* (September 14, 2004). According to Ebeling, Director's "greatest influence was through his teaching . . . during which he helped change how an entire generation of econo-mists and lawyers thought about government regulation and the impact of anti-trust laws on market competition" (p. 2). Also see Coase's biographical entry on Director in the *Palgrave Dictionary of Economics and the Law*, and this writer's obituary of Director in the November 2004 edition of *Liberty*.

Ronald Coase, "Law and Economics at Chicago," *Journal of Law and Econom-ics* (April 1993), includes discussion of Simons, Director, and Coase's own work. Coase writes that "both in and out of the classroom, Director was extremely ef-fective as a teacher, and he had a profound influence on the views of some of his students and . . . colleagues" (pp. 246–7). Also see Stephen Stigler, "Aaron Direc-tor Remembered," and Sam Peltzman, "Aaron Director's Influence on Antitrust Policy," both in the *Journal of Law and Economics* (October 2005).

Robert Pitofsky (ed.), *How the Chicago School Overshot the Mark: The Effect of Con-servative Economic Analysis on U.S. Antitrust* (Oxford: Oxford University Press, 2008), is a valuable collection from a diverse array of perspectives. F. M. Scherer writes: "Director encouraged legal and economic scholars at Chicago to investigate criti-cally the facts, assumptions, and theories underlying important antitrust doc-trines. Those investigations often identified weaknesses in the foundations and sometimes showed that the emperor had no clothes. The train of scholarly work has been of enormous benefit to all of us" (p. 31).

Among the best discussions of Hayek, though brief, are included in the work of Robert Skidelsky, including the second and third volumes of his Keynes bi-ography, *The Economist as Saviour 1920–1937* (New York: Penguin Books, 1994) and *Fighting for Britain 1937–1946* (London: Macmillan, 2000). Skidelsky describes Hayek in the latter as a "philosopher of liberalism" (p. 550). In a *Times Literary Supplement* (September 20, 1996) review of Andrew Gamble's *Hayek: The Iron Cage of Liberty*, Skidelsky writes that Hayek was "the dominant intellectual influence of the last quarter of the twentieth century" and that "the theory of spontaneous order is Hayek's finest achievement" (pp. 4–5).

By way of contrast, Nicholas Wapshott, *Keynes Hayek: The Clash that Defined Modern Economics* (New York: W. W. Norton, 2011), is a very misconceived work that completely misunderstands and misstates the relationship between Hayek and Keynes, giving far too much credence to Hayek's technical economic, as op-posed to political and philosophical, thought. As a technical economist, Hayek was only a minor figure. The *Economist* said in 2001: "Hayek was not much of a technical economist, as Keynes and Mr. Friedman in their different ways under-stood. But he was a social philosopher of rare system and power" (in Warren J. Samuels, Jeff E. Biddle, and John B. Davis (eds.), *A Companion to the History of Eco-nomic Thought* [Malden, MA: Blackwell Publishing, 2003], p. 335).

Perhaps the best work to appear to date on Hayek's comprehensive thought is Edward Feser (ed.), *The Cambridge Companion to Hayek* (Cambridge: Cambridge University Press, 2006). Almost all of the contributions are excellent, and some are exceptional; those by Andrew Gamble, Chandran Kukathas, and Gerald Gaus should be read by all serious students of Hayek. This work is a landmark in Hayek scholarship and covers all phases of his life and career.

The memoir of Hayek's last and longtime secretary, Charlotte Cubitt, *A Life of Friedrich August von Hayek* (Bedfordshire, UK: Authors OnLine, 2006), is an essential and illuminating portrayal of Hayek's final years. Among the most recent works on Hayek is Robert Leeson (ed.), *Hayek: A Collaborative Biography, Part 1. Influences, from Mises to Bartley* (Basingstoke, UK: Palgrave Macmillan, 2013). For a comprehensive presentation of Hayek's thought, see Bruce Caldwell, *Hayek's Challenge: An Intellectual Biography* (Chicago: University of Chicago Press, 2004). Caldwell is among the leading Hayek scholars and has written many articles on Hayek that deserve to be anthologized.

Of somewhat earlier works on Hayek, among the best is Graham Walker, *The Ethics of F. A. Hayek* (Lanham, MD: University Press, 1986). Walker writes from the perspective of a conservative Catholic. As such, he is attracted to and repelled by aspects of Hayek's thought. Walker accurately observes that Hayek was often far closer in ultimate philosophical perspective to the collectivists he derided than to the liberals he praised. Walker writes that Hayek was a "thoroughgoing naturalist. He firmly rejects any notion of transcendence . . . Ethics are fully immanent, fully of this world, fully the result of the process of cultural evolution. They have no transcendent, immutable, or eternal referent" (p. 35). However, unlike most "naturalists-materialists" as Walker terms them, Hayek did not believe in the power of individual reason to replace God. Thus, his thought has not been as susceptible to political excess as the thought of many other naturalists-materialists. For Hayek, the self-generating order replaces both God and a divinelike individual reason.

Jacob Viner, "Hayek on Freedom and Coercion," *Southern Economic Journal* (January 1961), is a review of *The Constitution of Liberty*. Viner noted that Hayek's "positive proposals for government action in the 'welfare' field . . . [are] a substantial enough program to destroy any claims Hayek may have to the *laissez faire* label" (p. 236).

Arthur Seldon (ed.), *Agenda for a Free Society: Essays on Hayek's* The Constitution of Liberty (London: Institute of Economic Affairs, 1961), is an early appraisal of Hayek's work by ten British economists, some of whom knew him. Arthur Shenfield wrote in his contribution that *The Constitution of Liberty* was "one of the great books of our time, profound in analysis, ample in scholarship, noble in spirit. . . . So complete a study of its subject could be attempted by few men in our world" (p. 51). With respect to social welfare, Michael Fogarty observed that Hayek "accepts without question the need for a minimum of public assistance or poor relief" (p. 121).

Anthony de Crespigny, "F. A. Hayek, Freedom for Progress," in de Crespigny and Kenneth Minogue (eds.), *Contemporary Political Philosophers* (London: Methuen, 1975), is an excellent brief introduction to Hayek's thought based mostly on *The Constitution of Liberty*. De Crespigny remarks that for Hayek, "freedom is to be valued not so much from the standpoint of the individual as from that of society" (p. 57). Fritz Machlup (ed.), *Essays on Hayek* (New York: New York University Press, 1976), is a collection with much of interest. Arthur Shenfield concluded: "Few other scholars, if any, have adorned the social sciences in our time as Hayek has done" (p. 176).

Calvin M. Hoy, *A Philosophy of Individual Freedom: The Political Thought of F. A. Hayek* (Westport, CT: Greenwood Press, 1984), is a short but stimulating presentation emphasizing Hayek's ethical thought. Hoy's discussion is provocative for the pithy summaries he makes of Hayek's work: "Without understanding the importance of prices in Hayek's political philosophy, one cannot understand Hayek's argument" (p. 81); "Freedom is possible only within a market order. . . . [T[his order can persist only if individuals are governed by law, that is, abstract rules of conduct" (p. 119); "Problems involving civil liberties receive too little attention from Hayek. . . . Hayek somewhat surprisingly does not much discuss the related ideas of resistance, rebellion, or revolution" (pp. 122–123).

Jim Tomlinson, *Hayek and the Market* (London: Pluto Press, 1990), is a perceptive and sympathetic, yet critical, account of Hayek from a British social democrat: "The basic paradox of . . . [Hayek's] evolutionism, that history has allegedly 'gone wrong' with the rise of collectivism over the last 100 years, and yet this has been accompanied by the most rapid population growth ever, supposedly the measure of evolutionary progress, is not resolved" (p. 122). Theodore A. Burczak, *Socialism after Hayek* (Ann Arbor: University of Michigan Press, 2006), is a work by a socialist intellectual to create a "'libertarian Marxist' conception of socialism" (p. 3) built upon Hayek's insights on the division of knowledge.

There is, as yet, no comprehensive history of the University of Chicago. Works from which information may be obtained include the valuable Edward Shils (ed.), *Remembering the University of Chicago: Teachers, Scientists, and Scholars* (Chicago: University of Chicago Press, 1991), and Hanna Holborn Gray (comp.), *One in Spirit: A Retrospective View of the University of Chicago on the Occasion of Its Centennial* (Chicago: University of Chicago Press, 1991). Shils, a great sociologist at Chicago, also contributed mightily to its historiography—*Remembering the University of Chicago* is a vital place to start for anyone interested in almost any aspect of Chicago's intellectual contributions. The essay on Viner by Samuelson is of particular value for light it sheds on Chicago economists generally. *One in Spirit* is of worth for its general history of the university rather than for its specific history of economics. Gray remarks in her preface that the University of Chicago has "change[d] American higher education as none other has" (p. ix).

Ron Chernow, *Titan: The Life of John D. Rockefeller, Sr.* (New York: Vintage Books, 1998), contains this observation: "Earlier in the century, Rockefeller inspired more prose than any other private citizen in America, with books about him tumbling forth at a rate of nearly one per year. . . . [H]e was the most famous American of his day" (p. xiii). Chernow also notes, of Rockefeller's involvement with the University of Chicago: "As a philanthropist, Rockefeller chose to cultivate a wise detachment from his creations and Harper that he saw himself as a silent partner in the operation" (p. 126).

William H. McNeill, *Hutchins' University: A Memoir of the University of Chicago 1919–1950* (Chicago: University of Chicago Press, 1991), contains valuable information on the Hutchins era. Mortimer J. Adler, *Reforming Education: The Opening of the American Mind* (New York: Collier, 1990), contains Adler's valuable 1941 piece, "The Chicago School," which referred, at that time according to Adler, to the entire thought emanating from the university as a whole. There was no reference to a specifically economic Chicago school.

Mary S. Morgan, *The History of Econometric Ideas* (Cambridge: Cambridge University Press, 1990); R. J. Epstein, *A History of Econometrics* (Amsterdam: North-Holland, 1987); and Clifford Hildreth, *The Cowles Commission in Chicago, 1939–1955*

(Berlin: Springer-Verlag, 1986)—in addition to providing more general histories—have background on the Cowles Commission at Chicago and its interaction with the economics department. Also see Carl F. Christ, "The Cowles Commission's Contributions to Econometrics at Chicago, 1939–1955," *Journal of Economic Literature* (March 1994).

Ben Seligman, *Main Currents in Modern Economics* (New York: Free Press, 1962), has an early section on Friedman, "Theory as Ideology." Here, after discussing the Keynesianism of Alvin Hansen, Seligman wrote (without referring to a "Chicago school"): "The viewpoint represented by . . . Hansen was not . . . well received in certain academic circles. This has been especially so at the University of Chicago, where Frank Knight, Jacob Viner, Henry Simons, Lloyd Mints, George Stigler, and Milton Friedman have built with great vigor and forcefulness a tradition emphasizing the virtues of pure competition . . . One of the sharpest exponents of this outlook has been Milton Friedman." Seligman made the perceptive comments, paraphrasing Friedman in the first instance, that the "quantity theory of money now was heading the counter-revolution against Keynes," and Friedman saw "economic instability . . . as basically monetary instability" (pp. 673, 678, 681).

Mark Blaug, *Economic Theory in Retrospect,* 5th ed. (Cambridge: Cambridge University Press, 1997; 1st ed., 1962), has been a textbook in the history of economic thought for more than fifty years. Blaug's summary of Smith's views on government was that "Smith was not satisfied to argue that a free market economy secures the best of all possible worlds. He was very much preoccupied with the specification of the exact institutional structure that would guarantee the beneficent operation of market forces . . . the *Wealth of Nations* should remind us that the benefits of competition call for more than *laissez faire.* It was not for nothing that Adam Smith spoke of *political* economy" (p. 62, emphasis in original).

Henry William Spiegel, *The Growth of Economic Thought,* 3rd ed. (Durham, NC: Duke University Press, 1991), is among the leading histories of economic thought. Spiegel also adopted the view of Adam Smith's position on appropriate government activities presented here:

> Although he [Smith] endorsed *laissez faire,* a careful examination of *The Wealth of Nations* reveals that he assigned to government a substantial variety of tasks. . . .
> [H]e endorses the regulation of paper money and banking, public enterprise in transportation, patents and copyrights, usury laws, public education, and even the grant of a temporary monopoly to a company in search of new trade in remote regions (p. 256).

Spiegel also wrote: "Smith was not a doctrinaire advocate of *laissez faire,* a quality that he shares with Viner" ("Jacob Viner," in Eatwell, Milgate, and Newman (eds.), *The New Palgrave: A Dictionary of Economics,* vol. 4, p. 812).

George H. Nash, *The Conservative Intellectual Movement in America since 1945* (Wilmington, DE: Intercollegiate Studies Institute, 1996; 1st ed., 1976), remains the authoritative work in its field. Nash writes that in 1945: "Among the various academic classical liberals, probably the most notable were Professors Henry C. Simons and Frank H. Knight of the University of Chicago—the nucleus of the nascent Chicago School in economics" (p. 14). As noted in the text here, Nash characterizes as "radical libertarian anarchists" (p. 313) the lineal philosophical predecessors of many of those who now sit atop the Republican Party and its constituent organizations. The influence of Mises, Rothbard, and Rand is considerable. But their thought should not be confused with classical liberalism, irrespective of terminology. They were no-government absolutists. Nash notes that "Knight favored more extensive governmental involvement in the economy" (p. 418, n. 196) than other classical liberals.

John Kenneth Galbraith, *Economics in Perspective: A Critical History* (Boston, MA: Houghton Mifflin, 1987), remarked of the period from about the mid-1930s to mid-1940s that Knight and Simons were "the best-known American proponents of the classical orthodoxy at the time" (p. 188). With respect to Smith, Galbraith said: "Though Smith did not see or completely foresee the Industrial Revolution in its full capitalist manifestation, he did observe with great clarity the contradictions, the obsolescence, and, above all, the socially confining self-interest in the old order. If he was a prophet of the new, he was even more an enemy of the old. Nor can one read *Wealth of Nations* without sensing his joy in afflicting the comfortable, causing distress to those who professed the convenient and traditional ideas and policies of his time" (p. 59).

Murray N. Rothbard, *Economic Thought Before Adam Smith, An Austrian Perspective on the History of Economic Thought,* vol. I (Cheltenham,UK: Edward Elgar, 1995), also shares the view of Smith presented here. Rothbard wrote that, for Smith, laissez-faire is "only a qualified presumption rather than a hard-and-fast rule" (p. 465) and that Smith supported public education, the Navigation Acts (which required that trade between Great Britain and its colonies be aboard British shipping), regulation of currency, public works, the Post Office, some building codes, and restrictions on the rate of interest. Rothbard noted the "particularly lengthy list of taxes advocated by Adam Smith" and his "proposals to levy heavy taxes on luxurious consumption. Thus he called for heavier highway tolls on luxury carriages than on freight wagons, specifically to tax the 'indolence and vanity of the rich,'" and also noted Smith's "call for a heavy tax on distilleries, in order to crack down on hard liquor" (p. 466). Smith would not be considered a libertarian today, and he wrote 250 years ago!

In their calls for radical, revolutionary change in society, contemporary libertarians are closer to the scope of societal change sought by Karl Marx, though in the opposite direction, than by classical liberals. Contemporary libertarians should not be considered the lineal philosophical descendants of such classical liberals and historical libertarians as Locke, Hume, Smith, Bentham, Mill, Marshall, Keynes, Viner, Knight, Simons, and the younger and middle-aged Hayek and Friedman. Rather, contemporary libertarians are the illegitimate offspring of true classical liberals. Hatred of government never was a core attribute of historical classical liberalism, and historical classical liberals were emphatic defenders of scientific truth, particularly for their times. They were the vanguards of their societies, not the most reactionary and illiberal elements. Rothbard also called Smith a "dubious partner of *laissez faire*" (p. 532) and noted that in the German literature there was wide discussion of *"Das AdamSmithProblem"*—"the big gap between the natural rights-*laissez faire* views" in Smith's earlier work and "the more qualified views" (p. 471) in *The Wealth of Nations*. Though a crackpot ideologically, Rothbard's scholarly historical work was not without value.

Lionel Robbins, *A History of Economic Thought* (Princeton, NJ: Princeton University Press, 1998), also recognized Smith's classical liberalism as opposed to contemporary libertarianism, commenting that Smith was not a "dogmatic supporter" of the "night watchman theory of the State." Indeed, Robbins went as far as to say that Keynes's "definition of the functions of the State runs in almost the same words" (pp. 152–153) as Smith's. Robbins took Hayek to task for his inclusion of Bentham and the other utilitarians as "false" individualists in the stream of continental rationalists: "I will confess unashamedly that I do not think that the main drift of nineteenth century English Utilitarian thought tends to a liberalism which, in any sense intelligible to me, deserves the appellation 'false'" ("Hayek on Liberty," *Economica* [February 1961], p. 71).

Emma Rothschild, *Economic Sentiments: Adam Smith, Condorcet, and the Enlightenment* (Cambridge, MA: Harvard University Press, 2001), is a beautifully written book presenting Smith in the Enlightenment tradition. She offers these comments, and quotes from Smith:

> Smith himself was tolerant . . . of some wage regulation: "When the regulation . . . is in favor of the workmen, it is always just and equitable; but it is sometimes otherwise when in favor of the masters." . . . Smith argued for high wages, more generally, on grounds of equity: "No society can surely be flourishing and happy, of which the far greater part of the members are poor and miserable. It is but equity, besides, that they who feed, clothe, and lodge the whole body of the people, should have such a share of the produce of their own labour as to be themselves tolerably well-fed, clothed, and lodged" (pp. 61–62).

She notes, too, that in the final edition of his *Theory of Moral Sentiments*, published just weeks before his death, Smith commented on the "'corruption of our moral sentiments' which follows from the disposition 'almost to worship the rich and the powerful'" (p. 56). In his unpublished lectures on jurisprudence, Smith held that "the poor laborer 'supports the whole frame of society,' yet is 'himself possessed of a very small share and is buried in obscurity'; that 'it may very justly be said that the people who clothe the whole world are in rags themselves'; or that 'laws and government may be considered . . . in every case as a combination of the rich to oppress the poor.' He is tolerant of government interference, especially when the object is to reduce poverty" (p. 69).

Samuel Fleischacker, *On Adam Smith's* Wealth of Nations (Princeton, NJ: Princeton University Press, 2004), presents a view similar to Rothschild:

> It is not surprising that students and admirers of Smith were prominent among those who, in the wake of the French Revolution, called for a drastic diminution of the right to inherit property . . . [H]e contributed to the change in moral outlook that made possible the modern notion of distributive justice, the notion used to justify socialism and welfare state liberalism. . . . [I]t was . . . Smith's students and admirers who proposed some of the most important programs for using government funds to help the poor in the 1790s (pp. 198, 201).

Also in this line of interpretation is Ian McLean, *Adam Smith, Radical and Egalitarian: An Interpretation for the Twenty-First Century* (New York: Palgrave Macmillan, 2007), who observes that "Smith is hostile to primogeniture and entail" (p. 93). Gerald P. O'Driscoll (ed.), *Adam Smith and Modern Political Economy* (Ames: Iowa State University Press, 1979), is an excellent collection of essays on Smith on the occasion of the bicentennial of *The Wealth of Nations,* most of which were presented at the University of California, Santa Barbara.

Sherryl Davis Kasper, *The Revival of Laissez-Faire in American Macroeconomic Theory* (Cheltenham, UK: Edward Elgar, 2002), presents the work of Frank Knight, Henry Simons, Friedrich Hayek, Milton Friedman, James Buchanan, and Robert Lucas. She emphasizes Lucas: "Ultimately the majority of macro-economists chose to replace Keynesian economics with the new classical theory developed by... Lucas" (p. 145). At the same time, she does not make the case that the work of Lucas and Buchanan has been significant in public policy. Kasper's original research is valuable.

David Harvey, *A Brief History of Neoliberalism* (Oxford: Oxford University Press, 2005), observes that the neoliberal movement

> remained on the margins of both policy and academic influence until the troubled years of the 1970s. At that point it began to move centre-stage, particularly in the US and Britain, nurtured in various well-financed think-tanks (offshoots of the Mont Pelerin Society, such as the Institute of Economic Affairs in London and the Heritage Foundation in Washington), as well as through its growing influence within the academy, particularly at the University of Chicago, where Milton Friedman dominated. Neoliberal theory gained in academic respectability by the award of the Nobel Prize in economics to Hayek in 1974 and Friedman in 1976 (p. 22).

Mark Skousen, *Vienna and Chicago: Friends or Foes? A Tale of Two Schools of Free-Market Economics* (Washington, DC: Capital Press, 2005), compares Austrian and Chicago economics. He writes: "If the Austrian school was not going to dethrone the Keynesian model in the academic world, who would step up? The answer came ultimately from an exceptional figure, an individual who almost single-handedly engineered a 'counterrevolution' in macroeconomics, demolished the Keynesian monolith, and helped restore the classical model of Adam Smith" (p. 61): Friedman. Skousen also has a chapter on Friedman in *The Making of Modern Economics: The Lives and Ideas of the Great Thinkers,* 2nd ed. (Armonk, NY: M. E. Sharpe, 2009). In *The Big Three in Economics: Adam Smith, Karl Marx and John Maynard Keynes* (London: M. E. Sharpe, 2007), Skousen writes that Smith "wrote a book for the welfare of the average working man. In his *magnum opus,* he assured the reader that his model for economic success would result in 'universal opulence which extends itself to the lowest ranks of the people'" (pp. 6–7).

Monica Prasad, *The Politics of Free Markets: The Rise of Neoliberal Economic Policies in Britain, France, Germany, and the United States* (Chicago: University of Chicago Press, 2006), is an incisive account from a mainstream perspective of political and economic developments in leading economies primarily in the 1980s. Prasad notes: "The most important legacy of the neoliberal period under Reagan was the introduction of large-scale deficits as a sustained feature of American politics" (p. 11), and:

> There is a folk theory of the neoliberal revolution that places academic economists at its center, but the historical record shows that academic economists overwhelmingly rejected the policies that both Reagan and Thatcher actually implemented. Instead, the process involved politicians settling upon specific policies for their own reasons and then seeking out those who could provide intellectual legitimacy for those policies, even if they were at the fringes of their profession (p. 21).

This work is a useful and well-written antidote to triumphalist libertarian and conservative presentations of the era—the truth undoubtedly lies somewhere in between.

Alessandro Roncaglia, *The Wealth of Ideas: A History of Economic Thought* (Cambridge University Press, 2006), is a work by a leading Italian historian of economic thought. Roncaglia calls attention to Viner's work on Smith in the provenance of the free market tradition at the University of Chicago (p. 125, n. 23 and p. 151, n. 64), noting that Smith allowed a significant role for government. With respect to later developments, Roncaglia states: "Among those who show faith in the equilibrating powers of the market and hostility to state intervention in the economy, the Chicago school is prominent. Milton Friedman . . . is the recognized leader of this school" (p. 484).

Brian Doherty, *Radicals for Capitalism: A Freewheeling History of the Modern American Libertarian Movement* (New York: Public Affairs, 2007), is the best history of postwar libertarianism. Doherty presents enlightening and entertaining information and perspectives on many issues and reveals the "radical" nature of contemporary libertarianism in the very title of his book. He tells a revealing anecdote from the Cato Institute's Tom Palmer about one of the mainstays of the contemporary libertarian movement, the Ludwig von Mises Institute: "Mises Institute president Rockwell's personal website . . . is overbrimming with pro-Confederacy, anti-American material . . . , as well as writings by people who (in other venues) are unacceptably racist or so traditionally Christian they call for stoning of sinners according to Old Testament rules" (p. 607). In a 2013 profile of Rand Paul, *New York Times* reporters Sam Tanenhaus and Jim Rutenberg write that when one of them contacted the Mises Institute for a tour, Rockwell "asked him to leave, saying he was 'part of the regime'" ("Rand Paul's Mixed Inheritance," *New York Times* [January 26, 2014], p. 21). Milton Friedman described the Mises Institute as "just as intolerant a bunch as you can find" (in J. Daniel Hammond, "An Interview with Milton Friedman on Methodology," in Samuels and Biddle [eds.], *Research in the History of Economic Thought and Methodology,* vol. 10, p. 102).

There is much information in *Radicals for Capitalism* that is not collected anywhere else in one place. Doherty has a good discussion of the possible evolution of the contemporary libertarian movement in the direction of what is here called classical liberalism (pp. 584–586). Doherty's review of this writer's collection of essays by Friedman, "The Increasingly Libertarian Milton Friedman" (reason.

com, November 20, 2012), emphasizes the extent to which Friedman became more radical as he aged.

Karen Ilse Horn, *Roads to Wisdom, Conversations with Ten Nobel Laureates in Economics* (Cheltenham, UK: Edward Elgar, 2009), contains an interesting interview with, among others, Paul Samuelson: "There is one thing that I'm not very happy about, even though I understand it. It's that the profession has gone very much to the right ideologically. And guess who was the most important person responsible for that. . . . Milton Friedman" (p. 53). Horn coaxes out Samuelson's final appraisal of his old friend: "Milton Friedman never made a mistake in his whole life. That's remarkable, isn't it? He is as bright a guy as you would ever meet. But I don't think he realizes the tremendous number of mistakes he made" (p. 49).

Steven F. Hayward, *The Age of Reagan: The Conservative Counterrevolution 1980–1989* (New York: Three Rivers Press, 2009), remarks of Reagan's tax cuts that he was "following the attitude of his favorite contemporary economist, Milton Friedman, who liked to say that he was for any tax cut at any time for any reason" (pp. 66–67). For Friedman's own statement of this position, see "Friedman on the Surplus," *Hoover Digest* (Spring 2001), p. 163.

Agnar Sandmo, *Economics Evolving: A History of Economic Thought* (Princeton, NJ: Princeton University Press, 2011), holds: "Among Keynes' critics none was more influential than the American economist Milton Friedman . . . Friedman was among the twentieth century economists who were best known among the general public . . . [H]is policy recommendations have had a strong influence on policymakers in many countries, particularly during the last quarter of the 20th century" (pp. 417, 419, 420).

Jeffrey A. Miron, *Libertarianism from A to Z* (Philadelphia, PA: Basic Books, 2010), is a fine example of contemporary libertarianism. Miron writes: "The principles of libertarianism point toward legalizing drugs and prostitution, replacing public schools with vouchers, and eliminating farm subsidies, trade restrictions, and middle-class entitlements. Libertarianism opposes regulation of guns, child labor, campaign finance, unions, financial markets, and more. Libertarianism would leave abortion policy to state governments, terminate foreign policy interventions, and get government out of the marriage business" (p. 1).

Allan H. Meltzer, *Why Capitalism?* (Oxford: Oxford University Press, 2012), is another work in the same genre. Meltzer's comment, "In many countries, the upper-income groups have increased their share of income for a decade or more. The principal reason is that returns to education dominate the change" (p. 81), is inaccurate. The argument of contemporary libertarians and their allies that the increasing inequality since the 1980s is the result of the schools—federal tax policy since that time has had nothing to do with it—is self-serving. Schools are important, and merit further attention, but this does not mean that the principal reason for the increase in the income of the wealthy in recent decades is because of changes in schooling during this period. It is because of changes in tax policy: specifically, reducing marginal income and estate tax rates.

A more extensive and scholarly work on contemporary libertarianism is Tom G. Palmer, *Realizing Freedom: Libertarian Theory, History, and Practice* (Washington, DC: Cato Institute, 2009). Also see Palmer, *After the Welfare State* (Ottawa, IL: Jameson Books, 2012), a briefer presentation.

David Boaz, *The Libertarian Mind: A Manifesto for Freedom* (New York: Simon & Schuster, 2015), is the work of a true and honest libertarian neo-anarchist and radical. Boaz writes: "How far could taxes be reduced? The libertarian goal is a society free of coercion. . . . Since taxation is coercive, the ultimate libertarian goal is to eliminate it. . . . [W]e have a great deal of government spending and taxation to roll back before we get to the point where the only remaining taxation goes to support the legitimate functions of government. At that point, maybe we will be able to see how even the remaining coercive taxation can be eliminated" (pp. 283–284). As an interim goal, he here suggests taxation and spending equal to 5 percent of gross domestic product as the appropriate extent of all government, including national defense.

Daniel Stedman Jones, *Masters of the Universe: Hayek, Friedman, and the Birth of Neoliberal Politics* (Princeton, NJ: Princeton University Press, 2012), is an ambitious and negative appraisal of the tie between political and economic ideas and public policy in the period approximately from 1950 to 2000. According to Jones: "The neoliberal breakthrough came in the seemingly unlikely realm of technical economic policy . . . The most consistent, systematic, and significant alternative economic strategy to Keynesian demand management and fine-tuning was the monetarism developed by Milton Friedman" (pp. 180, 201); "The crudeness of postwar Chicago neoliberal economic theory left a painful imprint on the social fabric of Britain and the United States after 1980 through the economic policies of the Thatcher and Reagan administrations" (pp. 268–269). Jones notes that "neoliberalism differed from the classical liberalism of Adam Smith" (p. 87).

Nobel laureate in economics Daniel Kahneman writes in *Thinking, Fast and Slow* (New York: Farrar, Straus and Giroux, 2011) that as "interpreted by the important Chicago school of economics, faith in human rationality is closely linked to an ideology in which it is unnecessary to protect people against their choices. Rational people should be free, and they should be responsible for taking care of themselves" (p. 411).

Nobel laureate Joseph E. Stiglitz, who was chairman of the Council of Economic Advisers under President Bill Clinton, writes in *The Price of Inequality: How Today's Divided Society Endangers Our Future* (New York: W. W. Norton, 2012) that, though in his view for its harmful effect, "the influence of the Chicago school should not be underestimated" (p. 44). Stiglitz has these comments on Friedman: "While his pioneering work on the determinants of consumption rightly earned him a Nobel Prize, his free-market beliefs were based more on ideological conviction than on economic analysis" (p. 257). With respect to Smith, Stiglitz says: "Adam Smith . . . was far more skeptical about the ability of markets to lead to efficient outcomes than his latter-day followers" (p. 363). In *The Great Divide: Unequal Societies and What We Can Do about Them* (New York: W.W. Norton, 2015), Stiglitz writes: "It shouldn't be a big surprise that some of the wealthiest Americans are promoting an economic fantasy in which their further enrichment is beneficial to everyone" (p. 421).

Brink Lindsey, *Human Capitalism* (Princeton University Press, 2013), includes these comments on encouraging economic growth: "The issue isn't really 'big' versus 'small' government. Economic dynamism can coexist with relatively high levels of social spending and a strong regulatory apparatus, and the absence of those manifestations of 'big government' is no guarantee of a vibrant and prosperous economy" (pp. 75–76).

Brink Lindsey, *Low-Hanging Fruit Guarded by Dragons: Reforming Regressive Regulation to Boost U.S. Economic Growth* (Washington, DC: Cato Institute, 2015), is an insightful analysis calling for reform of copyright and patent laws, and increased high-skilled immigration to the United States. He comments with respect to some of his proposals: "Restoration of an earlier status quo, rather than radical change, is the aim of these suggested policy moves" (p. 14). This same remark could be applied more broadly to policy proposals contained in the present book.

Edmund Fawcett, *Liberalism: The Life of an Idea* (Princeton, NJ: Princeton University Press, 2014), says: "No economist did more than Milton Friedman to shift the focus of public debate from keeping employment high to holding inflation low" (p. 373). Thomas Piketty, *Capital in the Twenty-First Century* (Cambridge, MA: Harvard University Press, 2014), makes these remarks: "Saving capitalism did not require a welfare state or tentacular government: the only thing necessary was a well-run Federal Reserve. . . . The work of Friedman and other Chicago school economists fostered suspicion of the ever-expanding state and created the intellectual climate in which the conservative revolution of 1979–1980 became possible" (p. 549).

Robert Van Horn has established himself in recent years as the leading archival researcher of multiple figures associated with Chicago economics. In particular, see his "Henry Simons's Death," *History of Political Economy* (Fall 2014); "Hayek's Unacknowledged Disciple: An Exploration of the Political and Intellectual Relationship of F. A. Hayek and Aaron Director," *Journal of the History of Economic Thought* 35 (03) (2013); and "Chicago's Shifting Attitude toward Concentrations of Business Power (1934–1962)," *Seattle University Law Review* (Summer 2011). He writes in "Hayek's Unacknowledged Disciple" that *The Road to Serfdom* should "not be read as a critique of planning *tout court*, but only as a critique of planning that undermined effective competition," noting that "Hayek advocated planning *for* competition" (p. 278). Van Horn quotes from Director's review of The Road to Serfdom that a liberal society requires government to improve the "rules of the game to increase the effectiveness of competition, monetary management to promote economic stability," and "measures to alleviate the lot of those 'who, in the great lottery of life, have drawn a blank'" (p. 282)—the classical liberal view.

In the preface, I make reference to previous works of my own on the development of classical liberal and libertarian political and economic thought in the twentieth century. These include *Friedrich Hayek: A Biography* (New York: Palgrave, 2001), *Hayek's Journey: The Mind of Friedrich Hayek* (New York: Palgrave Macmillan, 2003), *Milton Friedman: A Biography* (New York: Palgrave Macmillan, 2007), and, as editor, *The Indispensable Milton Friedman: Political and Economic Essays* (Washington, DC: Regnery, 2012). The first three of these have extensive bibliographical essays. Also see my "The Increasingly Libertarian Milton Friedman: An Ideological Profile," *Econ Journal Watch* (January 2014), for a presentation of the evolution of his thought.

NOTES

PREFACE

1. Milton Friedman in Lanny Ebenstein (ed.), *The Indispensable Milton Friedman* (Washington, DC: Regnery, 2012), p. 149.

INTRODUCTION: HISTORICAL BACKGROUND OF CHICAGONOMICS

1. Jeremy Bentham, *A Fragment on Government and an Introduction to the Principles of Morals and Legislation* (Oxford: Basil Blackwell, 1948), p. 3.
2. Jacob Viner, *The Long View and the Short: Studies in Economic Theory and Policy* (Glencoe, IL: Free Press, 1958), p. 215.
3. Adam Smith in William Ebenstein and Alan (Lanny) Ebenstein, *Great Political Thinkers: Plato to the Present,* 6th ed. (Fort Worth, TX: Harcourt College Publishers, 2000), p. 495.
4. Ibid., p. 494.
5. Adam Smith in Michael Lind, *Land of Promise: An Economic History of the United States* (New York: Harper, 2012), p. 49.
6. Viner, *The Long View and the Short,* p. 234.
7. Adam Smith in ibid., p. 237.
8. Ibid., p. 241.
9. Adam Smith in ibid., p. 243.
10. Adam Smith in ibid., pp. 243-244.
11. See, in general, "The Functions of Government," ibid., pp. 231-245.
12. Nicholas Phillipson, *Adam Smith: An Enlightened Life* (New Haven, CT: Yale University Press, 2010), p. 2.
13. Thomas Sowell in Gerald P. O'Driscoll (ed.), *Adam Smith and Modern Political Economy* (Ames: Iowa State University Press, 1979), p. 5.
14. James Buchanan in ibid., p. 117.
15. John Maynard Keynes in Ebenstein, *Great Political Thinkers,* p. 797. Keynes added: "Adam Smith, of course, was a Free Trader and an opponent of many

eighteenth century restrictions on trade. But his attitude towards the Navigation Acts and the Usury laws shows that he was not dogmatic. Even his famous passage about 'the invisible hand' reflects the philosophy which we associate with [William] Paley rather than the economic dogma of *laissez faire*. . . . Adam Smith's advocacy of the 'obvious and simple system of natural liberty' is derived from his theistic and optimistic view of the order of the world" (ibid.).

16. Friedrich Hayek, *Individualism and Economic Order* (University of Chicago Press, 1948), p. 1.

17. Adam Smith in Viner, *The Long View and the Short,* pp. 217-218.

18. I am indebted for the formulation of these successful reforms to Viner, *The Long View and the Short,* p. 227. Note, too, that it really was the utilitarians who brought Smith's reforms to fruition:

> In October 1808, in an article in the *Edinburgh Review,* James Mill noted, with curiosity and regret "the great difficulty with which the salutary doctrines of political economy are propagated in this country." Between 1776, the year in which Adam Smith published his *Wealth of Nations,* and 1817, the year in which Ricardo published his *Principles of Political Economy and of Taxation,* not a single complete treatise on political economy appeared in England. Adam Smith remained the only authority, and he was little heeded (Elie Halévy, *The Growth of Philosophic Radicalism* [Boston, MA: Beacon, 1955], pp. 264-265).

Halévy's work is, of course, a locus classicus of classical liberalism.

19. Jacob Viner, "Bentham and J. S. Mill: The Utilitarian Background," *American Economic Review* (March 1949), p. 362. This writer's father was a colleague of Viner at Princeton. Viner wrote in inscribing an offprint of "Bentham and J. S. Mill" to my father: "To William Ebenstein With the Warm Regards of Jacob Viner" (in the possession of author). My father, as far as I know, did not know Frank Knight, but they both contributed to a symposium on John Stuart Mill, Carl J. Friedrich (ed.), *Liberty, Nomos IV* (New York: Atherton, 1962). This writer's mother was a student at the University of Chicago in the 1930s, though not in economics. Her family slightly knew university president Robert Hutchins.

20. Viner, "Bentham and J. S. Mill," p. 362.

21. Henry Simons, *Economic Policy for a Free Society* (Chicago: University of Chicago Press, 1948), p. 105.

22. George Stigler, *The Economist as Preacher and Other Essays* (Chicago: University of Chicago Press, 1982), p. 143.

23. Friedrich Hayek, *The Fatal Conceit: The Errors of Socialism* (Chicago: University of Chicago Press, 1988), p. 107.

24. Milton Friedman in Annelise Anderson and Dennis L. Bark (eds.), *Thinking about America: The United States in the 1990s* (Stanford, CA: Hoover Institution Press, 1988), p. 457. David Friedman writes: "A more nearly correct version of libertarianism would owe more to Bentham than to Rawls" ("Natural Rights," *Cato Unbound: A Journal of Debate* [April 6, 2012]).

25. Simons, *Economic Policy for a Free Society,* p. 325.

26. Jeremy Bentham in Alan (Lanny) Ebenstein, *The Greatest Happiness Principle: An Examination of Utilitarianism* (New York: Garland, 1991), p. 45.

27. Jeremy Bentham, *An Introduction to the Principles of Morals and Legislation*, edited by J. H. Burns and H. L. A. Hart (London: Methuen, 1982), p. 11.
28. John Stuart Mill, *Utilitarianism, On Liberty, and Considerations on Representative Government* (1863; repr.; London: J. M. Dent & Sons, 1972), p. 17.
29. Ayn Rand, *The Fountainhead* (New York: Plume, 1994), pp. 281-282.
30. E.g., James A. Dorn, "Equality, Justice, and Freedom: A Constitutional Perspective," *Cato Journal* (Fall 2014).
31. Milton Friedman in Michael Albert, *Life After Capitalism* (London: Verso, 2003), p. 77.
32. Mill, *Utilitarianism*, p. 14.
33. John Maynard Keynes in Ebenstein, *Great Political Thinkers*, p. 796.
34. Richard Hofstadter, *Social Darwinism in American Thought*, revised ed. (Boston: Beacon Press, 1955), p. 4.
35. Ibid., pp. 4-5.
36. Hayek emphasized that Darwin was influenced by classical liberal writers, including Malthus and Smith, when formulating his biological theories. Sylvia Nasar notes that Malthus's work "inspired Charles Darwin and other founders of evolutionary theory" (*Grand Pursuit: The Story of Economic Genius* [New York: Simon & Schuster, 2011], p. 4).
37. Herbert Spencer in *John Stuart Mill: His Life and Works* (Boston: James R. Osgood, 1873), p. 38.
38. Ibid., p. 74.
39. Charles Darwin, *The Descent of Man* (New York: Plume, 2007), p. 157.
40. John Maynard Keynes in Ebenstein, *Great Political Thinkers*, p. 796.
41. John D. Rockefeller in Eric F. Goldman, *Rendezvous with Destiny: A History of Modern American Reform* (New York: Vintage Books, 1977), pp. 71-72.
42. Herbert Spencer in John Kenneth Galbraith, *Economics in Perspective: A Critical History* (Boston: Houghton Mifflin, 1987), p. 121.
43. William Graham Sumner in A. J. Beitzinger, *A History of American Political Thought* (Charlottesville, VA: Ibis Publishing, n.d.), p. 405.
44. William Graham Sumner in Galbraith, *Economics in Perspective*, pp. 122-123.
45. John Stuart Mill, *On Liberty*, (London: Penguin, 1988), pp. 69-70.
46. Ludwig von Mises in Brian Doherty, *Radicals for Capitalism: A Freewheeling History of the Modern American Libertarian Movement* (New York: Public Affairs, 2007), p. 83.
47. Ibid.

CHAPTER 1. ROCKEFELLER'S UNIVERSITY AND
THE DEPARTMENT OF POLITICAL ECONOMY

1. Milton Friedman in William Breit and Barry T. Hirsch (eds.), *Lives of the Laureates: Eighteen Nobel Economists*, 4th ed. (Cambridge: MIT Press, 2004), p. 66.
2. John D. Rockefeller in Ron Chernow, *Titan: The Life of John D. Rockefeller, Sr.* (New York: Vintage Books, 1998), p. 68.
3. Ibid., p. 308.
4. William Rainey Harper in ibid., p. 307.
5. John D. Rockefeller in ibid., p. 310.

6. Ibid., p. 493.

7. Harry S. Ashmore, *Unseasonable Truths: The Life of Robert Maynard Hutchins* (Boston, MA: Little, Brown, 1989), p. 57.

8. John S. Brubacher and Willis Rudy, *Higher Education in Transformation: A History of American Colleges and Universities*, 4th ed. (New Brunswick, NJ: Transaction, 1997), p. 378.

9. Ibid., p. 193.

10. Mortimer J. Adler, *Reforming Education: The Opening of the American Mind* (New York: Collier, 1990), p. 23.

11. Chernow, *Titan*, p. 317-318.

12. William H. McNeill, *Hutchins' University: A Memoir of the University of Chicago 1929-1950* (Chicago: University of Chicago Press, 1991), p. 53.

13. Ibid., p. 52.

14. William Rainey Harper in Adler, *Reforming Education*, p. 24.

15. Ibid.

16. James Laurence Laughlin in Milton Friedman, "James Laurence Laughlin," in John Eatwell, Murray Milgate, and Peter Newman (eds.), *The New Palgrave Dictionary of Economics*, vol. 3 (London: Macmillan, 1987), p. 139.

17. Johan Van Overtveldt, *The Chicago School: How the University of Chicago Assembled the Thinkers Who Revolutionized Economics and Business* (Chicago, IL: Agate, 2007), p. 48.

18. J. Laurence Laughlin (ed.), John Stuart Mill, *Principles of Political Economy* (New York: D. Appleton, 1885), "Introductory. A Sketch of the History of Political Economy."

19. Ibid.

20. Ibid., "Preface," "Introductory."

21. Ibid., "Introductory."

22. Ibid.

23. Ibid.

24. J. Laurence Laughlin, *The Elements of Political Economy* (New York: American Book, 1887), p. 349.

25. Richard M. Ebeling, "Milton Friedman and the Chicago School of Economics," *Freeman* (December 2006), p. 2.

26. For an excellent presentation of Malthus's role in creating economics as the "dismal science," see Sylvia Nasar, *Grand Pursuit: The Story of Economic Genius* (New York: Simon & Schuster, 2011).

27. Thorstein Veblen, *The Theory of the Leisure Class* (New York: Modern Library, 1934), p. 68.

28. Thorstein Veblen, *The Vested Interests and the Common Man* (New York: Viking Press, 1946), p. 160.

29. Stuart Chase in ibid., p. xiv.

30. Thorstein Veblen, *Essays in Our Changing Order* (New York: Viking Press, 1934), on front cover.

31. Thorstein Veblen in Ben Seligman, *Main Currents in Modern Economics* (New Brunswick, NJ: Transaction, 1990), p. 136.

32. Mitchell was led to his statistical approach through his early focus on Veblen. Mitchell wrote in a letter: "This feeling has been growing upon me as

I have realized how slight an impression Veblen's work has made upon other economists. . . . I often find that the only real answer lies in doing a lot of work with statistics" (in David Seckler, *Thorstein Veblen and the Institutionalists* [Boulder: Colorado Associated University Press, 1975], p. 103).

33. Wesley Clair Mitchell in Lanny Ebenstein (ed.), *The Indispensable Milton Friedman* (Washington, DC: Regnery, 2012), pp. 126-127.

34. Thomas A. Stapleford, "Positive Economics for Democratic Policy: Milton Friedman, Institutionalism, and the Science of History," in Robert Van Horn, Philip Mirowski, and Thomas A. Stapleford (eds.), *Building Chicago Economics: New Perspectives on the History of America's Most Powerful Economics Program* (Cambridge: Cambridge University Press, 2011), pp. 6-7.

35. James Heckman in William Breit and Barry T. Hirsch (eds.), *Lives of the Laureates,* 4th ed. (Cambridge: MIT Press, 2004), pp. 321-322.

36. Russell Kirk in Carl T. Bogus, *Buckley: William F. Buckley Jr. and the Rise of American Conservatism* (New York: Bloomsbury Press, 2011), p. 139.

37. John East in George W. Carey (ed.), *Freedom and Virtue: The Conservative/Libertarian Debate* (Wilmington, DE: ISI Books, 2004), p. 85.

38. Brink Lindsey, *The Age of Abundance: How Prosperity Transformed America's Politics and Culture* (New York: HarperCollins, 2007), p. 319.

39. John Locke, *A Letter Concerning Toleration* (1689; repr., Oxford: Basil Blackwell, 1946), p. 123.

40. Henry Simons, *Economic Policy for a Free Society* (Chicago: University of Chicago Press, 1948), p. 318.

41. Paul T. Homan, *Contemporary Economic Thought* (New York: Harper and Brothers, 1928).

42. John U. Nef, "James Laurence Laughlin (1850-1933), *Journal of Political Economy* (February 1934), p. 2.

43. Malcolm Rutherford, *The Institutionalist Movement in American Economics, 1918-1947* (Cambridge: Cambridge University Press, 2011), p. 125.

44. A. W. Coats, "The Origins of the 'Chicago School(s)'?" *Journal of Political Economy* (October 1963), p. 489.

45. George Stigler, *Memoirs of an Unregulated Economist* (Chicago: University of Chicago Press, 2003 [1988]), p. 22.

46. Milton Friedman in Ebenstein, *Indispensable Milton Friedman,* p. 35.

47. Coats, "Origins," p. 492.

48. John D. Rockefeller in Chernow, *Titan,* p. 325.

CHAPTER 2. JACOB VINER AS CLASSICAL LIBERAL

1. Henry W. Spiegel, "Jacob Viner," in John Eatwell, Murray Milgate, and Peter Newman (eds.), *The New Palgrave: A Dictionary of Economics,* vol. 4 (London: Macmillan, 1987), p. 812.

2. It is interesting to observe that when, in the 1962 preface to *Capitalism and Freedom,* Friedman listed the "teachers, colleagues, and friends" at Chicago to whom he "owe[d] the philosophy expressed in this book," he did not include Viner—those whom Friedman identified were Frank Knight, Henry Simons, Lloyd Mints, Aaron Director, Friedrich Hayek,

and George Stigler (*Capitalism and Freedom* [Chicago: University of Chicago Press, 2002], p. xvi).

3. Paul A. Samuelson, "Jacob Viner," in Edward Shils (ed.), *Remembering the University of Chicago: Teachers, Scientists, and Scholars* (University of Chicago Press, 1991), p. 538.

4. James M. Buchanan, "Foreword," in Frank H. Knight, *Freedom and Reform: Essays in Economics and Social Philosophy* (Indianapolis, IN: LibertyPress, 1982), p. ix.

5. Dieter Plehwe, "Introduction," in Philip Mirowski and Dieter Plehwe (eds.), *The Road from Mont Pelerin: The Making of the Neoliberal Thought Collective* (Cambridge, MA: Harvard University Press, 2009), p. 29.

6. Don Patinkin, *Essays On and In the Chicago Tradition* (Durham, NC: Duke University Press, 1981), p. 44.

7. Eugene Rotwein, "Jacob Viner and the Chicago Tradition," *History of Political Economy* (Summer 1983), p. 265.

8. Samuelson, "Jacob Viner," p. 534.

9. Jacob Viner, *The Long View and the Short: Studies in Economic Theory and Policy* (Glencoe, IL: Free Press, 1958), pp. 244-245.

10. Jacob Viner, *Essays on the Intellectual History of Economics* (Princeton, NJ: Princeton University Press, 1991), pp. 219, 200.

11. Viner, *Long View and the Short*, p. 122.

12. Ibid., p. 134.

13. Robert Van Horn, Philip Mirowski, and Thomas A. Stapleford (eds.), *Building Chicago Economics: New Perspectives on the History of America's Most Powerful Economics Program* (Cambridge: Cambridge University Press, 2011), p. xix.

14. Ross B. Emmett (ed.), *The Elgar Companion to the Chicago School of Economics* (Cheltenham, UK: Edward Elgar, 2010), p. 3.

15. J. Daniel Hammond, "The Development of Post-War Chicago Price Theory," in ibid., p. 7.

16. David Laidler, "Chicago Monetary Traditions," in ibid., p. 77.

17. Angus Burgin, *The Great Persuasion: Reinventing Free Markets since the Depression* (Cambridge, MA: Harvard University Press, 2012), p. 15.

18. Martin Bronfenbrenner, "Observations on the 'Chicago School(s),'" *Journal of Political Economy* (February 1962), pp. 72-73.

19. Jacob Viner in Patinkin, *Essays On and In the Chicago Tradition*, p. 266.

20. Jacob Viner in Arthur I. Bloomfield, "On the Centenary of Jacob Viner's Birth: A Retrospective View of the Man and His Work," *Journal of Economic Literature* (December 1992), p. 2058.

21. Ibid.

22. Ross B. Emmett, "How Should We Think of the Success of the Chicago School of Economics?" in Warren J. Samuels, Jeff E. Biddle, and Ross B. Emmett (eds.), *Research in the History of Economic Thought and Methodology* (Bingley, UK: JAI Press, 2008), p. 48.

23. Ross Emmett in Johan Van Overtveldt, *The Chicago School* (Chicago: Agate, 2007), p. 9.

24. Bloomfield, "On the Centenary of Jacob Viner's Birth," p. 2058.

25. Donald Winch in William J. Baumol and Ellen V. Seiler, "Jacob Viner," *International Encyclopedia of the Social Sciences,* vol. 18, *Biographical Supplement,* ed. David L. Sills (New York: Free Press, 1979), p. 783.

26. Burgin, *The Great Persuasion,* p. 35. George Nash also notes the negative influence that some believe Mises had and continues to have on causes he advocated. Nash quotes a 1944 article by Henry Simons that, as a result of his immoderation, Mises was "perhaps the worst enemy of his own libertarian cause" (in *The Conservative Intellectual Movement in America* [New York: Basic Books, 1976], p. 351).

27. J. Ronnie Davis in Milton Friedman, "Comments on the Critics," *Journal of Political Economy* (October 1972), p. 937.

28. Robert J. Gordon (ed.), *Milton Friedman's Monetary Framework: A Debate with His Critics* (Chicago: University of Chicago Press, 1974), p. 166.

29. Ibid., p. 165.

30. Ibid.

31. Ibid., p. 167.

32. Samuelson, "Jacob Viner," p. 543.

33. Paul A. Samuelson, "Jacob Viner, 1892-1970," *Journal of Political Economy* (January-February 1972), p. 6.

34. Paul Samuelson in Michael Szenberg, Aron A. Gottesman, and Lall Ramrattan, *Paul A. Samuelson: On Being an Economist* (New York: Jorge Pinto Books, 2005), p. 16.

35. Milton Friedman in William Breit and Roger L. Ransom, *The Academic Scribblers,* 3rd ed. (Princeton, NJ: Princeton University Press, 1998), p. 226.

36. Milton Friedman in William Breit and Barry T. Hirsch, *Lives of the Laureates,* 4th ed. (Cambridge, MA: MIT Press, 2004), p. 70. In his obituary of Viner, Friedman called him "one of the great teachers and scholars of our time and all times" ("In Memoriam Jacob Viner, 1892-1970," *American Economic Review* [March 1971], p. 247).

37. Jacob Viner, *Religious Thought and Economic Society* (Durham, NC: Duke University Press, 1978), p. 176.

38. Donald Winch, "Jacob Viner as Intellectual Historian," in Warren J. Samuels (ed.), *Research in the History of Economic Thought and Methodology,* vol. 1 (Greenwich, CT: JAI Press, 1983), p. 2.

39. John McDonald, "The Economists," *Fortune* (December 1950), p. 111.

40. Lionel Robbins, *Jacob Viner, 1892-1970* (Princeton, NJ: Princeton University Press, 1970), pp. 1-2.

41. Lionel Robbins, *Autobiography of an Economist* (London: Macmillan, 1971), p. 220.

42. Gary Becker in Karen Ilse Horn, *Roads to Wisdom, Conversations with Ten Nobel Laureates in Economics* (Cheltenham, UK: Edward Elgar, 2009), p. 139.

43. Gary S. Becker, "George Joseph Stigler," *Journal of Political Economy* (October 1993), p. 761.

44. Ibid.

45. Ross B. Emmett (ed.), *The Chicago Tradition in Economics 1892-1945,* vol. 6 (London: Routledge, 2002), p. vii-viii.

46. Ibid., p. vii.

47. Mark Blaug in ibid., p. vii.
48. Henry Spiegel, *The Growth of Economic Thought,* 3rd ed. (Durham, NC: Duke University Press, 1991), p. 642.
49. Rotwein, "Jacob Viner and the Chicago Tradition," pp. 266-267, 278.
50. Bloomfield, "On the Centenary of Jacob Viner's Birth," p. 2082.
51. William J. Baumol, "Jacob Viner at Princeton," *Journal of Political Economy* (January-February 1972), p. 12.
52. Jacob Viner in Rotwein, "Jacob Viner and the Chicago Tradition," p. 277.
53. Adam Smith in John Rae, *Life of Adam Smith,* with an Introduction by Jacob Viner (Fairfield, NJ: Augustus M. Kelley, 1977), p. 31. It is hard to imagine many contemporary libertarians referring to reformers and legislators in so highly positive a light, which again calls attention to the extent of divergence between contemporary libertarians and Smith, Viner, and other classical liberals.
54. Jacob Viner in Rotwein, "Jacob Viner and the Chicago Tradition," p. 277.

CHAPTER 3. FRANK KNIGHT BEFORE CHICAGO

1. Don Patinkin, *Essays On and In the Chicago Tradition* (Durham, NC: Duke University Press, 1981), p. 24.
2. Horace S. Knight, "The Early Education of My Father, Based Partly on a Paper by Donald Dewey" (1986), p. 2. I am indebted to Rose Friedman for providing me a copy of this manuscript.
3. Ibid.
4. Ibid.
5. Joseph Dorfman in Richard S. Howey, "Frank Hyneman Knight and the History of Economic Thought," in Warren J. Samuels (ed.), *Research in the History of Economic Thought and Methodology,* vol. 1 (Greenwich, CT: JAI Press, 1983), p. 182.
6. Horace Knight, "The Early Education of My Father."
7. Ibid.
8. Ibid.
9. Howey, "Knight and the History of Economic Thought," p. 165.
10. James Buchanan, "Frank Knight," in Edward Shils (ed.), *Remembering the University of Chicago* (Chicago: University of Chicago Press, 1991), p. 247.
11. George Stigler, "In Memoriam: F. H. Knight," *American Economic Review* (December 1973), p. 1047. This obituary is sometimes misattributed to Milton Friedman.
12. Alvin Johnson in Horace Knight, "The Early Education of My Father."
13. Ibid.
14. Howey, "Knight and the History of Economic Thought," p. 165.
15. Horace Knight, "The Early Education of My Father."
16. Howey, "Knight and the History of Economic Thought," p. 170.
17. Frank H. Knight, *Risk, Uncertainty and Profit* (Boston, MA: Houghton Mifflin, 1921), p. ix.
18. Allyn Young in Charles P. Blitch, *Allyn Young: The Peripatetic Economist* (London: Routledge, 1995), p. 121.

19. Frank Knight in ibid., p. 121.
20. Allyn Young in ibid., p. 162. Knight later revised Young's essay on the history of economics written for the *Encyclopedia of the Social Sciences* and published it in his *On the History and Method of Economics: Selected Essays* (Chicago: University of Chicago Press: 1956).
21. Knight, *Risk, Uncertainty and Profit*, p. ix.
22. Angus Burgin, *The Great Persuasion: Reinventing Free Markets since the Depression* (Cambridge, MA: Harvard University Press, 2012), p. 42.
23. Friedrich Hayek, *Studies in Philosophy, Politics and Economics* (Chicago: University of Chicago Press, 1967), p. 198.
24. Ross B. Emmett (ed.), *The Chicago Tradition in Economics 1892-1945*, vol. VII (London: Routledge, 2002), p. vii.
25. Knight, *Risk, Uncertainty and Profit*, p. ix.
26. Ibid., pp. 8, 201.
27. Ibid., pp. 16-17.
28. Milton Friedman, *Essays in Positive Economics* (Chicago: University of Chicago Press, 1953), p. 7.
29. Knight, *Risk, Uncertainty and Profit*, p. x.
30. Ibid., pp. 5-6.
31. Frank Knight in Patinkin, *Essays On and In the Chicago Tradition*, p. 25.
32. Ibid., p. 14.
33. Ibid., p. xxviii.
34. Rose Friedman, conversations with author.
35. Knight, *Risk, Uncertainty and Profit*, p. 31.
36. Frank Knight, *Freedom and Reform: Essays in Economics and Social Philosophy* (Indianapolis, IN: LibertyPress, 1982), pp. 61-62.
37. Knight, *On the History and Method of Economics*, p. 9.
38. Knight, *Freedom and Reform*, p. 478.
39. Burgin, *The Great Persuasion*, pp. 41-43.
40. Horace Knight, "The Early Education of My Father."

CHAPTER 4. CHICAGOAN AND AUSTRIAN
ECONOMICS IN THE 1930s

1. Elizabeth S. Johnson and Harry G. Johnson, *The Shadow of Keynes: Understanding Keynes, Cambridge and Keynesian Economics* (Oxford: Basil Blackwell, 1978), p. 151.
2. Paul A. Samuelson, "Jacob Viner," in Edward Shils (ed.), *Remembering the University of Chicago: Teachers, Scientists, and Scholars* (Chicago: University of Chicago Press, 1991), p. 536.
3. Edward Shils, *Portraits: A Gallery of Intellectuals* (Chicago: University of Chicago Press, 1997), pp. 31-34.
4. James M. Buchanan, "Frank H. Knight," in Shils, *Remembering the University of Chicago*, p. 244.
5. John Maynard Keynes in J. Ronnie Davis, *The New Economics and the Old Economists* (Ames: Iowa State University Press, 1971), p. 112.
6. Allen Wallis, "George Stigler," *Journal of Political Economy* (October 1993), p. 775.

7. Henry C. Simons, *Economic Policy for a Free Society* (Chicago: University of Chicago Press, 1948), p. 41.

8. Milton and Rose D. Friedman, *Two Lucky People: Memoirs* (Chicago: University of Chicago Press, 1998), p. 40.

9. Business cycle historian Robert Gordon remarked that the "monetary over-investment theory in the particular form developed by the Austrian school is a highly sophisticated explanation which impresses the reader both by its theoretical subtlety and also by its lack of touch with reality" (*Business Fluctuations*, 2nd ed. [New York: Harper & Brothers, 1961], p. 358).

10. Friedrich Hayek, *Monetary Theory and the Trade Cycle* (1932; New York: Augustus M. Kelley, 1966), p. 19.

11. Ibid., p. 20.

12. Friedrich Hayek, *Prices and Production* (New York: August M. Kelley, 1967), p. 162.

13. Milton Friedman interview (see appendix). Friedman said in another interview with respect to the practical influence of Austrian economics: "I think the Austrian business cycle theory has done the world a great deal of harm. If you go back to the 1930s, which is a key point, here you had the Austrians sitting in London, Hayek and Lionel Robbins, and saying you just have to let the bottom drop out of the world. You've just got to let it cure itself. You can't do anything about it. You will only make it worse. . . . I think by encouraging that kind of do-nothing policy both in Britain and in the United States, they did harm" (Gene Epstein, "Mr. Market," *Hoover Digest* [1999, no. 1]).

14. Lionel Robbins, *Autobiography of an Economist* (London: Macmillan, 1971), pp. 154-155.

15. Herbert Stein, "Henry C. Simons," in David L. Sills (ed.), *International Encyclopedia of the Social Sciences*, vol. 14 (New York: Macmillan and Free Press, 1968), pp. 334, 335.

16. Herbert Stein, *On the Other Hand . . . : Essays on Economics, Economists, and Politics* (Washington, DC: American Enterprise Institute, 1995), p. 244.

17. George J. Stigler, *Memoirs of an Unregulated Economist* (Chicago: University of Chicago Press, 1988), p. 181.

CHAPTER 5. HENRY SIMONS AND PROGRESSIVE TAXATION

1. Edmund W. Kitch (ed.), "The Fire of Truth: A Remembrance of Law and Economics at Chicago, 1932-1970," *Journal of Law and Economics* (April 1983), pp. 177, 179.

2. Sherryl D. Kasper, "Henry Calvert Simons," in Ross Emmett, *The Elgar Companion to the Chicago School of Economics* (Cheltenham, UK: Edward Elgar, 2010), p. 335.

3. Friedrich Hayek in Bruce Caldwell, "The Chicago School, Hayek, and Neoliberalism," in Robert Van Horn, Philip Mirowski, and Thomas A. Stapleford (eds.), *Building Chicago Economics* (Cambridge: Cambridge University Press, 2011), p. 306.

4. Angus Burgin, *The Great Persuasion: Reinventing Free Markets since the Depression* (Cambridge, MA: Harvard University Press, 2012), p. 241, f. 142.

5. Henry Simons, *Economic Policy for a Free Society* (Chicago: University of Chicago Press, 1948), p. 1.

6. Burgin, *The Great Persuasion*, p. 39. The use of the term "libertarian" to describe the political movement now going by that name is also ascribed to Dean Russell. See, in particular, his essay, "Who Is a Libertarian?": "Here is a suggestion: Let those of us who love liberty trade-mark and reserve for our own use the good and honorable word 'libertarian'" (*The Freeman* [May 1, 1955]). This is probably the truer ascription, as Simons's work did not reach a popular audience, nor was it in a line with postwar libertarianism.

7. Simons, *Economic Policy for a Free Society*, pp. 29-30.

8. Ibid., p. 105.

9. Adam Smith in Emma Rothschild, *Economic Sentiments: Adam Smith, Condorcet, and the Enlightenment* (Cambridge, MA: Harvard University Press, 2001), p. 45.

10. Jeremy Bentham, *An Introduction to the Principles of Morals and Legislation* (1789; London: Methuen, 1982), pp. 14-15.

11. John Stuart Mill in Lanny Ebenstein, *The Greatest Happiness Principle: An Examination of Utilitarianism* (New York: Garland, 1991), p. 233.

12. George Stigler, *Memoirs of an Unregulated Economist* (Chicago: University of Chicago Press, 1985), p. 149.

13. See William Ebenstein, *Great Political Thinkers: Plato to the Present*, 4th ed. (New York: Holt, Rinehart and Winston, 1969): "Socialism is not an outside invasion of the citadel of capitalism, but a product of capitalism itself. The struggle between the two is a family affair" (p. 762).

14. Allen Wallis and George Stigler, "Professor Simons' Book," *New York Times* (December 24, 1934), p. 22. Allen Wallis and George Stigler, "Problems of Competition," *New York Times* (December 7, 1934), p. 12.

15. Milton Friedman in Paul A. Samuelson and William A. Barnett (eds.), *Inside the Economist's Mind: Conversations with Eminent Economists* (Oxford: Blackwell Publishing, 2007), p. 120.

16. Wallis and Stigler, "Professor Simons' Book."

17. Jacob Viner in Robert Van Horn, "Reinventing Monopoly and the Role of Corporations," in Van Horn, Mirowski, and Stapleford, *Building Chicago Economics*, p. 231, n. 13.

18. Simons, *Economic Policy for a Free Society*, p. 5.

19. Ibid. p. 6.

20. Ibid.

21. Ibid., pp. 51-53.

22. Ibid., p. 57.

23. Ibid., p. 65.

24. Ibid., p. 321.

25. Ibid., pp. 66, 67.

26. Ibid., p. 68.

27. Ibid., p. 76.

28. Ibid., pp. 75-77.

29. Ibid., p. 321.

30. Friedrich Hayek in Robert Van Horn and Philip Mirowski, "The Rise of the Chicago School of Economics and the Birth of Neoliberalism," in Philip

Mirowski and Dieter Plehwe (eds.), *The Road from Mont Pelerin: The Making of the Neoliberal Thought Collective* (Cambridge, MA: Harvard University Press, 2009), p. 142.

31. Friedrich Hayek, *Hayek on Hayek* (Chicago: University of Chicago Press, 1994), p. 127. Hayek also said of Chicago economists: "Simons I should have had great hope for, and his death was a catastrophe" (p. 144).

32. Ibid., pp. 111-115, 121.

33. William Breit and Roger L. Ransom, *The Academic Scribblers,* 3rd ed. (Princeton, NJ: Princeton University Press, 1998), p. 208.

34. Herbert Stein, *On the Other Hand . . . : Essays on Economics, Economists, and Politics* (Washington, DC: American Enterprises Institute, 1995), p. 245.

CHAPTER 6. COWLES COMMISSION AND KEYNES

1. Henry Simons in Ronald Coase, "Law and Economics at Chicago," *Journal of Law and Economics* (April 1993), pp. 244-245.

2. George J. Stigler, *Memoirs of an Unregulated Economist* (Chicago: University of Chicago Press, 1988), pp. 148-150.

3. Paul A. Samuelson, "Jacob Viner," in Edward Shils (ed.), *Remembering the University of Chicago: Teachers, Scientists, and Scholars* (Chicago: University of Chicago Press, 1991), p. 538.

4. Aaron Director in Henry Simons, *Economic Policy for a Free Society* (Chicago: University of Chicago Press, 1948), p. v.

5. Martin Bronfenbrenner, "Observations on the 'Chicago School(s),'" *Journal of Political Economy* (February 1962), p. 72.

6. John Maynard Keynes, *The Economic Consequences of the Peace* (New York: Penguin, 1988), p. 254.

7. John Maynard Keynes in Robert Skidelsky, *John Maynard Keynes: The Economist as Savior, 1920-1937* (New York: Viking Penguin, 1994), p. 235.

8. John Maynard Keynes, *The General Theory of Employment, Interest, and Money* (New York: Harcourt Brace Jovanovich, 1964), pp. 379-380.

9. Jacob Viner, "Mr. Keynes on the Causes of Unemployment," *Quarterly Journal of Economics* (November 1936), p. 147.

10. Don Patinkin, *Essays On and In the Chicago Tradition* (Durham, NC: Duke University Press, 1981), p. 299.

11. Frank Knight in ibid., p. 300.

12. John Maynard Keynes in ibid.

13. Frank Knight in ibid., p. 301.

14. Lester Telser, interview, by Lanny Ebenstein, June 10, 2004, Chicago.

15. Lawrence Klein in William Breit and Barry T. Hirsch, *Lives of the Laureates,* 4th ed. (Cambridge, MA: MIT Press, 2004), p. 19.

16. Milton Friedman in J. Daniel Hammond, "An Interview with Milton Friedman on Methodology," in Warren J. Samuels and Jeff Biddle (eds.), *Research in the History of Economic Thought and Methodology,* vol. 10 (Greenwich, CT: JAI Press, 1992), p. 110.

17. Gary Becker in Milton Friedman, *Milton Friedman on Economics: Selected Papers* (Chicago: University of Chicago Press, 2007), pp. 182, 186.

18. Milton and Rose D. Friedman, *Two Lucky People: Memoirs* (Chicago: University of Chicago Press, 1998), p. 197.
19. Milton Friedman, interview by Lanny Ebenstein in Stanford, California, July 2004.
20. Box 7, folder 4, Friedman Archive, Hoover Institution on War, Revolution and Peace, Stanford, California.
21. Milton Friedman in Carl F. Christ, "The Cowles Commission's Contributions to Econometrics at Chicago, 1939-1955," *Journal of Economic Literature* (March 1994), p. 46.
22. Robert M. Solow, "Cowles and the Tradition of Macroeconomics," in Alvin K. Klevorick (ed.), *Cowles Fiftieth Anniversary Volume* (1983).
23. Melvin W. Reder, "Chicago School," in John Eatwell, Murray Milgate, and Peter Newman (eds.), *The New Palgrave Dictionary of Economics,* vol. 1 (London: Macmillan, 1991), p. 415.
24. William Frazer, *Power and Ideas: Milton Friedman and the Big U-Turn,* vol. 2 (Gainesville, FL: Gulf/Atlantic, 1998), p. 706.
25. In Christ, "Cowles Commission's Contributions," pp. 34-35.
26. Ibid., p. 35.
27. Patinkin, *Essays On and In the Chicago Tradition,* p. 17.
28. Jacob Marschak in F. A. Hayek, *The Road to Serfdom,* vol. II in *The Collected Works of F. A. Hayek* (University of Chicago Press, 2007), pp. 251–52.
29. Frank Knight in F. A. Hayek, *The Road to Serfdom,* vol. II in *The Collected Works of F. A. Hayek* (University of Chicago Press, 2007), pp. 249–50.
30. Herbert Stein, *On the Other Hand . . . : Essays on Economics, Economists, and Politics* (Washington, DC: American Enterprise Institute, 1995), p. 220.
31. Hunter Crowther-Hayek, *Herbert A. Simon: The Bounds of Reason in Modern America* (Baltimore, MD: Johns Hopkins University Press, 2005), p. 124.

CHAPTER 7. THE CHICAGO SCHOOL OF ECONOMICS

1. Robert Van Horn and Philip Mirowski, "The Rise of the Chicago School of Economics and the Birth of Neoliberalism," in Philip Mirowski and Dieter Plehwe (eds.), *The Road from Mont Pelerin: The Making of the Neoliberal Thought Collective* (Cambridge, MA: Harvard University Press, 2009), pp. 140, 143.
2. Henry Simons in ibid., p. 145.
3. Paul Douglas, *In the Fullness of Time* (New York: Harcourt Brace Jovanovich, 1972), p. 128.
4. Milton and Rose D. Friedman, *Two Lucky People: Memoirs* (Chicago: University of Chicago Press, 1998), p. 197.
5. Friedman-Ebenstein interview, Stanford, California, July 2004.
6. According to Bruce Caldwell: "Though many parts of Friedman's essay are consistent with the logical empiricism of his time, his preoccupation with prediction and his insistence that the 'realism of assumptions' is immaterial are not" (*Beyond Positivism: Economic Methodology in the Twentieth Century* [London: George Allen & Unwin, 1982], p. 184). For an exchange between this writer and Caldwell largely considering issues of methodology, see this writer's review of Caldwell's *Hayek's Challenge* (Chicago: University of Chicago

Press, 2004), Caldwell's response, and my reply in the 2005 first volume and edition of the *NYU Journal of Law & Liberty*, pp. 304-312. I write there: "Prediction is the most vital component of scientific discourse . . . where there is no prediction, there is no science," and characterize my own position as "predictive positivism" (pp. 304-305).

7. Milton Friedman to C. W. Guillebaud (February 1, 1949), Box 6, Folder 6, Friedman Archive, Hoover Institution on War, Revolution and Peace, Stanford, California. Friedman remarked in a 2000 interview: "I go back to what Alfred Marshall said about economics: Translate your results into English and then burn the mathematics. I think there's too much emphasis on mathematics as such" (in Paul A. Samuelson and William A. Barnett [eds.], *Inside the Economist's Mind: Conversations with Eminent Economists* [Oxford: Blackwell Publishing, 2007], p. 132). For this writer's views on mathematical methodology in economics, see Alan (Lanny) Ebenstein, "The Poverty of Samuelson's Economics," *Liberty* (April 2003).

8. Milton Friedman, *Essays in Positive Economics* (Chicago: University of Chicago Press, 1953), p. 15.

9. Ibid., p. 91.

10. Milton Friedman, letter to author (March 27, 2003).

11. Johan Van Overtveldt, *The Chicago School: How the University of Chicago Assembled the Thinkers Who Revolutionized Economics and Business* (Chicago, IL: Agate, 2007), p. 27.

12. Milton Friedman, "Comment on Katona and Fisher" (August 28, 1949), Box 40, Folder 2, Friedman Archive, Hoover Institution on War, Revolution and Peace, Stanford, California, pp. 1-2.

13. Ibid., p. 3.

14. Milton Friedman in J. Daniel Hammond, "An Interview with Milton Friedman on Methodology," in Warren J. Samuels and Jeff Biddle (eds.), *Research in the History of Economic Thought and Methodology*, vol. 10 (Greenwich, CT: JAI Press, 1992), p. 109.

15. Don Patinkin, *Essays On and In the Chicago Tradition* (Durham, NC: Duke University Press, 1981), p. 16.

16. In William Frazer, *Power and Ideas: Milton Friedman and the Big U-Turn*, vol. 1 (Gainesville, FL: Gulf/Atlantic, 1988), p. 3.

17. Milton Friedman in John McDonald, "The Economists," *Fortune* (December 1950), p. 111.

18. J. Daniel Hammond, *Theory and Measurement: Causality Issues in Milton Friedman's Monetary Economics* (New York and Cambridge: Cambridge University Press, 1996), p. 41.

19. "Wallis Years at the University of Rochester," transcript of interviews with William H. Meckling (University of Rochester Library, Rochester, NY, 1976), p. 40.

20. "*Free to Choose*: A Conversation with Milton Friedman," *Imprimis* (July 2006), pp. 5-7.

21. Lanny Ebenstein, *Milton Friedman: A Biography* (New York: Palgrave Macmillan, 2007), p. 43.

22. Milton Friedman in Hammond, *Theory and Measurement*, p. 1.

23. Milton Friedman in Paul A. Samuelson and William A. Barnett, *Inside the Economist's Mind: Conversations with Eminent Economists* (Oxford: Blackwell Publishing, 2007), p. 143.

24. Randall E. Parker, *Reflections on the Great Depression* (Northampton, MA: Edward Elgar, 2002), pp. 54-55.

25. John McDonald, "The Economists," *Fortune* (December 1950), p. 113.

26. Ibid., pp. 113, 126.

27. Ibid., p. 128.

28. D. Gale Johnson-Ebenstein interview (2001).

29. John Davenport in Friedman, *Memoirs*, p. 160.

30. Lester Telser-Ebenstein interview, June 10, 2004, Chicago.

31. Henry W. Spiegel, "Jacob Viner," in John Eatwell, Murray Milgate, and Peter Newman (eds.), *The New Palgrave: A Dictionary of Economics*, vol. 4 (1987), p. 813.

32. George Stigler, "Comment," *Journal of Political Economy* (February 1962), p. 70

33. Paul A. Samuelson, "Milton Friedman," *Newsweek* (October 25, 1976), p. 89.

34. Melvin W. Reder, "Chicago Economics: Permanence and Change," *Journal of Economic Literature* (March 1982), pp. 10, 32.

35. Van Overtfeldt, *The Chicago School*, p. 27.

36. David Rockefeller, *Memoirs* (New York: Random House, 2003), p. 88.

37. Gary Becker in Edward Shils (ed.), *Remembering the University of Chicago: Teachers, Scientists, and Scholars* (Chicago: University of Chicago Press, 1991), p. 143.

38. Robert Lucas in William Breit and Barry T. Hirsch (eds.), *Lives of the Laureates: Eighteen Nobel Economists*, 4th ed. (Cambridge, MA: MIT Press, 2004), p. 281. Lucas reveals here the extent of his methodological differences with Friedman: "I loved [Samuelson's] *Foundations*. Like so many others in my cohort, I internalized its view that if I couldn't formulate a problem in economic theory mathematically, I didn't know what I was doing. I came to the position that mathematical analysis is not one of many ways of doing economic theory: it is the only way. Economic theory *is* mathematical analysis. Everything else is just pictures and talk" (p. 279, emphasis in original).

39. Daniel Patrick Moynihan in Steven F. Hayward, *The Age of Reagan* (New York: Random House, 2001), p. 524.

40. George Shultz-Ebenstein interview (September 30, 2013).

41. Edmund W. Kitch (ed.), "The Fire of Truth: A Remembrance of Law and Economics at Chicago, 1932-1970," *Journal of Law and Economics* (April 1983), pp. 177-178, 211, 219.

42. George Stigler in Robert Leeson, *The Eclipse of Keynesianism: The Political Economy of the Chicago Counter-Revolution* (New York: Palgrave, 2000), pp. 52-53.

43. Ibid., pp. 51-52.

44. Edward Nik-Khah, "George Stigler, the Graduate School of Business, and the Pillars of the Chicago School," in Robert Van Horn, Philip Mirowski, and Thomas A. Stapleford (eds.), *Building Chicago Economics: New Perspectives on the History of America's Most Powerful Economics Program* (Cambridge: Cambridge University Press, 2011), p. 117.

45. Milton Friedman in J. Daniel Hammond and Claire H. Hammond (eds.), *Chicago Price Theory: Friedman-Stigler Correspondence, 1945-1957* (London: Routledge, 2006), p. 5.

46. Ibid., pp. 4-5.
47. George Stigler in ibid., p. 19.
48. Milton Friedman in ibid., p. 21.
49. Milton Friedman and George Stigler in ibid., p. 148.
50. George J. Stigler, *Five Lectures on Economic Problems* (New York: Macmillan, 1950).
51. Ibid., p. 42.
52. Milton Friedman in Hammond and Hammond, *Chicago Price Theory*, pp. 78-79.
53. George Stigler, *The Essence of Stigler* (Stanford, CA: Hoover Institution Press, 1986), p. 343.
54. George Stigler, *The Economist as Preacher and Other Essays* (Chicago: University of Chicago Press, 1982), p. 130.
55. Ibid., p. 169.

CHAPTER 8. CHICAGO ECONOMISTS IN ACADEMIA

1. Martin Bronfenbrenner, "Contemporary American Economic Thought," *American Journal of Economics and Sociology* (July 1950), p. 487.
2. Edward Hastings Chamberlin, *Towards a More General Theory of Value* (Oxford: Oxford University Press, 1957), p. 296.
3. H. Laurence Miller, "On the 'Chicago School of Economics,'" *Journal of Political Economy* (February 1962), p. 67.
4. George Stigler, *Memoirs of an Unregulated Economist* (Chicago: University of Chicago Press, 2003), pp. 148-150.
5. Mary Ann Dzuback, *Robert M. Hutchins: Portrait of an Educator* (Chicago: University of Chicago Press, 1991), p. 160.
6. Miller, "On the 'Chicago School,'" p. 67.
7. William J. Baumol, review of Don Patinkin, *Essays On and In the Chicago Tradition, Journal of Political Economy* (December 1983), p. 1082.
8. "Goldwater's Economists," *Newsweek* (August 31, 1964).
9. George Stigler in William Breit and Barry T. Hirsch, *Lives of the Laureates,* 4th ed. (Cambridge: MIT Press, 2004), p. 85.
10. Paul A. Samuelson, *Economics,* 10th ed. (New York: McGraw-Hill, 1976), p. 848.
11. Paul Samuelson in Mark Skousen, "The Perseverance of Paul Samuelson's Economics," *Journal of Economic Perspectives* (Spring 1997), p. 142.
12. Ibid.
13. Ibid.
14. Todd G. Buchholz, *New Ideas from Dead Economists* (New York: Plume, 1999), p. 241.
15. Milton Friedman, *Friedman on Galbraith* (Vancouver, BC: Fraser Institute, 1977), pp. 15, 23-24, 30.
16. John Kenneth Galbraith, *The New Industrial State* (Boston, MA: Houghton Mifflin, 1967), p. 124.
17. John Kenneth Galbraith, *Economics in Perspective: A Critical History* (Boston, MA: Houghton Mifflin, 1987), pp. 271, 274.

18. Milton Friedman, *Milton Friedman's Monetary Framework: A Debate with His Critics,* edited by Robert J. Gordon (Chicago: University of Chicago Press, 1974), pp. 77, 88.
19. James Tobin in Henry Spiegel and Warren J. Samuels, *Contemporary Economists in Perspective* (Greenwich, CT: JAI Press, 1984), p. 246.
20. Friedman, *Monetary Framework,* p. 143.
21. Harry G. Johnson, "The Keynesian Revolution and the Monetarist Counter-Revolution," *American Economic Review* (May 1971), pp. 9-11.
22. Robert Leeson, "Patinkin, Johnson, and the Shadow of Friedman," *History of Political Economy* (Winter 2000), pp. 746-747.
23. Milton Friedman in ibid., p. 753.
24. Milton Friedman in Robert Leeson, *Keynes, Chicago and Friedman,* vol. 1 (London: Pickering & Chatto, 2003), p. x.

CHAPTER 9. LAW AND ECONOMICS, AND POLITICAL PHILOSOPHY

1. Melvin W. Reder, "Chicago Economics: Permanence and Change," *Journal of Economic Literature* (March 1982), p. 7.
2. Ronald Coase, "Law and Economics at Chicago," *Journal of Law and Economics* (April 1993), p. 247.
3. George Stigler, *Memoirs of an Unregulated Economist* (Chicago: University of Chicago Press, 2003), p. 158.
4. Milton and Rose D. Friedman, *Two Lucky People: Memoirs* (Chicago: University of Chicago Press, 1998), p. 50.
5. Coase, "Law and Economics at Chicago," p. 247.
6. Ibid.
7. Robert Van Horn, "Reinventing Monopoly and the Role of Corporations," in Robert Van Horn, Philip Mirowski, and Thomas A. Stapleford (eds.), *Building Chicago Economics: New Perspectives on the History of America's Most Powerful Economics Program* (Cambridge: Cambridge University Press, 2011), pp. 228-229.
8. Richard Ebeling, "Aaron Director and the Market for Goods and Ideas," *Freeman* (November 2004), p. 2.
9. Milton Friedman in J. Daniel Hammond, *Theory and Measurement: Causality Issues in Milton Friedman's Monetary Economics* (Cambridge: Cambridge University Press, 1996), p. 114.
10. Arjo Klamer (ed.), *Conversations with Economists: New Classical Economists and Opponents Speak Out on the Current Controversy in Macroeconomics* (Totowa, NJ: Rowman & Allanheld, 1984), p. 181.
11. Edmund W. Kitch (ed.), "The Fire of Truth: A Remembrance of Law and Economics at Chicago, 1932-1970," *Journal of Law and Economics* (April 1983), p. 185.
12. J. Daniel Hammond, *Theory and Measurement: Causality Issues in Milton Friedman's Monetary Economics* (New York and Cambridge: Cambridge University Press, 1996), p. 113., *Theory and Measurement,* p. 113.
13. Kitch, "The Fire of Truth," pp. 183-184.
14. Lionel Robbins in Coase, "Law and Economics at Chicago," p. 244.

15. Paul Samuelson, correspondence to author, June 30, 2005.
16. Paul Samuelson in Karen Ilse Horn, *Roads to Wisdom, Conversations with Ten Nobel Laureates in Economics* (Cheltenham, UK: Edward Elgar, 2009), p. 46.
17. Friedman, *Memoirs*, p. v.
18. Steven N. S. Cheung, "Ronald Harry Coase," in John Eatwell, Murray Milgate, and Peter Newman (eds.), *The New Palgrave: A Dictionary of Economics*, vol. 1 (London: Macmillan, 1987), p. 456.
19. Ludwig von Mises in Friedrich Hayek (ed.), *Collectivist Economic Planning* (London: Routledge & Kegan Paul, 1935), pp. 87-88.
20. Ludwig von Mises, *Human Action: A Treatise on Economics, 3rd revised edition (Chicago: Henry Regnery, 1966), p. 698.*
21. Ludwig von Mises in Hayek, *Collectivist Economic Planning*, p. 110.
22. Bruce Caldwell, *Hayek's Challenge: An Intellectual Biography* (Chicago: University of Chicago Press, 2004), p. 325.
23. Friedrich Hayek, *Individualism and Economic Order* (Chicago: University of Chicago Press, 1948), pp. 50, 54.
24. Bettina Bien Greaves, correspondence to author (February 18, 1999).
25. See Alan (Lanny) Ebenstein, *Edwin Cannan—Liberal Doyen* (London: Routledge/Thoemmes, 1997).
26. UCLA Oral History Program, "Nobel Prize Winning Economist Friedrich A. von Hayek" (1983), p. 395.
27. Charlotte E. Cubitt, *A Life of Friedrich August von Hayek* (Bedfordshire, UK: Authors Online, 2006), p. 211.
28. Ibid., p. 285.
29. Friedrich Hayek, *Hayek on Hayek* (Chicago: University of Chicago Press, 1994), p. 126.
30. Ronald Hamowy, "F. A. Hayek, On the Occasion of the Centenary of His Birth," *Cato Journal* (Fall 1999), p. 285.
31. John Stuart Mill, *On Liberty* (1859), ch. 3.
32. Friedrich Hayek, *The Constitution of Liberty* (Chicago: University of Chicago Press, 1960), p. 31.
33. Ibid., p. 394.
34. Ibid., pp. 86-87.
35. James M. Buchanan, *Better than Plowing and Other Personal Essays* (Chicago: University of Chicago Press, 1992), p. 77.
36. Alexander Hamilton, James Madison, and John Jay, *The Federalist* (Oxford: Basil Blackwell, 1948), p. 265.
37. James M. Buchanan and Gordon Tullock, *The Calculus of Consent: Logical Foundation of Constitutional Democracy* (Ann Arbor: University of Michigan Press, 1962), p. 303.
38. Ibid., p. 306.

CHAPTER 10. HAYEK AT CHICAGO:
PHILOSOPHER OF CLASSICAL LIBERALISM

1. George H. Smith, *The System of Liberty: Themes in the History of Classical Liberalism* (Cambridge: Cambridge University Press, 2013): "One must appreciate this

broad conception of the free market, which includes far more than tangible goods, if one wishes to understand the passionate commitment of many liberals [libertarians] to competition and their *unbridled hatred* of government interference" (p. 172, emphasis added); Yaron Brook, in Mallory and Elizabeth Factor (eds.), *The Big Tent: The Story of the Conservative Revolution as Told by the Thinkers and Doers Who Made It Happen* (New York: Broadside Books, 2014): "Today, a significant portion of the libertarian movement believes in anarchy. This belief manifests itself not only in direct arguments for no government, but also in a hatred of government, a resentment of all government functions" (p. 133); and Rand Paul, in ibid.: "Returning to a more libertarian conservatism would return us to a sharply more limited government and radically more pro-freedom agenda"; and "If the GOP is the party of smaller government, we must also be the party that is suspicious of government at every juncture" (pp. 347, 355).

2. By the "younger" Hayek, I do not intend the Hayek of seventeen to twenty-four years of age or so who identified himself as a socialist. Rather, by the "younger" Hayek I mean Hayek from the time he returned to Vienna from the United States in 1924 until he published *The Road to Serfdom* twenty years later. The middle-aged Hayek, then, would be another thirty years or so, until he received the Nobel Prize in 1974. The late Hayek would be from 1974 until his death in 1992.

3. Friedrich Hayek, *The Collected Works of F. A. Hayek,* vol. 3 (Chicago: University of Chicago Press, 1991), p. 34.

4. Friedrich Hayek, *The Road to Serfdom* (1944; London: Routledge & Kegan Paul, 1986), pp. 13, 27-29. Henry Simons remarked in a 1939 speech: "The scheme of policy for which I plead may be called *laissez faire,* for historical reasons; but a modern program of *laissez faire* cannot be a do-nothing program by any name" (in Sherryl Davis Kasper, *The Revival of* Laissez-Faire *in American Macroeconomic Theory* [Cheltenham, UK: Edward Elgar, 2002], p. 36).

5. Friedrich Hayek, *Hayek on Hayek* (Chicago: University of Chicago Press, 1994), p. 116.

6. George H. Nash, *The Conservative Intellectual Movement in America* (New York: Basic Books, 1976), pp. 313, 315-316, 318.

7. Friedrich Hayek, *The Constitution of Liberty* (Chicago: University of Chicago Press, 1960), pp. 257, 222.

8. Ibid., pp. 257-258.

9. Ibid., pp. 375, 259.

10. Ibid., p. 258.

11. Ibid., p. 141.

12. Ibid., p. 144.

13. Ibid., p. 223.

14. Ibid.

15. Ibid., pp. 225, 354-355.

16. Ibid., p. 229.

17. Ibid., p. 217.

18. Ibid., p. 227.

19. Ibid., pp. 224-225.
20. Ibid., p. 231.
21. David Glasner, *Commentary* (October 1992), p. 50.
22. Anthony de Jasay, *Critical Review* (Spring 1989), p. 296.
23. Geoffrey Vickers, "Controls for Freedom," *Futures* (August 1979), p. 347.
24. Hans-Hermann Hoppe in Christoph Frei and Robert Nef (eds.), *Contending with Hayek* (Bern: Peter Lang, 1994), p. 127.
25. Ludwig von Mises, "Liberty and Its Antithesis," *Christian Economics* (August 1, 1960), pp. 1, 3.
26. Lionel Robbins, "Hayek on Liberty," *Economica* (February 1961), pp. 69-70, 78.
27. Friedrich Hayek, *Studies in Philosophy, Politics and Economics* (Chicago: University of Chicago Press, 1967), p. 121.
28. Milton Friedman, *Capitalism and Freedom* (Chicago: University of Chicago Press, [1962] 1982), p. 2.
29. Ibid., p. 4.
30. Ibid., p. 3.
31. Hayek, *The Constitution of Liberty*, pp. 404-405.

CHAPTER 11. FRIEDMAN AS ECONOMIST AND PUBLIC INTELLECTUAL

1. Milton Friedman in Lanny Ebenstein, *Hayek's Journey: The Mind of Friedrich Hayek* (New York: Palgrave Macmillan, 2003), pp. 168-169.
2. Paul Krugman, "Who Was Milton Friedman?" *New York Review of Books* (February 15, 2007).
3. Warren Samuels, review of *Two Lucky People*, in Warren J. Samuels and Jeff E. Biddle (eds.), *Research in the History of Economic Thought and Methodology*, vol. 18-A (New York: JAI, 2000), pp. 242-243.
4. Agnar Sandmo, *Economics Evolving: A History of Economic Thought* (Princeton, NJ: Princeton University Press, 2011), pp. 417, 420.
5. Milton and Rose D. Friedman, *Two Lucky People: Memoirs* (Chicago: University of Chicago Press, 1998), p. xii.
6. Milton Friedman, *Capitalism and Freedom* (Chicago: University of Chicago Press, 1962), pp. 1-2.
7. Jeremy Bentham, *An Introduction to the Principles of Morals and Legislation* (London: Methuen, 1982), p. 12.
8. Friedman, *Capitalism and Freedom*, p. 195.
9. John Stuart Mill, *Utilitarianism, On Liberty, and Considerations on Representative Government* (1859; London: J. M. Dent & Sons, 1972), p. 58.
10. Friedman, *Capitalism and Freedom*, p. 4.
11. Mill, *On Liberty*, ch. 3.
12. Friedman, *Capitalism and Freedom*, p. 11.
13. George H. Nash, *The Conservative Intellectual Movement in America* (Wilmington, DE: Intercollegiate Studies Institute, 1996), pp. 267, 270, 189.
14. Melvin W. Reder, "Chicago Economics: Permanence and Change," *Journal of Economic Literature* (March 1982), p. 35.

15. Milton Friedman, *Dollars and Deficits: Inflation, Monetary Policy and the Balance of Payments* (Englewood Cliffs, NJ: Prentice-Hall, 1968), p. 18.

16. Milton Friedman, letter to author (June 1, 2005).

17. "Interview with Milton Friedman," *Technos Quarterly* (Spring 1996), final quote.

18. Milton Friedman, *Essays in Positive Economics* (Chicago: University of Chicago Press, 1953), p. 134.

19. Milton Friedman and George J. Stigler, *Roofs or Ceilings? The Current Housing Problem* (Irvington-on-Hudson, NY: Foundation for Economic Education, 1946), p. 6.

20. Milton Friedman in Beatrice Cherrier, "The Lucky Consistency of Milton Friedman's Science and Politics, 1933-1963," in Robert Van Horn, Philip Mirowski, and Thomas A. Stapleford (eds.), *Building Chicago Economics: New Perspectives on the History of America's Most Powerful Economics Program* (Cambridge: Cambridge University Press, 2011), p. 361.

21. Friedman, *Capitalism and Freedom,* pp. 195, 169.

22. Nash, *The Conservative Intellectual Movement,* p. 187.

23. Milton and Rose Friedman, *Free to Choose* (New York: Harcourt Brace Jovanovich, 1980), pp. 136-137.

24. Herbert Stein, "Adam Smith Did Not Wear an Adam Smith Necktie," *Wall Street Journal* (April 6, 1994).

25. Herbert Stein, *Governing the $5 Trillion Economy* (New York: Oxford University Press, 1989), pp. 2, 10.

26. George P. Shultz, "The Practical Milton Friedman," *Hoover Digest* (Fall 2006, no. 4), pp. 13, 16-17.

27. George Shultz, interview by Lanny Ebenstein, September 30, 2013.

28. Adam Smith in William Ebenstein and Alan (Lanny) Ebenstein, *Great Political Thinkers: Plato to the Present,* 6th ed. (Fort Worth, TX: Harcourt College Publishers, 2000), p. 494.

29. Friedman and Friedman, *Free to Choose,* p. 5.

30. Friedman, *Memoirs,* p. 390.

31. "Economic Strategy for the Reagan Administration: A Report to President-Elect Reagan from His Coordinating Committee on Economic Policy" (November 16, 1980) (copy obtained by author from George Shultz).

32. Ibid., p. 1. I have written "restrain" rather than "restraining," "reduce" rather than "reducing," and "conduct" rather than "conducting" in the text here.

33. Ibid., p. 2.

34. Ibid., p. 10.

35. Ibid., p. 2.

36. Milton Friedman, "Freedom's Friend," *Wall Street Journal* (June 11, 2004).

37. Martin Anderson, *Revolution* (New York: Harcourt Brace Jovanovich, 1988), p. 172.

38. Edwin Meese, interview by Lanny Ebenstein, 1996. In a later contact, Meese reaffirmed the intellectual significance of Friedman to the Reagan administration (Edwin Meese–Ebenstein conversation [December 7, 2012]).

39. Edwin Meese III, *With Reagan: The Inside Story* (Washington, DC: Regnery, 1992), p. 127.

40. George Shultz, interview with Lanny Ebenstein, 2013.
41. William Niskanen in Robert J. Samuelson, *The Great Inflation and Its Aftermath* (New York: Random House, 2008), p. 115.
42. David Stockman, conversation with Lanny Ebenstein, April 13, 2013.
43. Rich Thomas, "The Magic of Reaganomics," *Newsweek* (December 16, 1988), p. 33.
44. Angus Burgin provides these thoughts on the transition from classical liberalism to contemporary libertarianism exemplified and led by Friedman:

> Frank Knight, Jacob Viner, and Henry Simons . . . , Wilhelm Ropke . . . , and Friedrich Hayek and Lionel Robbins . . . all recognized a broad scope for the government to intervene, with beneficial effects, in the working of the economy and the distribution of goods. All of them manifested reservations about the effects of unhindered competition and . . . skepticism toward the social and political viability of *laissez faire*. In the case of Friedman, as Krugman accurately observed, it is "extremely hard" to find places where he "acknowledged the possibility that markets could go wrong, or that government intervention could serve a useful purpose." The universality of Friedman's belief in the efficacy of free markets exceeded even that of the nineteenth century theorists . . . His was not a Spencerian or Sumnerian world in which free markets dealt crushing blows to some in order to contribute to the greater advancement of humanity. Rather, it was one in which incontrovertible benefits redounded, in a display of spectacular bounty, to people of all kinds and in all situations. He represented markets as an unremitting good. [*The Great Persuasion* (Cambridge, MA: Harvard University Press, 2012), pp. 184-185]

CHAPTER 12. THE 1980s CRESCENDO AND CONTEMPORARY LIBERTARIANISM

1. Paul Samuelson in Arnold Beichman, *Wall Street Journal* (November 17, 1994), p. A-21.
2. Ibid.
3. Ibid.
4. Paul Samuelson and William Nordhaus, *Economics,* 13th ed. (New York: McGraw-Hill, 1989), p. 837.
5. Lee Edwards, "Still Bowing to the God That Failed," *Intercollegiate Review* (Fall/Winter 2004), p. 9.
6. John Kenneth Galbraith in J. Daniel Hammond, "Markets, Politics, and Democracy at Chicago: Taking Economics Seriously," in Robert Van Horn, Philip Mirowski, and Thomas A. Stapleford (eds.), *Building Chicago Economics: New Perspectives on the History of America's Most Powerful Economics Program* (Cambridge: Cambridge University Press, 2011), p. 60.
7. Ibid.
8. Lester Thurow in Edwards, "Still Bowing," pp. 9-10.
9. Paul Kennedy, *The Rise and Fall of the Great Powers* (New York: Vintage, 1989), p. 429.

10. John Maynard Keynes, "Activities 1940-1946," in Donald Moggridge (ed.), *Collected Works of John Maynard Keynes,* vol. XXVII (London: Macmillan, 1980), pp. 385-387.
11. Robert Skidelsky, *John Maynard Keynes: The Economist as Saviour 1920-1937* (New York: Penguin Books, 1994), pp. 228-229.
12. Robert Skidelsky, *John Maynard Keynes: Fighting for Britain 1937-1946* (London: Macmillan, 2000), p. 550.
13. William Ruger, *Milton Friedman* (New York: Continuum, 2011), p. 96.
14. Angus Burgin, *The Great Persuasion: Reinventing Free Markets since the Depression* (Cambridge, MA: Harvard University Press, 2012); Brian Doherty, "The Increasingly Libertarian Milton Friedman," http://reason.com/archives/2012/11/20/the-increasingly-libertarian-milton-frie (November 20, 2012); J. Daniel Hammon in Ruger, *Milton Friedman,* p. 16.
15. Milton Friedman, *Capitalism and Freedom* (Chicago: University of Chicago Press, 1982), pp. 4, 34, 191.
16. Ibid., pp. 199, 85-86, 96.
17. Milton Friedman, "The Case for Choice," in K. L. Billingsley (ed.), *Voices on Choice: The Education Reform Debate* (San Francisco, CA: Pacific Research Institute, 1994), p. 94.
18. Milton and Rose Friedman, *Two Lucky People: Memoirs* (Chicago: University of Chicago Press, 1998), p. 628.
19. Milton Friedman in Richard Vedder, *Going Broke By Degree: Why College Costs Too Much* (Washington, DC: AEI Press, 2004), p. 127.
20. Milton Friedman, interview by Brian Doherty, "Best of Both Worlds," *Reason* (June 1995).
21. Ibid.
22. Milton Friedman, correspondence to author (September 26, 2001).
23. Milton Friedman, interview by Russell Roberts, *Library of Economics and Liberty* (Liberty Fund: September 4, 2006).
24. Burgin, *The Great Persuasion,* p. 198.
25. Friedrich Hayek, *Law, Legislation and Liberty,* vol. III (Chicago: University of Chicago Press, 1979), p. 147.
26. James J. Heckman in William Breit and Barry T. Hirsch (eds.), *Lives of the Laureates,* 4th ed. (Cambridge, MA: MIT Press, 2004), p. 308.
27. Ibid., pp. 320-321.
28. Milton Friedman, *Essays in Positive Economics* (Chicago: University of Chicago Press, 1953).
29. James J. Heckman, *Giving Kids a Fair Chance* (Cambridge, MA: MIT Press, 2013), pp. 40-41.

CONCLUSION: CURRENT APPLICATIONS OF CHICAGONOMICS

1. Peter Boettke recalls Knight's student James Buchanan saying: "It takes varied reiteration to force alien concepts upon reluctant minds" (in *Living Economics* [Oakland, CA: Independent Institute, 2012], p. 28).

2. Stephen M. Caliende, *Inequality in America: Race, Poverty, and Fulfilling Democracy's Promise* (Boulder, CO: Westview Press, 2015), p. 48. Approximately 22 percent of Americans under age eighteen live in poverty at this time, including 35 percent of Hispanics under eighteen and 38 percent of African American children and youth. More than 40 percent of children under eighteen at the current time in the United States live in single-parent, female-headed households.

3. Stephen Moore, "The U.S. Tax System: Who Really Pays?" *Issues 2012* (Manhattan Institute for Public Policy, August 2012), p. 3 (Figure 3).

4. Ibid., p. 4 (Figure 4).

5. Ibid., p. 4 (Figure 3).

6. There are many others than Moore who present the inegalitarian nature of contemporary American society, though from a different perspective. See, for example, Joseph E. Stiglitz, *The Price of Inequality: How Today's Divided Society Endangers Our Future* (New York: W. W. Norton, 2012); Robert B. Reich, *Beyond Outrage: What Has Gone Wrong with Our Economy and Our Democracy, and How to Fix It* (New York: Vintage Books, 2012); and Jacob S. Hacker and Paul Pierson, *Winner-Take-All Politics: How Washington Made the Rich Richer—And Turned Its Back on the Middle Class* (New York: Simon & Schuster, 2010).

7. Michael Tanner, "Inequality Myths," *National Review Online* (May 14, 2014).

8. E. N. Wolff, "Recent Trends in Household Wealth in the United States: Rising Debt and the Middle-Class Squeeze—An Update to 2007," Levy Economics Institute of Bard College (2010).

9. Harry G. Johnson, "The Keynesian Revolution and the Monetarist Counter-Revolution," *American Economic Review* (1971), p. 3.

10. Moore, "Who Really Pays?" p. 5.

11. Ibid., p. 4 (Figure 4).

12. Ibid., pp. 1-2.

13. Walter Williams, "Parting Company," creators.com (December 30, 2013).

14. In this writer's one or two interactions with Professor Williams, he has been kind and thoughtful. He provided a positive endorsement for my collection of Friedman essays, *The Indispensable Milton Friedman*.

15. John Stossel, "Equality versus Liberty," *Santa Barbara News-Press* (January 8, 2014), p. A7. Stossel comments elsewhere: "Friedman won the Nobel Prize in 1976 for his technical work in consumption analysis and monetary theory. But his real impact came through his popular writings in books and magazines" ("Milton Friedman Day," creators.com [July 30, 2007]). This is exactly the opposite of Friedman's view—he emphasized his scholarly work.

16. John Stossel, "What, Exactly Is Fair?" *Santa Barbara News-Press* (March 12, 2015), p. A2

17. Matthew Gardner, "With State Tax Reform, First Do No Harm," *Santa Barbara News-Press* (February 4, 20130), p. A7.

18. Christopher Howard, *The Hidden Welfare State* (Princeton, NJ: Princeton University Press, 1997).

19. David Cay Johnston, "The Fortunate 400," *Reuters* (June 6, 2012).

20. These views are held by individuals associated with leading conservative and libertarian think tanks, including the American Enterprise Institute,

the Heritage Foundation, and the Cato Institute. This writer is an adjunct scholar at Cato, but does not share these views.

21. I am indebted to Henning Bohn for his incisive analysis of Reagan tax policy.

22. Moore, "Who Really Pays?" pp. 3, 4 (Figures 3 and 4).

23. Ibid., p. 3 (Figure 3). It bears noting that Moore's predictions with respect to what the influence of higher taxes starting in 2013 would be were quite in error: "Here is what will happen if nothing is done about extending the Bush-era tax cuts and abolishing Obamacare taxes: . . . it will push the stock market lower, contract the real economy, and possibly contribute to a double-dip recession like the one that Americans suffered under President Jimmy Carter" (pp. 6-7). In fact, since 2013, with higher tax rates, the stock market has reached all-time highs, economic growth has continued, and unemployment has substantially declined.

24. William Ebenstein, *Today's Isms: Communism, Fascism, Capitalism, Socialism* (New York: Prentice-Hall, 1954), p. 142.

25. Milton Friedman, correspondence with author (June 1, 2005).

26. Ibid.

27. Ibid.

28. Milton Friedman, conversations with author (1996-2005).

29. "The Richest People in America," *Forbes* (October 20, 2014), p. 16.

30. Wolff, "Recent Trends in Household Wealth in the United States."

31. William Ebenstein, *Today's Isms*, p. 98.

32. I am indebted to David Beaver for this point.

33. David Boaz, *The Libertarian Mind: A Manifesto for Freedom* (New York: Simon & Schuster, 2015), p. 17.

34. Herb Stein, *On the Other Hand . . . : Essays on Economics, Economists, and Politics* (Washington, DC: American Enterprise Institute, 1995), p. 50.

35. Joseph E. Stiglitz, *The Price of Inequality: How Today's Divided Society Endangers Our Future* (New York: W.W. Norton, 2012), p. 298, n. 19. Separately, this writer has calculated average annual US economic growth rates between 1948 and 1980 and between 1981 and 2009 as 3.7 percent and 2.8 percent, respectively.

36. Boaz, *The Libertarian Mind*, p. 283.

37. Lord Acton in Friedrich Hayek, *The Constitution of Liberty* (Chicago: University of Chicago Press, 1960), p. 395. Acton's views—nourished by scholarship, nuanced, and complex—pointed toward classical liberalism. He also wrote in "The History of Freedom in Antiquity" (1877), the lecture from which Hayek quoted, that the appropriate activities of government include giving "indirect help to fight the battles of life by promoting the influences which prevail against temptation—religion, education, and the distribution of wealth." He supported democracy as an important element in government legitimacy and effectiveness. In the best tradition of conservative communitarianism, he emphasized the group as well as the individual: "Pericles held that every Athenian who neglected to take his part in the public business inflicted an injury on the commonwealth. . . . The instrument of his sway was the art of speaking. He governed by persuasion.

Everything was decided by argument in open deliberations, and every influence bowed before the ascendency of mind." Acton supported government activity "for education, for practical science, for the indigent and helpless, or for the spiritual needs of man" (Lord Acton, *The History of Freedom and Other Essays* [London: Macmillan, 1909], pp. 4, 10, 17).

INTERVIEW WITH MILTON FRIEDMAN
ON FRIEDRICH HAYEK

1. Friedman said in another interview: "Have the Misesians in any way stopped saying exactly what they were saying for fifty years? Not a word of it. They keep on repeating the same nonsense. What they call scientific work isn't scientific work at all. Because they regard facts as ways of illustrating theory, not as ways of testing theory. So their scientific work is from any point of view useless" (in J. Daniel Hammond, "An Interview with Milton Friedman on Methodology," in Warren J. Samuels and Jeff Biddle [eds.], *Research in the History of Economic Thought and Methodology*, vol. 10 [Greenwich, CT: JAI Press, 1992], p. 102).

    He said, in yet another interview, with this writer, in November 2000:

    > FRIEDMAN: . . . Hayek retains, he's not as bad as Mises. But he retains a large element of the praxeological approach of Mises, that knowledge comes from us inside. That we have sources of data we can rely on, and we can reach truth by. As Mises would say, facts can illustrate theories, but they can't test theories.
    >
    > EBENSTEIN: I just think it's a nonsensical view.
    >
    > FRIEDMAN: I think it's an utterly nonsensical view. I've never been able to understand how anybody could accept it.

INDEX

Acton, Lord, 208, 266–7n37
Adler, Mortimer, 22–3
Agricultural Adjustment Act (AAA), 46, 89
American Economic Association, 92, 137
  Francis A. Walker Award, 52, 221
  Friedman as president of, 138, 172
  John Bates Clark Medal, 134, 171, 221
  Knight as president of, 118
  and Laughlin, 26
  Mitchell's 1924 presidential address to, 31
  Schultz as president of, 138
  Stigler as president of, 128, 138
  Viner as president of, 52
Anderson, Martin, 181–2
antigovernmentism, 7, 40, 158, 165–6, 191
Arrow, Kenneth, 138
Ashmore, Harry, 21–2
Austrian school of economics, 43, 45, 74–7, 118, 145–6, 251n13

Bartley, Robert, 181, 225
Baumol, William, 51, 132
Beaver, David, 266n32
Becker, Gary, 50, 94, 102, 120, 122, 138

Beichman, Arnold, 185
Bentham, Jeremy, 1–2, 7, 81–2, 193
  and classical liberalism, 17, 27, 194, 202
  and egalitarianism, 9
  influence of, 1–2, 7–9
  on interest of the community, 170
  Introduction to the Principles of Morals and Legislation, An, 9
  and Mill, 9, 11
  and social reform, 8
  and voting, 8
  on utility, 9
Bernanke, Ben, 18, 117
Blaug, Mark, 50, 234
Bloomfield, Arthur, 45, 51
Boaz, David, 207, 240
Boettke, Peter, 229, 264n1
Bohn, Henning, 266n21
Bork, Robert, 140
Boulding, Kenneth, 78
Breasted, James, 35
Breit, William, 90, 226
Bronfenbrenner, Martin, 44, 78, 95, 130
Brook, Yaron, 259–60n1
Brunner, Karl, 143
Buchanan, James, 6, 39, 70–1, 138, 151–3, 222, 225, 237
Buchholz, Todd, 134–5

Buckley, William F., 158
Building Chicago Economics (Van Horn, Mirowski, and Stapleford), 43, 220–1
Bullock, Charles Jesse, 57
Burgin, Angus, xi, 45, 63, 67, 80–1, 189, 191, 263n44
    Great Persuasion, The, 43–4, 220
Burns, Arthur, 110, 176
    Measuring Business Cycles (with Mitchell), 102
business cycles, 71–2, 102, 116–17, 134, 146
Business Cycles (Mitchell), 30
Busby, John, xi

Cannan, Edwin, 18, 147, 194
Caldwell, Bruce, 146, 232, 254n6
Casier, Bob, xi
Cato Institute, 207, 266n20
Chamberlin, Edward, 84, 94, 97, 118–19, 131
Chase, Stuart, 29
Chernow, Ron, 21, 23, 233
"Chicago Plan" for monetary reform, 72
Chicago school of economics
    in academia, 131–9
    early references to "Chicago school," 22, 94–5, 119–20
    "first," 39–44, 84–6, 94, 144
    first reference in an academic journal, 130–1
    post-war Chicago school, 43, 45, 80, 83–4, 93–5, 100–1, 108–9, 120–3, 133, 144
    "two Chicago schools," 39, 44, 84, 94
    Viner on, 44–5
Clark, John Bates, 34–5, 65
Clark, John Maurice, 26, 34–6, 63
classical liberalism
    contemporary libertarianism compared with, 31–4, 154–6, 165–6, 194–6
    and egalitarianism, 85, 91
    and Friedman, 18, 127, 165, 170–1, 174, 187–91

and Hayek, 18, 101, 118, 127, 142, 145, 154–67, 185, 187–9, 191–2
and Keynes, 18, 98
and Knight, 18, 39–40, 45–6, 66–7, 70, 193–4, 225
Mises on, 17
and Mont Pelerin Society, 118, 120, 146, 174
move to contemporary libertarianism, 187–93
and post-war Chicago school, 43, 117
principles of, 31–4, 48–9, 87, 90, 156–7, 164–6, 194–6
and Simons, 18, 34, 45–6, 80–7, 90–1, 109, 142, 194
and Stein, 177
and Stigler, 127
theoretical tradition of, 1–18
and Viner, 18, 39–40, 44–6, 48–9, 78, 194
Coase, Ronald, 124, 138, 140–2, 144, 231
Coats, A. W., 36–7, 226
Cockett, Richard, 212, 228
Columbia University, 30–1, 35, 78, 110
Colwell, E. C., 132
Committee on Social Thought, 36, 80, 93, 95, 101, 118, 132, 148–9
Communism, 73, 100, 172, 185–8
commutative (procedural) justice, 85
Constitution of Liberty, The (Hayek), 149–51, 154–5, 158–64, 166–7, 208, 214–15, 232
Contemporary Economic Thought (Homan), 120
contemporary libertarianism, 31–4, 39–42, 85, 134, 154–7, 159, 165–6, 177, 187–91, 194–6
Cowles Commission, 92–3, 95, 99–107, 111, 114, 136, 233–4
Cox, Garfield, 72
Crowther-Heyck, Hunter, 107
Cubitt, Charlotte, 148, 223, 231

Darwin, Charles
    Descent of Man, 15

influence of, 13–17, 29–30
influenced by Malthus, 27
Origin of Species, 13–14
Spencer and, 15–16
See also social Darwinism
Davenport, Herbert, 35
Davenport, John, 120
Davis, J. Ronnie, 47, 71–2, 93, 226
de Crespigny, Anthony, 232
de Jasay, Anthony, 162
Debreu, Gerard, 138
DeLong, J. Bradford, 225
Dewey, John, 35
Director, Aaron, 71–2, 77–8, 153,
   230–1, 241
early years and education of, 141
as founder of *Journal of Law and
   Economics,* 143
and Free Market Study, 142
Friedman on, 143–4, 213, 219
and Hayek, 105, 118, 213
influence of, 140–1, 143–4
and post-war Chicago school, 43,
   45, 80, 83–4, 93–5, 100, 108–9,
   144
return to Chicago, 142
teaching of, 69, 140–1, 143–4
division (specialization) of labor, 2–3,
   77, 91, 147, 172
Doherty, Brian, 17, 189, 238–9
Dorfman, Joseph, 57, 120
*Economic Mind in American Civilization,
   The,* vol. v, 222
Douglas, Paul, 69, 71, 111, 144

earned income tax credit, 176,
   206
East, John, 33
Ebeling, Richard, 26, 143, 228
Ebenstein, Lanny, 241, 254–5n6,
   255n7
Ebenstein, William, 205–6, 243n19,
   252n13
econometrics, 71, 92–3, 100–107,
   111–12, 114–15
"economics," etymology of, 27
Edwards, Lee, 186

egalitarianism, 2, 4–6, 9–11, 32, 66,
   82–7, 126, 128, 150, 174–6, 183,
   196, 203. *See also* inequality of
   income and wealth
Eisenhower, Dwight D., 110
Emmett, Ross, xi, 43–5, 50, 63
Chicago Tradition in Economics 1892–1945
   (editor), 224
*Elgar Companion to the Chicago School of
   Economics,* 221
*Frank Knight and the Chicago School in
   American Economics,* 224
introduction to *Selected Essays by Frank
   H. Knight,* 224
empiricism, 30–2, 73–5, 92–3, 101,
   114–15, 169, 183, 190–3, 211
enlightened self-interest, 2
evolution, theory of, 14, 29–30, 167.
   See also social Darwinism
exchange rates, 96, 123, 130, 173,
   177–8

Fabian Society, 12, 24
Farma, Eugene, 139
Fawcett, Edmund, 241
Fawcett, Henry, 14–15
Federal Reserve, 24, 47–8, 52, 75–7,
   110, 134, 173, 176
Federalist, The, 152
Feser, Edward, 231
Fiorito, Luca, 224
fiscal policy, 39, 46–7, 71, 74–6,
   96–8, 106–7, 116, 134–5, 143,
   172–4, 181, 195
Fleischacker, Samuel, 236
Fogel, Robert, 138
Ford, Gerald, 77, 176
Foundation for Economic Education
   (FEE), 126
Frazer, William, 103, 227
Freedman, Craig, 229
Friedman, David, 243n24
Friedman, Milton
as academic economist, 130–8
advisor to Goldwater, 123, 133,
   168–9
advisor to Nixon, 133, 176, 178, 182

advisor to Reagan, 133, 172, 176–83
and Austrian school, 74–5, 251n13,
    267n1
Capitalism and Freedom, 134, 165–6,
    170–1, 175, 189–90
on Chicago school, 101, 131
on Chicago economics department,
    36 7
and classical liberalism, 11, 18, 31,
    127, 165, 170–1, 174, 187–91
and Communism, 172
and Cowles Commission, 95,
    100–7, 112
on Director, 143–4
early career of, 110–11
early views, 11, 18, 127–8, 155, 165,
    170–1, 174, 187–91
emphasis on prediction, 112–15
and exchange rates, 123, 130, 173,
    177–8
and Galbraith, 135–6
on gay rights, 205
on the Great Depression, 47, 116,
    172–3
on Hayek, 168, 209–17, 251n13
hired at Chicago, 132
on income and wealth inequality,
    11, 174–6
influenced by Viner, 48, 64
John Bates Clark Medal received
    by, 171
on Keynes, 210, 212, 214, 216–17
later views of, 18, 166, 188–91, 220
"Methodology of Positive
    Economics, The," 64, 115
Monetary History of the United States, A,
    48, 136
and monetary theory and policy, 48,
    64, 115–17, 172–4
and neoanarchism, 18, 165–6
Nobel Prize in Economics received
    by, 121, 138, 172
and post-war Chicago school, 40,
    43, 45, 83–4, 94, 101, 108–9,
    130–8
as public intellectual, 123, 168–72,
    191, 196

on public policy avocation, 169–70
Roofs or Ceilings? (with Stigler), 174
Samuelson on, 134, 218–19
on social welfare policy, 203–4
and socialism, 83, 115–16
and taxation, 11
teaching of, 69, 219
two career phases of, 123, 168–9
at University of Chicago, 21
and use of "libertarianism," 31
and utilitarianism, 170, 204
Friedman, Rose Director, 94, 140–2,
    144, 169–70, 190, 249n2,
    250n34
Free to Choose (with Milton), 175, 178,
    181–2
on Knight, 65, 70, 141
as student at Chicago, 65, 70, 77–8,
    141

Galbraith, John Kenneth, 117, 134–6,
    186–7
*Economics in Perspective: A Critical
    History,* 235
New Industrial State, The, 135–6
Gardner, Matthew, 201
*General Theory of Employment, Interest, and
    Money, The* (Keynes), 96–9, 106
George Mason University, 77, 199
Gideonse, Harry, 72, 132
Glasner, David, 161–2
gold standard, 24, 96, 215–16
Goldwater, Barry, 123, 133, 168–9
Great Depression, 43, 46–8, 71–8, 83,
    107, 116, 118, 130, 172–3. *See also*
    New Deal
*Great Persuasion: Reinventing Free Markets
    since the Depression, The* (Burgin),
    43–4, 220. *See also* Burgin,
    Angus
Guillebaud, C. W., 112

Haavelmo, Trygve, 138
Hacker, Jacob S., 265n6
Hale, George E., 35
Hamilton, Walton, 35–6
Hammond, Claire, xi, 125, 227–8

Hammond, J. Daniel, xi, 43, 101, 115, 125–6, 189, 227, 264n14
Hansen, Alvin, 119
Hansen, Lars Peter, 139
happiness, 2–3, 5–9, 11, 17, 27, 55, 68, 82–3, 151, 206
Hardy, Charles, 35, 63
Harper, William Rainey, 19–23, 222
Hart, Albert, 78
Harvard University, 22, 24, 38, 57, 62, 70, 101, 119, 135
Harvey, David, 237
Hayek, Friedrich
  on Bentham, 9
  and classical liberalism, 17–8, 101, 118, 127, 142, 145, 154–67, 185, 187–9, 191–2
  and Committee on Social Thought, 80, 101, 118, 132, 148–9, 212, 223
  and conservatism, 166–7
  Constitution of Liberty, The, 149–51, 154–5, 158–64, 166–7, 208, 214–15, 232
  early views, 73–6, 90, 177, 194, 196
  "Economics and Knowledge," 146–7
  and "false" individualism, 7
  Fatal Conceit, 218
  free market views of, 149–51
  and Friedman, 179, 182, 185
  Friedman on, 168, 209–17, 251n13
  on government's role, 73–6
  influence of, 52, 144–6, 184–5
  and Keynes, 188–9, 210
  on Knight, 63
  later views of, 18, 187–9, 191–2, 195
  and libertarianism, 154–61, 164, 166
  marriages of, 148–9, 210
  and Mont Pelerin Society, 118, 146
  and neoanarchism, 18
  Nobel Prize for Economics received by, 182, 185, 213–14
  Prices and Production, 210, 214, 217–18
  Road to Serfdom, The, 89, 105–6, 109, 141, 147–8, 155–7, 164, 171, 185, 188
  and Simons, 89
  and socialism, 146, 155–8, 163
  teaching of, 211–12
  and use of "libertarianism," 31
Hayek, Larry, xi
Hayward, Steven F., 239
Heckman, James, 18, 33, 138, 192–3
  Giving Kids a Fair Chance, 193
Hobbes, Thomas, 26–7, 55
Hofstadter, Richard, 13
Homan, Paul, 35, 120
Hoover, Kenneth R., 223
Hoppe, Hans-Hermann, 162
Horn, Karen Ilse, 239
Howey, Richard, 60–1
Hoxie, Robert, 35–6
Hoy, Calvin M., 232–3
Hume, David, 61, 81, 164, 194
Hurwicz, Leonid, 139
Hutchins, Robert Maynard, 21–2, 109, 132

imperfect competition, theory of, 44, 84, 97, 99, 117, 128, 153
income and wealth distribution, 4, 11, 39, 77, 84–8, 128, 200–3, 207, 228
inequality of income and wealth, 10–11, 77, 81–7, 94, 126, 150, 174–5, 196–203, 205. See also egalitarianism
Irwin, Douglas W., 223

James, Jerry, xi
John Bates Clark Medal, 134, 171
Johnson, Alvin, 35, 59–62
Johnson, D. Gale, 78, 119–20
Johnson, Harry, 69, 137, 198, 215
Johnson, Lyndon B., 207
Jones, Daniel Stedman, 240
Jones, Homer, 77, 110, 133
Jordan, Virgil, 29
Journal of Law and Economics, 143–4
Journal of Political Economy, 26, 28, 52, 71, 120, 131, 223–4

Kahneman, Daniel, 240

Kasper, Sherryl, xi, 80, 221, 237,
	260n4
Kay, John, xi
Kemp, Jack, 181
Kennedy, John, 207
Kennedy, Paul, 187
Kern, William S., 224
Kershner, Frederick, 56–9, 67–8,
	224
Keynes, John Maynard, 15, 52
	and classical liberalism, 18, 98, 194
	on Darwinism, 13
	Economic Consequences of the Peace, The,
		95
	End of Laissez Faire, The, 95
	Friedman on, 210, 212, 214,
		216–17
	General Theory of Employment, Interest,
		and Money, The, 96–9, 106
	and Hayek, 188–9, 210
	influence of, 106, 117–19
	and Knight, 98–9
	on laissez faire, 6–7
	and socialism, 97
	Tract on Monetary Reform, A, 95–6
	Treatise on Money, A, 95, 216
	and Viner, 98–9
Keynesianism, 44, 71, 75–6, 78, 90,
	97, 99–101, 106, 117–19, 133–7,
	237, 240
Kirk, Russell, 33
Kitch, Edmund W., 230
Klein, Lawrence, 100, 103, 138
Klein, Naomi, 229–30
Knight, Frank, 77, 93, 110–11, 124–5,
	130
	Buchanan on, 70–1
	and classical liberalism, 18, 39–40,
		45–6, 66–7, 70, 193–4, 225
	as co-editor of Journal of Political
		Economy, 52, 71
	as a colleague, 53
	and Cowles Commission, 99–100,
		103
	Ethics of Competition, The, 77, 133
	and "first" Chicago school, 78, 80,
		84, 94, 100–1, 108, 121–2

and fiscal and monetary policy,
	46–7, 72
free market views of, 43, 45–6,
	65–7, 71
Freedom and Reform, 225
hired at Chicago, 69–70
influence on Buchanan, 151–3
influence on Hayek, 147
on liberalism, 225
and Keynes, 98–9
and Mill, 59, 61, 64–5
Milton Friedman on, 143
reader's report on The Road to
	Serfdom, 105–6
religious views of, 67–8
Risk, Uncertainty and Profit, 62–4, 67,
	70, 77
Rose Friedman on, 65, 70, 141
and Simons, 72, 109
on Smith, 66, 179
teaching of, 53–4, 70, 118–19
and utilitarianism, 153
and Viner, 63, 67, 69–72
Knight, Horace, 54, 56–7
Koopmans, Tjalling, 102, 138
Krueger, Maynard, 89
Krugman, Paul, 18, 169, 230

Laffer, Arthur, 180–1
Laidler, David, 43
Lange, Oskar, 100
Laughlin, James Laurence, 23–6, 28,
	30, 35–7, 221–2
	edition of Mill's Principles of Political
		Economy, 24–6
	Elements of Political Economy, 26
	founder of Journal of Political Economy,
		26
Leeson, Robert, xi, 125, 137, 228–9,
	232
Leland, Simeon, 93
Lerner, Abba, 74
Levi, Edward, 140
Leviathan (Hobbes), 26–7
libertarianism, contemporary,
	31–4, 39–42, 85, 134, 154–7, 159,
	165–6, 177, 187–91, 194–6

Lichtenstein, Nelson, xi
Liebeler, Wesley, 144
Lindsey, Brink, 33, 240–1
Locke, John, 1
  and classical liberalism, 17, 81, 194, 202
  Second Treatise of Civil Government, 27
  on toleration, 33
London School of Economics (LSE), 46, 62, 74, 96, 105, 126, 141, 144, 147, 156, 163
Lucas, Robert, 122, 138, 256n38
Luhnow, Harold, 141

MacDougall, Peter, xi
macroeconomics, 28, 39, 96–8, 123, 173, 185, 187
Madison, James, 152
Malthus, Thomas, 6, 27, 59
Markowitz, Harry, 138
Marschak, Jacob, 105–6
Marshall, Alfred, 18, 34, 65, 81, 104, 112, 194, 255n7
Marshall, Leon, 35
Marx, Karl, 8, 235
Marxism, 18, 97, 166
mathematics, 25, 27–9, 31, 49, 64–5, 92–107, 112–14, 228–9
McDonald, John, 95, 118–19
McFadden, Daniel, 139
McLean, Ian, 237
McNeill, William, 23, 233
Mead, George Herbert, 35
Meese, Edwin, xi, 182, 262n38
Meltzer, Allan H., 239
Merriam, Charles, 35, 89
Michelson, Albert, 35
microeconomics, 28, 49–50, 123–4
Mill, James, 9, 11, 27
Mill, John Stuart, 1, 9–10, 81, 128, 193
  and classical liberalism, 17, 24, 194, 202
  and egalitarianism, 9–10, 82
  emphasis on genius, 12, 170
  on extinguishing poverty, 12–13
  Hayek and, 149–50
  and individualism, 13, 170

influence of, 11–12, 14–15
Knight and, 59, 61, 64–5
On Liberty, 11–12, 17, 24, 149–50, 170
Principles of Political Economy, 11, 24–6, 82
and secular utility maximization, 12–13
Utilitarianism, 12, 24
Miller, Lawrence, 94, 120, 131–2, 226
Miller, Merton, 138
Millis, Harry, 71–2, 92
Mints, Lloyd, 71–2, 80, 93, 101, 126
Miron, Jeffrey A., 239
Mirowski, Philip, xi, 43, 108–9
  Road from Mont Pelerin (with Plehwe), 221
Mises, Ludwig von, 17, 40, 45–6, 75, 151, 158, 162–3, 235, 238
  on classical liberalism, 17
  and contemporary libertarianism, 158, 165–6, 195
  Friedman on, 170, 209–11, 214–16, 218, 267n1
  Liberalism in the Classical Tradition, 17
  on socialism, 145–7
Mitchell, Wesley Clair, 18, 26, 30–1, 35–6, 101–2
  Business Cycles, 30
  founder of National Bureau of Economic Research, 30
  on justification of free market capitalism, 30–1
  Measuring Business Cycles (with Burns), 3, 102
  on Veblen, 245–6n32
monetary policy, 47, 71–2, 76–7, 84, 96–8, 106, 116, 118, 122
  and Friedman, 48, 64, 115–17, 172–4
monopoly, 81, 84, 94, 117, 119, 126–7, 142–3, 153, 190–2
Mont Pelerin Society, 118, 120, 146, 174
Moore, Stephen, 197–200, 202, 266n23

Moynihan, Daniel Patrick, 123
Mundell, Robert, 138, 181
Myerson, Roger, 139

Nasar, Sylvia, 244n36, 245n26
Nash, George, xi, 158, 171, 175, 234–5, 248n26
National Bureau of Economic Research, 30–1, 101–2, 110–11, 116
National Industrial Recovery Act (NIRA), 46, 88–9
Nef, John, 36–7, 71, 93
Nelson, Robert H., 224–5
neoanarchism, 18, 39, 154, 187
Nerozzi, Sebastiano, 224
New Deal, 71–2, 83, 111
    Agricultural Adjustment Act (AAA), 46, 89
    National Industrial Recovery Act (NIRA), 46, 88–9
    Tennessee Valley Authority, 89
New Economics and the Old Economists, The (Davis), 71
New York University, 77
Nik-Khah, Edward, 125, 220
Niskanen, William, 182
Nixon, Richard, 77, 110, 133, 138, 176, 178–9, 181–2
Nobel Prize, 19, 37, 138–9, 221
Nordhaus, William, 134–5
Nutter, Warren, 152

Obama, Barack, 159
On Liberty (Mill), 11–12, 17, 24, 149–50, 170

Park, Robert, 35
Patinkin, Don, 40, 44, 54, 98–9, 105, 114, 137, 227
Paul, Rand, 238, 259–60n1
Peck, Jamie, 220–1
Peltzman, Sam, xi, 120, 231
Phillipson, Nicholas, 6
Pierson, Paul, 265n6
Piketty, Thomas, 241
Pitofsky, Robert, 231

Plehwe, Dieter, 39–40
    Road from Mont Pelerin (with Mirowski), 221
Prasad, Monica, 237–8
Prescott, Edward, 139
price theory, 35, 46, 49, 51, 121–8, 132, 143–7, 151, 164, 172–3, 179, 215, 233
Princeton University, 44–5, 49–51, 56, 63, 84, 93
public policy
    and Chicago economists, 11, 28, 37, 71, 74, 77, 84, 118, 127, 133, 143, 192–3
    and classical liberalism, 27, 34, 156, 202
    and contemporary libertarianism, 32, 200–2
    and Friedman, 122, 133, 169–72, 176, 187, 204
    recommendations, 206–7

Rand, Ayn, 10–11, 165–6, 195
Ransom, Roger, 90, 226
Reagan, Ronald, 133, 138, 172, 176, 178–84, 186, 201, 207, 220, 226–7, 237–40
Reder, Melvin, 103, 121, 140, 171, 227
Reich, Robert, 18, 265n6
Republic (Plato), 26
Ricardo, David, 6, 9, 24, 27, 59
Rise and Fall of the Great Powers, The (Kennedy), 187
Risk, Uncertainty and Profit (Knight), 62–4, 67, 70, 77
Road to Serfdom, The (Hayek), 89, 105–6, 109, 141, 147–8, 155–7, 164, 171, 185, 188
Robbins, Lionel, 18, 43, 45–6, 74, 76, 141, 144
    and classical liberalism, 18, 194
    Friedman on, 209–10, 212
    on Hayek, 163–4
    History of Economic Thought, A, 236
    on Viner, 49–50
Robinson, Joan, 84, 97, 118–19
Rockefeller, David, 121–2

Rockefeller, John D., 15–16, 25, 37, 121
  and founding of University of
    Chicago, 19–22
Roden, Stan, xi
Roncaglia, Alessandro, 238
Roosevelt, Franklin D., 29, 46, 52,
  83, 90
Rothbard, Murray, 158, 195, 235
Rothschild, Emma, 236
Rotwein, Eugene, 40, 51, 223
Ruger, William, 189
Russell, Dean, 252n6
Rutherford, Malcolm, xi, 36
  Institutionalist Movement in American
    Economics, 1918–1947, 222

Samuels, Warren, xi, 169, 224
  Chicago School of Political Economy, The,
    222
Samuelson, Paul, 18, 44, 48, 69, 119,
  121, 125–6
  and classical liberalism, 18
  on Director, 144
  Economics (textbook), 134–5, 185–7
  first recipient of John Bates Clark
    Medal, 134
  Foundations of Economic Analysis, 134
  on Friedman, 218–19, 239
  Nobel Prize in Economics received
    by, 134, 138
  on Smith, 40–1
  on "two Chicago schools," 39, 44,
    84, 94
  on Viner, 40
Sandmo, Agnar, 169, 239
Sargent, Thomas, 139
Scherer, F. M., 231
Schlesinger, Arthur, Jr., 186–7
Scholes, Myron, 138
Schrock, Tom, xi
Schultz, Henry, 71–2, 93, 111, 138
Schultz, Theodore, 80, 138, 142
Schumpeter, Joseph, 120
Seckler, David, 222–3
Seldon, Arthur, 228, 232
Seligman, Ben, 234
Shils, Edward, 70, 224

Shultz, George, xi, 123, 138, 176–82,
  262n31
Simon, Herbert, 107, 138
Simons, Henry, 69, 71–2, 78, 93, 119,
  124
  on Bentham, 9, 81–2
  at Chicago Law School, 79, 108–9
  and Chicago Plan, 72
  and classical liberalism, 18, 34,
    45–6, 80–7, 90–1, 109, 142,
    194
  contributions of, 79–80
  on distribution of wealth and
    income, 11, 86–7, 94, 128
  Economic Policy for a Free Society, 81,
    130
  and egalitarianism, 81–2, 86–7,
    128
  and "first" Chicago school, 39,
    44–6, 94
  and Hayek, 89
  Hayek on, 253n31
  influence of, 77, 90–1, 95, 108–9,
    130
  and *laissez faire,* 43
  and libertarianism, 81
  on the National Recovery Act, 88
  Positive Program for Laissez Faire, A, 34,
    72–3, 83, 86–9
  and progressive taxation, 11, 43, 77,
    86, 88–9, 91, 202
  on Smith, 9, 81–2
  and socialism, 34, 81–2
  Stigler on, 124, 128
  and Viner, 67
Skidelsky, Robert, xi, 188–9, 231
Skousen, Mark, xi, 134, 237
Smith, Adam, 1–9, 11, 13, 17, 50, 196
  on division of labor, 3
  and egalitarianism, 4, 6
  on free market, 3–4
  on government activity, 4–6
  on happiness, 7
  influence on Laughlin, 24–5
  on progressive taxation, 5
  Theory of Moral Sentiments, 3, 7, 52
  as utilitarian, 7

Wealth of Nations, 3–5, 24, 27, 40–1, 82, 176

Smith, George H., 259–60n1

social conservatism, 155, 188, 203

social Darwinism, 13–16, 30

socialism, 15, 24, 34, 81–3, 89, 97, 99–100, 127, 195
  and Friedman, 83, 115–16
  and Hayek, 146, 155–8, 163

Solow, Robert, 103

Soviet Union, 172, 184–7

Sowell, Thomas, xi, 6, 122, 225–6

specialization (division) of labor, 2–3, 77, 91, 147, 172

Spencer, Herbert, 7, 13–17, 29, 77, 165, 195

Spiegel, Henry, xi, 38, 50, 120, 234

Sprinkel, Beryl, 182

Stapleford, Thomas, xi, 31, 43

Stein, Herbert, 77, 90–1, 106, 138, 176–7, 181, 207, 226

Steuart, James, 27

Stigler, George, 36, 69, 111, 118, 135, 225, 228, 230
  on Bentham, 9
  on Chicago school, 131–2
  and classical liberalism, 127
  on Director, 141, 143
  on economic equality, 126–8
  on Friedman, 141
  on Knight, 59, 77
  and post-war Chicago school, 40, 43, 84, 94, 101, 120–3, 133
  Roofs or Ceilings? (with Friedman), 174
  on Simons, 82–3, 128
  and taxation, 11
  teaching of, 125
  wit of, 123–4

Stigler, Stephen, xi, 231

Stiglitz, Joseph, 18, 207, 240, 265n6

Stockman, David, xi, 182

Stossel, John, 200, 265n15

Summers, Larry, 18, 230

Sumner, William Graham, 16, 24, 29

supply-side economics, 181. *See also* Reagan, Ronald

survival of the fittest, 13, 15–16, 30

Taussig, Frank, 38

taxation
  and earned income tax credit, 176, 206
  and income distribution, 4, 11, 39, 77, 84–8, 128, 200–3, 207, 228
  progressive, 5, 11, 43, 77, 86, 88–9, 91, 127, 195–6, 202, 205, 208

Tea Party, 158

Telser, Lester, xi, 100, 120

Tennessee Valley Authority, 89

Thatcher, Margaret, 172, 178, 182–5

Theory of Moral Sentiments (Smith), 3, 7, 52

Theory of the Leisure Class (Veblen), 28–30

Thomas, Rich, 183

Thurow, Lester, 186–7

Tobin, James, 134, 136–7

Tomlinson, Jim, 233

Truman, Harry S, 52

Tullock, Gordon, 152, 226

University of Chicago
  acceptance of Jewish students, 23
  architecture and Midway, 35
  Committee on Social Thought, 36, 80, 93, 95, 101, 118, 132, 148–9
  Department of Political Economy, 23–8, 35–6
  emphasis on graduate programs and research, 22–3
  faculty, 22–3
  founding of, 19–22
  location, 21
  and Nobel Prize recipients, 19, 37, 138–9, 221
  See also Chicago school of economics

University of Chicago Press, 23

University of Wisconsin (Madison), 95, 111, 205

utilitarianism, 1–2, 7, 9, 12, 17, 24, 27, 58, 82, 153, 170, 204

Utilitarianism (Mill), 12, 24

Valdés, Juan Gabriel, 229
Van Horn, Robert, xi, 43, 108–9,
    142–3
Van Overtveldt, Johan, xi, 24, 113, 121
    Chicago School, The, 221–2
Veblen, Thorstein, 26, 28–30, 35–6,
    117
    Theory of the Leisure Class, 28
    The Vested Interests and the Common
    Man, 29
Vickers, Geoffrey, 162
Viner, Jacob
    on Bentham, 8
    at Chicago, 26, 36, 38–49, 63, 67,
        69–72, 93–4, 153
    and "Chicago school," 44–5, 78,
        100, 119–22, 131
    and classical liberalism, 18, 39–40,
        44–6, 48–9, 78, 194
    as co-editor of *Journal of Political*
        Economy, 52, 71
    on Federal Reserve, 47–8
    on fiscal and monetary policy,
        46–7, 64
    Friedman on, 48, 143
    as government consultant, 52
    influence as a colleague, 51–2
    influence as a teacher, 48, 50–1
    influence as a scholar, 49–51
    Long View and the Short, The, 223
    and Keynes, 98–9
    and Knight, 63, 67, 69–72
    on monopoly, 84
    at Princeton, 44–5, 49–51, 63, 84,
        93, 108–9
    recipient of Francis A. Walker
        Award, 52

Religious Thought and Economic Society,
    49
and role of government, 4–5, 40–3,
    48–9, 84
and Simons, 67
on Smith, 3–5, 40–1, 52, 66
"United States as a 'Welfare State,'
    The," 52
and value of democracy, 42
Vining, Routledge, 152
Virginia school of political economy,
    152
Volker Fund, 141–2

Walker, Francis A., 65
Walker, Graham, 232
Wallis, Allen, 69, 77, 103, 111, 133, 138,
    142, 182
    on Friedman, 115
    and post-war Chicago school, 45,
        77, 80, 83–4, 100–1, 108
    on Simons, 73, 79, 83
Wanniski, Jude, 181
Wapshott, Nicholas, 231
Wealth of Nations (Smith), 3–5, 24, 27,
    40–1, 82, 176
Williams, Walter, 199–200, 265n14
Winch, Donald, xi, 45, 49
World's Fair of 1893 (Chicago), 20–1
World War I, 38, 95–6
World War II, 22, 60, 95, 111, 116,
    145, 212
Wright, Chester, 72, 93

Yale University, 22, 107, 136, 141, 187
Yellen, Janet, 18
Yntema, Theodore, 72, 84, 93
Young, Allyn A., 62, 250n20